INSIDE THE INVESTMENTS
OF WARREN BUFFETT

INSIDE THE
INVESTMENTS
OF WARREN
BUFFETT

TWENTY CASES

YEFEI LU

Columbia University Press
Publishers Since 1893
New York Chichester, West Sussex
cup.columbia.edu
Copyright © 2016 Yefei Lu
All rights reserved

Library of Congress Cataloging-in-Publication Data
Names: Lu, Yefei, author.
Title: Inside the investments of Warren Buffett : twenty cases / Yefei Lu.
Description: New York : Columbia University Press, 2016. | Includes
bibliographical references and index.
Identifiers: LCCN 2015048094 | ISBN 9780231164627 (cloth : alk. paper)
Subjects: LCSH: Buffett, Warren. | Capitalists and financiers—United States.
| Investments. | Portfolio management.
Classification: LCC HG172.B84 L8 2016 | DDC 332.6—dc23
LC record available at http://lccn.loc.gov/2015048094

Columbia University Press books are printed on permanent
and durable acid-free paper.
Printed in the United States of America

c 10 9 8 7 6 5 4 3 2 1

COVER DESIGN: Noah Arlow

To my love, Nora, and our beautiful daughter, Lily

CONTENTS

ACKNOWLEDGMENTS

This book would not have been possible without the support and contributions of numerous individuals, all of whom I would like to thank sincerely for their help.

First, I would like to thank Eddie Ramsden at the London Business School, who encouraged me to turn what was originally a personal research project into a full-fledged book. Without his vision on what was still missing, I would have concluded that there were already too many books written about Warren Buffett and would never have ventured to write about this topic in this form.

I want to thank Bridget Flannery-McCoy and Stephen Wesley at Columbia University Press, who directly worked with me and together spent countless hours giving me feedback and editing my writing. Thank you so much for your dedication to this project and for sharing your talent. Without you and the help of the entire Columbia University Press organization, this book, as it is written, would not have been possible.

Very important, I would like to acknowledge my current colleagues at Shareholder Value Management AG in Frankfurt, Germany for the critical role that they have individually played. Thank you, Frank Fischer and Reiner Sachs, for creating an organization that has provided me with both an amazing environment and the freedom to continually improve my understanding of value investing, without which I could not have written this book. You are, honestly, each in your own way, two of the most incredible and positive individuals I have ever had the opportunity to work with. I am especially thankful for the very significant time that you, Frank, have spent sharing with me your lessons learned in investing and many other things in life. Thank you also to my colleagues Suad Cehajic, Gianluca Ferrari, Ronny Ruchay, Simon Hruby, and Cedric Schwalm for our frequent discussions on this topic and for taking time out of your busy schedules to read my manuscript drafts and give me detailed feedback. Together, this organization and its individuals have added very significantly to what I know about value investing and about life.

I also would like to thank my previous colleagues at Forum Family Office in Munich. All the individuals in that organization, led by Dr. Burkhard Wittek, have taught me much of the remainder of what I know about value investing. Special thanks goes to Frank Weippert, Till Campe, Jeremie Couix, and Sasha Seiler, who even today are wonderful sparring partners for investment ideas and my valued peers in the German value investing community that I am glad to be a part of.

From this network, I also want to thank Norman Rentrop and Jens Grosse-Allermann, who host the yearly German investor get-together at the Berkshire Hathaway annual meeting. I have had the pleasure of attending on several occasions and have found this a great resource and service especially for the German value investor community.

I owe a significant debt to several other individuals: Rob Vinall of RV Capital, who helped review several chapters of this book and who over the years has taught me about many aspects of value investing for which I am grateful; Frederik Meinertsen of SEB, who took an interest in my rather academic work and gave valuable feedback on several parts of this book; Chris Genovese of Sanborn Maps, who was responsible for historical archiving of the company as of 2013, and who helped me significantly in my research for original materials for that company; Professor T. Lindsay Baker at Tarleton State University, who helped me greatly with the case study of Dempster Mill Manufacturing; and all the individuals, including Ralph Bull and Daniel Teston, who allowed me to use their artwork and photography in my book.

Finally, I want to thank my loving family, Nora, Lily, my parents Xuanyong and Lizhu, and my brother Felix, who have all supported me in this long endeavor, putting up with my countless hours typing away on my computer at home, at the beach, and everywhere in between. Thank you so much for your understanding, your patience, and your love.

INTRODUCTION

Over the last thirty years, Warren Buffett and his investment vehicle Berkshire Hathaway have become household names. Likewise, Omaha, Nebraska is no longer an unknown midwestern town for anyone in the investment community. Buffett's legendary investing performance has prompted small investors to want to invest just like him and many investment professionals seek to emulate his strategies. But what are Buffett's greatest investments and in which context did he make them? Moreover, what can we learn from his experience?

The focus of this book is to uncover answers to these questions by journeying through Buffett's investing career. Specifically, I look at the twenty investments Buffett made that I feel had the largest material impact on his trajectory. I selected a cross-section of different types of investments and investments I found especially informative. I also considered the relative size of each investment at the time it was made.

My approach in analyzing these key investments was to look at the detailed actions Buffett took when he made his investment decisions and try to understand from a third-party perspective what rationales he or any investor was likely to have seen in each situation. Where appropriate, I tried to take the perspective of an investment analyst studying the businesses at the same time in which Buffett did in order to highlight Buffett's unique standpoint. In this way, unlike the many biographical books written about Buffett, this book focuses on telling the story of Buffett only as it relates to his key investments. This book aims to extend beyond the various publications that contain significant information about Buffett's investments (including Buffett's own annual letters) by leveraging original source documents and other historical information where possible. My overall aim is to give readers a realistic analysis of the key investments that Buffett made and then have them draw their own insights and conclusions.

The book consists of three sections, ordered chronologically. The first section details five key investments that Buffett made between 1957 and 1968 when he ran Buffett Partnership Limited, the private investment partnership he managed before taking over Berkshire Hathaway. The second section details nine investments Buffett made between 1968 and 1990, the first two decades when Berkshire Hathaway served as his investment vehicle. The third and final section focuses on the period at Berkshire since 1990. A brief introduction to each section provides a picture of how each investment fits within Buffett's career as well as setting the broader investment context during that time period of the U.S. stock market, the primary market in which Buffett invested. Individual chapters in each section focus on the specific investments, treating each as a case study. The final section of the book reflects upon the broader evolution of Buffett as an investor. It also summarizes my overall learning from Buffett's investment philosophy and strategy based on my analysis of his twenty key investments.

Before I consider the Buffett's specific investments, I want to define the methodology I used in my analysis. In evaluating an investment, my approach was, first, to understand the qualitative factors and context of the investment and then its valuation. For the valuation, I accessed the intrinsic value based primarily on earnings that I considered the sustainable level of earnings for the company. Often this included adjustments made based on the cyclicality of a business. At times I adjusted for depreciation and amortization costs compared to maintenance capital expenditures (CAPEX), and at other times I simply used the last year's earnings. For the sake of consistency and simplicity, I chose to stick with EV/EBIT[1] based on the normalized figures mentioned above as the earnings-based valuation metric, referring to P/E[2] less frequently. In a few instances, where I felt it was warranted, I used an asset-based valuation instead of, or in addition to, the earnings-based valuation. The qualitative assessment and the valuation methodologies I have chosen are not the only ways to assess these companies. My analysis has a significant degree of interpretation, and

---

1. EV/EBIT ratio refers to Enterprise Value divided by Earnings Before Interest and Tax.

2. P/E ratio refers to Market Capitalization divided by nominal Earnings or Share Price divided by Earnings per Share.

certainly there are times when these interpretations could be improved by other adjustments that I did not make. In sum, however, this book aims to provide an accurate investment analysis of the companies based on the available data. Collectively, my analysis reflects my own best understanding and interpretation of Buffett's investment decisions.

INSIDE THE INVESTMENTS
OF WARREN BUFFETT

Part I

The Partnership Years (1957–1968)

Warren Buffett's investment career started in earnest in 1957, with the formation of his first investment partnership. Following two years of working as a securities analyst at the Graham-Newman Corporation and the well-documented experience of studying at the Columbia Business School under Benjamin Graham, Buffett established Buffett Partnership Limited (BPL) with the funding of a few friends, family, and close associates.[1]

While details of Buffett's investment thought process are much more widely documented later in his career, a few obvious themes can be discerned in his partnership years. Foremost is the focus on being a buyer at a good price. In his 1962 partnership letter, Buffett states that the cornerstone of his investment philosophy is to purchase assets at a bargain price, which he considers in the traditional Benjamin Graham view of low price versus intrinsic valuation—a fundamental assessment of a company's ability to generate cash flow or a company's value in assets. Second, Buffett adopts a strong view of a moving market; Mr. Market either overvalues or undervalues a company, but over the long run does pass around the intrinsic value. Third, Buffett also pays attention to investor psychology as pertains to who is investing in the market and what impact this investor thinking has. Specifically, he mentions several times the concept of whether investors have steady hands and the manias of different periods.

In running his partnership, Buffett kept secret his holdings during this period and adopted a black-box type of strategy with his limited partners. In the appendix of his 1963 year-end partnership letter he states, "We cannot talk about our current investment operations. Such an open-mouth policy could never improve our results and in some situations could seriously hurt us. For this reason, should anyone, including partners, ask us whether we are interested in any security, we must plead the Fifth Amendment."

The significant investments Buffett made during this time were a mix of value bets and corporate actions. At times BPL would invest up to 35 percent of its net assets into a single company and at times, given the opportunity, take a majority ownership stake in the company.

When Buffett ran his partnership during the late 1950s and 1960s, the United States was enjoying relatively calm and economically prosperous times: on the heels of the Korean War in the 1950s and in the midst of the Cold War at the beginning of the 1960s, the U.S. economy was less eventful than its politics. In the 1950s the Dow climbed from approximately 200 points in 1950 to roughly 600 points in 1960 (a 200 percent increase). Although there was a small recession at the beginning of the 1960s that saw the Dow pull back into the 530s in 1962 from a high in the 730s at the end of 1961 (a decrease of 27 percent), the Dow would rise again to over 900 by 1965 (a 70 percent increase from the low). The economy continued to grow through the Kennedy years, with signs of the first serious concerns only surfacing at the end of the 1960s when inflation rates started increasing ever more quickly. By the time Buffett closed his investment partnership in 1968, economic prosperity abounded to a level where he found it increasingly difficult to find the value investments that he was looking for. This was in fact one of the key rationales for ending his partnership amidst great performance.

The five investments discussed in part I of this book are the investments I deemed the most significant or otherwise most interesting during Buffett's partnership years.

1

1958: Sanborn Map Company

The history of the Sanborn Map Company is fascinating. In the 1860s a young surveyor by the name of D. A. Sanborn was hired by the Aetna Insurance Company to produce several maps of the city of Boston. Aetna used these maps to assess the fire insurance risks for specific buildings in the areas surveyed. The maps produced proved so successful that D. A. Sanborn started his own company, which came to be known as the Sanborn Map Company. Throughout the 1860s and 1870s, Sanborn expanded regionally, and by the late 1870s he had already mapped over fifty cities.[1] By the 1920s, Sanborn Maps had become the market leader in fire insurance mapping in the United States.

To better understand Sanborn Maps and what it produced, it is important to understand the fire insurance industry. Fire insurance had its origins in England after the Great Fire of 1666, which destroyed more than 13,000 houses in the city of London and made approximately 20 percent of London's inhabitants homeless. During the 1700s and 1800s, this industry migrated over to the United States, administered first by British companies that had the royal decree to operate this business, and later by American firms that pioneered the industry locally. By the late 1800s, fire insurance companies were prominent in larger cities such as Boston and Philadelphia. These companies underwrote risk and determined pricing by inspecting

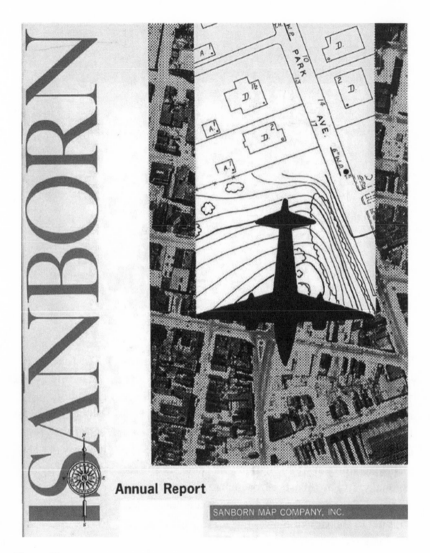

Figure 1.1.

the individual building in question for construction type, construction materials, number of windows, and other factors related to the structure including the surrounding structures. The methodology used thus required a field inspection by a professional surveyor. As field inspections were both time-consuming and very expensive, a company that produced maps with enough detail to assess fire risk appropriately had obvious advantages. First, rather than assessing one structure at a time, it was far more efficient to work through a block or even a city neighborhood at a time. More important, rather than using the generated information once for one insurer, a map had the advantage of scale; once produced, a map could be used by multiple insurance companies to assess the risk for the same set of underlying structures.[2] This is similar to, for example, the modern seismic exploration industry—the industry that generates the cartography necessary for oil companies to drill for oil offshore. Companies such as TGS-Nopec, for example, benefit from similar benefits of scale. TGS-Nopec conducts 2D and 3D surveys of ocean floor regions such as the Gulf of Mexico and then sells this information to major oil companies who are interested in drilling in the region. In the context of its time, Sanborn Maps' mapping was also very much aligned with the practice of multi-insurance; it was quite common for larger industrial structures to be insured by several insurance companies, each of whom only assumed a portion of the risk.

Although the initial cost of producing such detailed maps was extremely high, once Sanborn had invested the large up-front costs of mapping a city, its continued operations in a region were much less capital intensive. Often the continued work necessitated only a few surveyors in a region monitoring changes in roads and construction and sending this information to the Sanborn headquarters' cartography department to issue edits to the maps. This meant that as time went on, Sanborn would make very nice margins. However, if a competitor were to enter that same market and both Sanborn and the competitor had to share the revenues available from customers in the city, the smaller amount of revenues in a divided market would no longer justify the up-front investment of mapping. Hence, once Sanborn had mapped a city, no second competitor would enter a market. This second point left the industry ripe for consolidation.

Given this background, it is not difficult to understand how a well-run company like Sanborn Maps, which focused meticulously on training its staff to produce exacting and high-quality maps, and which was aggressive in its expansion both organically and later via acquisitions, would become very successful. Although there were several other mapping companies in the late 1800s, including the Jefferson Insurance Company, Hexamer & Locher, Perris & Brown (which merged with Sanborn in 1889), and the Dankin Map Company, Sanborn Maps was the dominant player by the 1920s.[3] One last fact that helped significantly in this transformation was the insurance companies' need for standardization. As insurance companies generally preferred to train their underwriters on one standard, a company that ensured a systematic surveying process on a national scale had the advantage.

By 1958, when Warren Buffett invested, Sanborn had been the dominant player in its industry for several decades. For an idea of the product that Sanborn produced, see figures 1.2 and 1.3 for copies of one of Sanborn's maps for the city of Boston, dated 1867.[4]

True to its original purpose of assisting in the estimation of fire risk for insurance companies, Sanborn's maps included details of not only streets and houses of a city but also such items as diameter of water mains underlying streets, number of windows, elevator shafts,

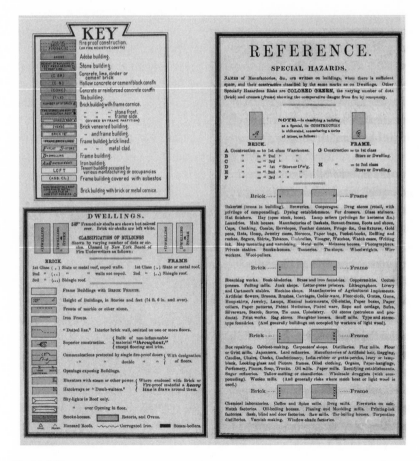

Figure 1.2.
Sanborn map of the city of Boston key (1867).

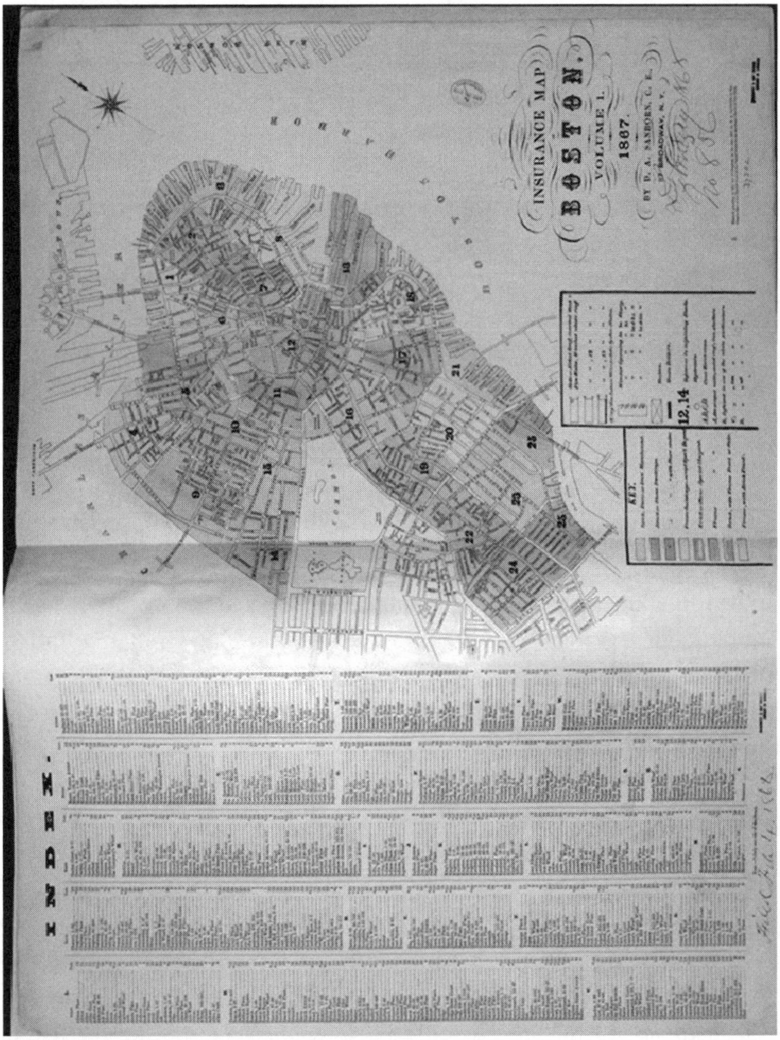

Figure 1.3.
Sanborn map of the city of Boston (1867). (D. A. Sanborn. *Insurance Map of Boston.*
Map. New York: 1867. From Library of Congress, *Sanborn Map Collections.*)

construction materials for buildings, and production lines for industrial
facilities. The commercial product sold to its customers would typically
be a large volume of maps that weighed approximately fifty or so pounds,
which would cover the detailed layouts for a particular city. In addition
to the initial cost of the volume, Sanborn charged a subscription fee for

its customers to keep their maps revised, which ran approximately $100 per year for a medium-sized city such as Omaha. While the uses of such detailed maps had expanded to include public utilities, mortgage companies, and tax authorities, it was known that as late as 1950, 95 percent of Sanborn's revenues still came from a core group of about thirty insurance companies.[5]

All things considered, Sanborn was a great business up to the 1950s. It provided a critical service to its customers and in return got steady and profitable recurring revenues. Unfortunately for Sanborn, in the 1950s a new technology was developed that offered a substitute for Sanborn's maps. Instead of using maps to gauge insurance risks based on structures and surroundings, insurance companies could now depend on algorithmic calculations based on financial information such as costs of the structures. This methodology was called "carding." Even more unfortunate for Sanborn, more and more insurance companies were using carding. By 1958, when Buffett began investing in Sanborn, profit margins had decreased dramatically for several years, and the share price had dropped to roughly $45 per share compared to the $110 per share it commanded in 1938 (a drop of almost 60 percent).[6] Referencing Buffett's annual letter to BPL shareholders, this occurred in the same timeframe that the Dow Industrial Index moved from about 120 to about 550 (an increase of 360 percent).

For someone considering investing in Sanborn Maps when Buffett was investing, the assessment likely would have been as follows: Sanborn was a near-perfect business for a long time, a sole provider of a critical service, with high returns on capital; however, in the last several years prior to 1958, the business had faced serious substitution by newer technology, which had clearly and significantly eroded its core business within the fire insurance industry. Despite its proud heritage, to an analyst who just started looking at the business, the business would have looked rather poor fundamentally as it seemed to be in a structural decline. Looking at the detailed financial information (see exhibit 1.1) for Sanborn Map Company (renamed First Pelham Corporation in 1959) contained in the original 1960 *Moody's Industrial Manual*, one could see that both gross profit and net income had been gradually declining since 1950. Net income had declined approximately 10 percent per annum for the period 1950–1958.

One area, however, where a more careful analysis would have revealed a somewhat different conclusion, which Buffett certainly picked up on, was that although declining, Sanborn Maps was far from a dead business.

Exhibit 1.1

Selected Financial Information on Sanborn Map Co. from the
Moody's Manual for 1960
First Pelham Corp.

History: Incorporated in New York, Feb. 8, 1876 as Sanborn Map and Publishing Co. In 1899, name changed to Sanborn-Perris Map Co. and to Sanborn Map Co. in Dec. 1901; present name adopted Dec. 31, 1959, see "Reorganization" below.

Reorganization—Name Change approved by stockholders Dec. 15, 1959 and effective Dec. 31 provided for transfer of map business to new New York company known as Sanborn Map Co., Inc.; change of corporate name to First Pelham Corp. and amendment of charter to extend powers and purposes of company to include trading in stock, bonds, and securities of other companies. As result, company became directly engaged only in managing its investment assets, including 315,000 common shares in new Sanborn Map received for operating assets.

Business: Since Dec. 31, 1959, invests in all types of securities. Owns entire stock of Sanborn Map Co., Inc. which operates former map business and properties.

Subsidiary: Sanborn Map Co., Inc., wholly-owned, surveys and publishes fire insurance and real estate maps of cities and towns throughout the U.S. and some of its territories. Sells principally to fire insurance companies and allied interests. Also mapping service in community planning, public utility records and market analysis. Publishing plant and main office located at Pelham, N.Y. Branch offices in Chicago and San Francisco, and sales offices in New York and Atlanta.

Officers: C.P. Herbell, Pres.; H.E. Oviatt, Vice-Pres. and Sec.; R.E. Kellner, C.F. Doane, Vice-Pres.; C.H. Carr, Asst. Vice-Pres.; F. H. Kleist, Treas.; D.G. Dobbins, Asst. Sec.

Directors: D.R. Ackerman, Esmond Ewing, H.H. Flagg, C.P. Herbell, H.W. Miller, H.E. Oviatt, W.B. Rearden, J.S. Taber, W.C. Ridgway, Jr., W.L. Nolen, J.A. North, L.A. Vincent, P.S. Brown, W.E. Buffett

No. of Stockholders: Dec. 31, 1959, 1,475.

No. of Employees: Dec. 31, 1959, 350.

Auditors: Child, Lawson & Leonard.

Office: 629 Fifth Ave., Pelham, N.Y.

Capital Stock: 1. First Pelham Corp. common; pay $25

OUTSTANDING—105,000 shares; par $25 (changed from $100 par, Oct., 1934, five $25 shares issued for each $100 share).

Table 1.1.
Income account, years ended Dec. 31

	1959	1958
Gross profit	$665,693	$706,168
Oper. expenses	533,573	542,765
Operating profit	132,120	163,403
Other income, net	228,013	242,862
Total income	360,133	406,265
Fed. income tax	77,608	103,400
Net income	282,526	302,866
Retain. earn., 1-1	1,664,749	1,659,351
Dividends	267,750	283,500
Pr. yr. tax adj., net	1,752	cr 1,465
Other deduct.	—	5,735
Prof. secur. sold	8	dr 9,698
Retain. earn., 12-31	1,681,281	1,664,749

Table 1.2.
Earnings, years to Dec. 31

	Gross profit ($)	Net income ($)	No. of shares	Earn. on com.
1959	665,693	282,526	105,000	2.69
1958	706,168	302,866	105,000	2.88
1957	774,785	372,185	105,000	3.54
1956	800,890	418,980	105,000	3.99
1955	1,151,648	537,078	105,000	5.12
1954	1,196,199	550,998	105,000	5.25
1953	1,170,047	513,223	105,000	4.89
1952	1,152,705	511,873	105,000	4.87
1951	1,216,617	537,742	105,000	5.12
1950	1,344,170	679,935	105,000	6.48

DIVIDENDS—(Payments since 1934 follow):

At the time of the 4 for 1 split-up in 1934, paid one share extra, in stock.

TRANSFER AGENT AND REGISTRAR—Marine Midland Trust Co., New York.

Source: Moody's Manual of Industrial and Miscellaneous Securities (1960), 915.

Table 1.3.
Balance sheet, as of Dec. 31

	1959	1958
Assets:		
Cash	$425,831	$227,852
Accts. receivable	444,430	414,860
Inventories	830,331	1,068,785
Prepayments	4,726	6,404
Total current	$1,705,319	$1,717,902
Fixed assets, net	154,356	155,540
Invest., cost[1]	2,601,873	2,592,706
Deferred charges	6,000	—
Total	$4,467,547	$4,466,148
Liabilities:		
Wages payable	$8,494	$6,908
Accounts payable	29,610	19,814
Fed. income tax	77,608	100,987
Other accr. tax	45,555	43,140
Total current	$161,267	$170,850
Deferred income	—	5,550
Capital stk. ($25)	2,625,000	2,625,000
Retained earnings	1,681,281	1,664,749
Total	$4,467,547	$4,466,148
Net current assets	$1,544,052	$1,547,052
Net tang. per sh.	$41.01	$40.85

[1]Mkt. value: 1959, $7,349,323; 1958, $6,972,884.

Table 1.4.

1935–36	$5.00	1937–39	$6.00	1940	$7.00
1941	5.00	1942–43	4.00	1944	4.25
1945	4.00	1946–47	4.50	1948–51	5.00
1952–55	4.50	1956	4.00	1957	3.50
1958	2.70	1959	2.55	1960*	0.60

*To Apr. 16.

Table 1.5.

Price range	1959	1958	1957	1956	1955
High	65	54 ¼	54	70	75
Low	52	37 ½	36	57	64

Referring to the financial data and services to customers in the boxes, we see that although the business had certainly been negatively affected by

---

Services to Customers
Sanborn

In order to familiarize our shareholders with the type of services performed by the company, some typical examples of assignments are mentioned briefly in the following paragraphs:

Design and produce for the Naval Facilities Engineering Command, Philadelphia, Pa., a Community Shelter Atlas of Lancaster County, Pa. This represents a graphic inventory of structure locations presently identified in the Civil Defense Program.

The land use inventory and resulting land use maps of the 149 square miles comprising Floyd County, Indiana.

Election district maps of New York City as a result of a new re-apportionment.

Brush Hazard Surveys at San Rafael Hills and Verdugo Mountains in the Los Angeles area requiring the inspection and listing of 16,000 structures; and in another area of more than 125 square miles extending from San Bernardino to Santa Barbara, Calif. More than 30,000 structures have been inspected and listed to date.

Original maps of Bethlehem Steel Company's new facilities at Burns Harbor Steel Plant and the Pinole Fabricating Works at Richmond, Calif., as well as the revision of existing Bethlehem Steel Company maps at Bethlehem, Johnstown and Lebanon, Pa.

Block counts totaling more than 4,000,000 housing units in the New York, Chicago, Dallas, Fort Worth, Houston, and San Antonio metropolitan areas. These counts are posted on appropriate maps for use in determining dealership territories for Avon Products, Inc.

The annual land use revision service and household count for the New York City Planning Commission.

The land use revision service and area computations of land use changes in Philadelphia for the Philadelphia City Planning Commission.

Thumbnail sketches for approximately 50 localities for a television service.

Distribution system maps compiled and drafted for American Water Works, Inc. and other water companies operating in the state of New York, New Jersey, Pennsylvania, and Kentucky.

Conversion of the twelve volume Portland, Ore. Insurance maps series to black and white format; adding real estate description to the existing maps sheets; and, the surveying of 120 additional sheets.

The custom surveying and publication of 30 Sanborn map sheets at Sioux City, Iowa; 25 sheets at Detroit, Mich.; and other sheets at Richmond and Coronado, Calif.

Our diagram service continued to expand during the year. In the educational field, we are diagramming new plans of Princeton and Yale Universities. We also have increased the number of customers using our diagram services for insurance and other related purposes.

Source: Sanborn Maps, *Annual Report FY 1966*, 3.

Mergers among insurance companies and innovations in underwriting procedures have diminished the use of maps in the insurance industry for the time being. This has made it necessary for us to become increasingly selective with respect to fire insurance map revision services to meet present day requirements. As a consequence our income from this industry has declined; but, on the other hand, the demand for custom inspection and map service from non-insurance categories has been increasing and will continue to do so in the future. From our studies, it seems inconceivable that there will not be a continuing need for our services in one form or another by the insurance companies in the years to come. We shall actively explore all possibilities in this direction.

Source: Sanborn Maps, *Annual Report FY 1966*, 4.

---

the emergence of the new technology (carding) in the mid-1960s more than in 1958, it is nevertheless the case that:

(a) Even then, there was still a portion of business that involved the traditional mapping services for insurance purposes; traditional mapping was not disappearing overnight and in fact had demanded revision services.

(b) There were always many alternative purposes for the surveying done by Sanborn Maps that were unaffected by the carding phenomenon.

Buffett himself noted in his annual letter to shareholders year-end 1960 that at the time, $500 million worth of fire insurance premiums were still underwritten by companies that utilized fire insurance maps, and Sanborn was still profitable, although its net income margin had decreased significantly over the years. Referring again to the Moody's document (see exhibit 1.1), we can see that the operating income from the historical Sanborn business had fallen to a bit above $100,000 by 1959, but that this figure seemed to be stabilizing. Specifically, a potential investor would have seen a stabilizing core business that generated around $100,000 per annum and some source of investment income of around $200,000 per annum. The key here seems to be that the Sanborn Map Company, during the time of Buffett's investment, was clearly still profitable.

The second part of the analysis focuses on valuation. With a market price of $45 per share and 105,000 shares outstanding, Sanborn Map Co. had a total market capitalization of $4.73 million. Even accounting for the significant inflation since 1960, this company was clearly a small cap company. Based on numbers provided in the partnership letter and those referenced previously ($100,000 income from the operating business and about $2 million in revenues),[7] Sanborn stock was valued at an unadjusted 2.4× revenues and 47× 1959 trailing full-year earnings. For a business in terminal decline, this definitely would not have looked cheap based on its earnings power alone. In fact, we would have to assume that net income would have to go back almost to its 1938 $500,000 level for the stock to be trading at earnings multiple of 10× (at a $45 share price), which I would consider more reasonable for a stock with such structural risk. Even at that valuation, without any other considerations, a normal investor would not be inclined to invest in a structurally declining business. This indicates that Buffett may have seen something in the fundamentals of the business that made it look significantly more attractive.

In his annual partnership letter of 1961, Buffett does allude to the possibility of improving the company's operations because management had been neglecting the core mapping business. Also, he seems to point to opportunities to repackage and reuse the plethora of available information collected by Sanborn Maps for a revised product offering that would be more usable for customers, indicating another positive possibility for the company. In any case, Buffett certainly would have deviated from the perception of an analyst who had taken a superficial look at Sanborn and dismissed it as a dying business due to the introduction of carding technology.

But the most interesting part in the investment case of Sanborn Maps was not in the operating business. What Buffett clearly saw, and where others may have not paid enough attention, would have been found in the balance sheet of Sanborn Maps in 1959.[8] This balance sheet reveals that Sanborn Maps had built a securities portfolio of bonds and stocks worth $7 million. This was more than the value of the entire company. Specifically, in his letter to the partnership, Buffett discusses a business with potential for being turned around, and that was trading at a negative value if one considered the value of the investment portfolio. He notes that this was the same company that twenty years before had been trading for roughly 18× P/E or $90 per share, excluding its investment portfolio at that time.

In the end, this was an opportunity Buffett decided was worth investigating. At one point he had invested roughly 35 percent of the net asset value of BPL in Sanborn. What I found especially interesting in Buffett's discussion was his detailed understanding of the lack of focus of the board of directors and their misalignment with the operational management. In my opinion, in this case, Buffett had a much more detailed understanding of the key stakeholders within the company than most investment analysts would have had. Specifically, he appeared to identify clear operational levers whereby the fundamental mapping business could be improved, which the management had not investigated simply due to a board of directors who were resistant to change. He states:

> Prior to my entry on the Board, of the fourteen directors, nine were prominent men from the insurance industry who combined held 46 shares of stock out of 105,000 . . . the tenth director was the company attorney, who held ten shares. The eleventh was a banker with ten shares who recognized the problems of the company, actively pointed them out, and later added to his holdings. . . . The [management] officers were capable, aware of the problems of the business, but kept in a subservient role by the Board of Directors.

To get to this value as well as release the value of the investment portfolio, Buffett turned his stake into a *control holding* by acquiring a majority in Sanborn between 1958 and 1961. In 1961 Buffett finalized his investment by successfully separating Sanborn Map Co. into two separate entities. First, he took clear steps to separate the stifling board of directors from the fundamental map business, which was subsequently left to pursue operational improvements. This entity also received a $1.25 million reserve fund of stocks and bonds as additional capital for the turnaround. Second, the remainder of the investment portfolio value was realized via an exchange of portfolio securities for Sanborn Maps stock, which involved approximately 72 percent of outstanding stock of Sanborn Maps. As a last sweetener, the deal also included a smart tax structuring, which further saved shareholders approximately $1 million in corporate capital gains tax.

When summarizing this investment, it seems that two key factors ultimately led to this investment. The obvious factor was the clear asset value present in the securities portfolio, which only required a way of realizing. Moreover, it cannot be ignored that the fundamental business, although in a structurally declining state, was not dead and not hemorrhaging cash, as is often the case with businesses trading below cash value. In fact, it was a business where Buffett likely saw potential for immediate improvement and possibly potential for a complete turnaround. In this case Buffett had to take a control position to be able to realize the value of the investment, which naturally also involved his deal-making abilities.

The story of Sanborn Maps did not end in the 1960s. Over the next decades, the company did in fact manage to build upon its historical fire insurance mapping services to create several different lines of business and survive as an operating entity. Unbeknownst to most investors, Sanborn Maps still existed in 2015 and operated up until 2011 as a subsidiary of the UK media conglomerate DMGT, when it was sold to its management in a management buyout. Today, some of its main services include geospatial data visualization, 3–D mapping, aerial photography, field data collection, software services related to storm water, forest inventory management, and assessment of insurance risks such as wildfire.[9] In fact, many of these services are directly related to Sanborn's historical business of mapping, data collection, and analysis.

2

1961: Dempster Mill
Manufacturing Company

Dempster Mill Manufacturing Company was founded in 1878 by Charles B. Dempster in Beatrice, Nebraska. After the Civil War, many people moved to the West to start new lives. Mr. Dempster believed that as these people settled down, they would have a need for windmills, water pumps, and other related machinery—and he wanted to be the person serving those needs.

At first, Dempster Mill was set up as a retail shop, and products were sourced through a distributor in Omaha, Nebraska. After 1885, Dempster began building its own production capabilities after Mr. Dempster decided that revenues would be even better if his company had its own brand and control over the quality of production. Between the late 1880s and the 1930s, Dempster Mill was one of several companies that pioneered the development of windmills and farm irrigation systems in the Great Plains, and many of their windmills (figure 2.2) became a part of the familiar farm landscape.[1]

Windmills in those days were the primary source of energy for operating water pumps, which brought up ground water for use in irrigation, feeding of livestock, and other essential water uses in operating a farm. In this sense, the windmills and their accompanying water system machinery were integral parts of land development at the time and an important

Figure 2.1.
Dempster Mill Manufacturing Co. pinback button from early 1900s. Photograph by
Ralph Bull.

investment for any settler. Dempster Mill was not the only company in this
industry, but it was one of a few successful ones that had a good reputation.
In addition to windmills, Dempster also built many related water systems,
such as pumps and irrigation machinery.

By the 1960s, windmills and their related accessories had declined
as a market. During and after the Great Depression, federal government
stimulus had helped extend the electricity grid to many parts of the rural

Figure 2.2.
Dempster Mill windmill. Photo used with permission from Daniel Teston, © 2013.

Midwest, which in turn led to electrical pumps replacing many functions of the windmill-driven water source. The main advantage of electrical pumps was that they could be turned on whenever water was needed, whereas with the windmill-driven pumps, a farmer had only the water provided in a reservoir, which was replenished by the windmills at an unpredictable rate. Hence, electrical pumps were more convenient.

In 1961, Dempster Mill Manufacturing was a business with $9 million in sales. It was in that year that Buffett first wrote about the company in his annual letter to Buffett Partnership Limited (BPL). In his 1961 letter, Buffett comments that the partnership had been building a stake in the company for the previous five years. While Dempster Mill had originally been acquired as a general value investment, it had become a control situation. By the end of 1961, BPL owned 70 percent of the company directly and another 10 percent indirectly through associates.

Before we discuss the financials, let us quickly sum up our understanding of the inherent business quality of Dempster Mill Manufacturing based on what we know. Although Dempster Mill operated in an industry that was not growing, this industry was not one that was going away immediately. First, as with all windmill companies, there were sales of new equipment as well as spare parts and servicing (aftersales). Any business that has aftersales is one with a long tail business; that is, there is a recurring revenue stream for a long period after the original equipment is sold. This revenue stream protects the business from a quick decline. By the 1960s Dempster Mill also had diversified into other industries. In addition to its original core business of selling windmills, it sold an assortment of agricultural equipment. This equipment included seed drills (machinery used for the planting of grains) as well as fertilizer applicators (machinery used to inject liquid fertilizers into soil). While this business must have been relatively small, it would have been a growing business in the 1960s.[2]

In 1961, Dempster Mill would have been mediocre but not terrible from a business quality perspective. Although its core windmill business, which had been an excellent business, was in decline, this decline was gradual because the business had services and spare parts revenue extending out for years after the original equipment was installed.[3] In addition, new products, some of which were in growing market segments, would also have given the company additional avenues to counteract the decline in its core business. Here it must be pointed out that although Dempster Mill had a strong brand name in the windmill business and few competitors, it did not enjoy such advantages in its new product categories. There were many competitors, some of whom were more well-known than Dempster Mill in the agricultural equipment space. Nevertheless, the evidence would have pointed to Dempster Mill as a business where good business execution would allow it to generate a return above its cost of capital.

Dempster Mill Manufacturing is one of the few investment cases where the Buffett Partnership Letters give us an extremely detailed account of the company's financials. Table 2.1 shows a summary of the balance sheet of Dempster Mill Manufacturing for year-ending 1961:

Table 2.1.
Consolidated balance sheet (1961)

Assets	Book figure	Valued @	Adjusted valuation	Liabilities	
Cash	$166	100%	$166	Notes payable	$1,230
Accts. rec. (net)	$1,040	85%	$884	Other liabilities	$1,088
Inventory	$4,203	60%	$2,522		
Ppd. exp., etc.	$82	25%	$21		
Current assets	$5,491		$3,593	Total liabilities	$2,318
Cash value life ins., etc.	$45	100 Est. net auction value	$45	Net work [sic] per books	$4,601
Net plant equipment	$1,383		$800	Net work [sic] as adjusted to quickly realizable values	$2,120
Total assets	$6,919		$4,438	Shares outstanding 60,146; adj. value per share	$35.25

Source: Warren Buffett to Buffett Partnership Limited, January 18, 1963, 6.
Note: 000s omitted.

Buffett lists the major items on the balance sheet. As table 2.1 shows, assets including cash, accounts receivables, inventory, prepaid expenses, PPE, and other items totaled $6.92 million. On the liabilities side, considering debt, accounts payables, and other liabilities, the book value was minus $2.32 million. Going by just the balance sheet, the total value of the business was $4.6 million, which represented $76.48 per share.

Buffett took an approach reminiscent of how Benjamin Graham must have looked at many investments that were based on asset values rather than earnings. Instead of going by book value, Buffett gives us an estimate of the fair value of the business by taking significant discounts in all assets where he felt that the book value may not be conservative enough: he applied a 15 percent discount to accounts receivable and a 40 percent discount to inventory. For liabilities, however, to be conservative, he assumed 100 percent of the book value. Using this approach, Buffett estimated that the fair value of the business to be about $35 per share.

Buffett does not give the specific figures on the income and earnings level of the business, but he does give us clues. He states: "The operations for the past decade have been characterized by static sales, low inventory turnover and virtually no profits in relation to invested capital."

This side comment on the business as one with "static sales" and "virtually no profits" is more significant than it first appears. What it means is that Dempster Mill was not a quickly deteriorating business, one that was losing cash. In fact, Dempster Mill still made a profit. As the box at the end of this chapter shows, this is consistent with the financial information from the 1960 *Moody's Industrial Manual*, which also showed that the business had positive earnings in 1958 and 1959. I will discuss why I find this significant in the next few paragraphs.

Buffett gives us the exact price he paid for Dempster Mill Manufacturing. In the 1962 year-end annual letter, he states that he began buying stock of the company several years prior at a price as low as $16 per share, and he had acquired the vast majority of his take in an off-market transaction for $30.25 in 1961. On average, the price he paid was $28 per share. At this valuation, Buffett had purchased the shares at a 63 percent discount to the book value per share and a 20 percent discount to his own conservatively calculated fair value. This is certainly a significant margin of safety.

While rare, it is not impossible to find companies that trade far below book value even today. The issue is that companies trading below book value are by no means guaranteed investments. Many times the companies that trade below book value are those that for one reason or another have net assets worth much less than what their book values may suggest.

In this particular investment case Buffett most likely saw two things very clearly. First, Dempster Mill, which could be dismissed at first glance as a dead business, was in fact not in the midst of suffering a quick collapse. The business had been stagnant and was not making much profit, but its decline was most likely gradual, and it was not bleeding cash. In fact, if anything, Dempster Mill was a business with a significant potential for operational improvements.

Moreover, the bulk of assets in this business were assets that could be sold and turned into cash. Specifically, the asset value assigned by Buffett was for the most part not in plant, property, and equipment, but rather in inventory and accounts receivables. Buffett must have known that the business would be able to realize this value within twelve to twenty-four months.

In this sense, Dempster Mill Manufacturing was in fact a classic net-net. If one adds up just its net current assets and subtract all liabilities, and then takes only two-thirds of this amount, the value would still exceed the stock price.[4] This is important because often companies that sell at great discounts to book value are companies where the book assets really have no way of being realized. An example of this would be a solar cell manufacturer who has a lot of production capacity on its books and whose replacement value could be very significant, but no one is likely to buy any of these assets because there is simply no demand for them.

In addition to purchasing a business at a great price with the reassurance that its fundamentals were not deteriorating quickly, Buffett employed a straightforward strategy. He saw an opportunity to improve operations in a company whose asset values could be realized through converting inventory to cash, and in turn, that cash could be used to invest. In order to do this, Buffett did not shy away from making this a control situation. With a 1961 year-end total asset under management of about $7.2 million, Dempster Mill represented a bit over 20 percent of the total assets of Buffett's partnerships based on his valuation of the business at $35 per share. Again, this was a big investment.

More should also be said about the management at Dempster Mill. When Buffett initially invested in the company, the management team was, simply put, not very capable. There were clear indications that the management had not pursued operational improvement opportunities that would have seemed fairly basic. One example was that the original managers had no differentiated pricing for replacement parts and the original equipment. A standard framework for a business with spare parts is to have higher prices for those replacement parts because they are sold to a captive audience who must choose those compatible components and are therefore less price-sensitive; this framework would allow better margins. Hence, when the subsequent management team introduced a differentiated pricing model, profits immediately increased with no loss on volumes.

Even though Buffett recognized the shortcomings of the original management team, he tried to work with them toward more effective use of capital and more efficient operations. However, after repeated failures, Buffett brought in his own management: a man named Harry Bottle. Buffett would

speak very positively about Bottle for the next few years in his annual letters. In his discussion of Bottle, Buffett seems to reflect how he assesses
management based on three main criteria:

(a) Key Performance Indicators ("KPIs"): Harry Bottle was incentivized
    through clear KPIs and managed the business based on key financial
    metrics. These included realizing a high percent of inventory into
    cash; reducing selling, general, and administrative costs by 50 percent;
    and shutting down unprofitable branches.
(b) Tackles "tough things first": Harry was a man who did not shy away
    from necessary action including the aforementioned disposal of un-
    profitable facilities. He also did not wait to dispose of or write off dead
    merchandise.
(c) Hardworking: Buffett described Harry Bottle as someone who was fo-
    cused on the tasks at hand; "I like dealing with someone who is not trying
    to figure how to get the fixtures in the executive washroom gold-plated."

The partnership letters of 1962 and 1963 reveal how Dempster's value
as calculated by Buffett's conservative discounting method rose from $35,
to $50, to $65. Table 2.2 shows the balance sheet as presented in the annual
letter for 1962.

Fundamental to this growth in value was Bottle's ability to realize
value from the assets at almost 100 percent of book value. A bit like in
a modern private equity setup, Bottle generated cash from the working
capital and used this to pay off most of the debt. Moreover, the cash
generated was subsequently used to build a portfolio of securities that
Buffett invested alongside his remaining investment portfolio. It seems
like Buffett drew on his experience with Sanborn Maps to value the ability to use cash to invest. By the time Buffett had the chance to exit this
position in late 1963 through a private transaction, the total value he was
able to realize on the investment was equal to about $80 per share: a
handsome profit.

Interestingly, in her biography on Buffett, Alice Schroeder reveals that
this experience was also one where Buffett learned that he very much disliked playing the role of the activist investor. Despite the superb gains in
this investment, the role he had to play in laying off personnel and selling off assets was one he did not want to repeat in the future.[5] It has been
said that this experience was the beginning of Buffett's preference for being
rather hands-off, both as a manager and as an investor.

Table 2.2.
Consolidated balance sheet (1962)

Assets	Book figure	Valued @	Adjusted valuation	Liabilities	
Cash	$60	100%	$60	Notes payable	$0
Marketable securities	$758	Mrkt. 12/31/62	$834	Other liabilities	$346
Accts. rec. (net)	$796	85%	$676	Total liabilities	$346
Inventory	$1,634	60%	$981		
Cash value life ins.	$41	100%	$41	Net worth: per books	$4,077
Recoverable income tax	$170	100%	$170		
Ppd. exp., etc.	$14	$25	$4	As adjusted to quickly realizable values add: proceeds from potential exercise of option to Harry Bottle	$3,125 $60
Current assets	$3,473		$2,766	Shares outstanding 60,146	
Misc. invest.	$5	100%	$5	Add: shs. potentially outstanding under option 2000; total shs. 62,146	
Net plant equipment	$945	Est. net auction value	$700	Adjusted value per share	$51.26
Total assets	$4,423		$3,471		

Source: Warren Buffett to Buffett Partnership Limited, January 18, 1963, 7.
Note: ooos omitted.

Exhibit 2.1

Dempster Mill Manufacturing Co.

History: Incorporated in Nebraska, June 15, 1886. Founded in 1878.
Florence Table & Mfg. Co. (Memphis, Tenn.), a former subsidiary, was liquidated in 1935.
In May, 1959, acquired Habco Mfg. Co.
Business: Company manufactures windmills, pumps, cylinders, water systems, centrifugal pumps, steel tanks, water supply equipment, fertilizer equipment, farm implements, etc.
Property: Factory occupies 8 acres of land in Beatrice, Neb. Branch houses located at Omaha, Neb.; Kansas City, Mo.; Sioux Falls, S.D.; Denver,

Colo.; Oklahoma City, Okla.; Des Moines, Ia.; and Amarillo and San Antonio, Tex.

Subsidiaries: Dempster Products Co., Habco Mfg. Co.

Officers: C. B. Dempster, Chmn. and Pres.; J. H. Thomsen, Exec. Vice-Pres. and Gen. Mgr.; E. R. Gaffney, R. E. Heikes, Vice-Pres.; C. A. Olson, Vice-Pres. and Treas.; A. M. Wells, Sec.

Directors: C. B. Dempster, J. H. Thomsen, E. R. Gaffney, R. E. Heikes, Hale McCown, G. S. Kilpatrick, C. R. Macy, R. C. Dempster, Beatrice, Nebr.; C. A. Olson, R. M. Green, Lincoln, Nebr.; W. E. Buffett.

Annual Meeting: First Monday in Feb.

No. of Stockholders: Nov. 30, 1959, 297.

No. of Employees: Nov. 30, 1959. 451.

Office: Beatrice, Neb.

Income Account, years ended Nov. 30:

Income account, years ended Nov. 30

	1959	1958
Net sales	$7,157,738	$6,108,556
Cost of sales*	5,453,331	4,776,200
Selling, etc., exp.	1,312,631	1,188,003
Operating profit	391,776	144,347
Other income	60,316	49,864
Total income	452,092	194,211
Other deductions	124,604	115,088
Income taxes	176,400	36,600
Special charges	5,063	16,724
Net profit	**146,025**	**25,799**
Prev. retain. earn.	3,108,013	2,600,258
Transf. fr. res.	—	500,000
Dividends	72,175	18,044
Ret. earn., 11–30**	3,181,863	3,108,013
Earn., com. share	$2.43	$0.43
No. of com. shares	60,146	60,146

*Incl. $95,068 (1958, $93,135) depr.
** $73,850 not restricted.

Secured Loan: Outstanding, Nov. 30, 1959, $350,000 6% notes due annually to Nov. 30, 1963; secured by first mortgage on plant at Beatrice, Neb., and by pledge of entire stock of Dempster Products Co. and notes for advances to subsidiary. Company may not pay dividends except from earnings after Nov. 30, 1958 or acquire stock, which would reduce retained earnings below $3,108,013.

Balance sheet as of Nov. 30

	1959	1958
Assets:		
Cash	$613,690	$399,809
U.S. govt. secur.	197,958	—
Receivables, net	562,421	657,639
Inventories*	2,595,181	2,336,960
Prepayments	69,447	70,809
Total current	$4,038,747	$3,465,217
Land, bldgs., etc.	2,643,494	2,607,944
Deprec. & amort.	1,551,897	1,458,226
Net property	1,091,597	1,149,718
Investments	243,075	35,076
Deferred fees	27,293	40,939
Goodwill, etc.	1	1
Total	$5,400,713	$4,690,951
Liabilities:		
Notes payable	50,000	—
Accounts payable	187,062	153,281
Accruals	248,414	201,758
Income taxes	174,283	18,808
Total current	$659,759	$373,847
Notes payable	350,000	—
Common stock	1,202,920	1,202,920
Capital surplus	6,171	6,171
Earned surplus	3,181,863	3,108,013
Total	$5,400,713	$4,690,951
Net current assets	$3,378,988	$3,091,370
Net tang. com. sh.	$73.00	$71.78

*At lower of estimated cost or replacement market.

Working capital must be maintained at not less than $2,750,000. At Nov. 30, 1959, $73,850 of retained earnings was not so restricted.

Capital Stock: 1, Dempster Mill Mfg. Co. common; par $20:

1920	$14.00	1921–1925	$6.00	1926–1930*	$7.00
1931	3.50	1932–1936	Nil	1937	6.25
1938–1942	5.00	1943	6.25	1944–1947*	6.00
1948–1949	7.50	1950	12.50	1951	11.00
1952–1955	6.00	1956	1.50		

*Also stock dividends: 1929, 5%; 1944, 20%.

AUTHORIZED—100,000 shares; outstanding, 60,146 shares; par $20 (changed from $100 to $20 par in Feb., 1956, five $20 shares issued for each $100 share).

VOTING RIGHTS—Has one vote per share.

DIVIDENDS—(payments since 1919 follow):

1956	0.90	1957	1.20
1958	0.30	1959	1.20

On $100 par shares:

	1959	1958	1957	1956*	1955
High	25 ½	18 ½	18 ½	23	115
Low	18 ½	14 ½	17	17	106

*$20 par shares; old $100 par, 110–110.

On $20 par shares:

Price Range—

Transfer Agent: Stock transferred and registered at company's office.

Source: *Moody's Manual of Industrial and Miscellaneous Securities* (1960), 217.

3

1964: Texas National Petroleum Company

I have included Texas National Petroleum Company as an investment to look at because it is one of the few cases of a *workout* that is explicitly discussed by Warren Buffett in his annual letters to shareholders. In effect, this was a merger arbitrage situation, which is of course still an area of focus for many investment funds that dabble in special situations investing.

In 1964, Texas National Petroleum Company was a relatively small producer of oil that was in the process of being acquired by Union Oil of California. To be more precise, Union Oil of California had already announced a formal offer with specific details of terms, but this had yet to be accepted by Texas National Petroleum. Hence the deal was announced but not completed.

As with any merger arbitrage deal, there are three factors that investors examining the company at the time would have taken into consideration. First, they would want to know the specific terms of the offer, for example, at what price, in which form, etc. Second, they would want to know the time-lines involved, such as the stage that the merger is at and how many months the deal is expected to take until it is completed. Third, investors would want to understand what the risks are of the deal falling apart. This collapse could be due to regulatory approvals needed, shareholder approvals from both the acquirer and the acquired, or other specific stipulations specified in the terms of the offer.

In a sense, merger arbitrage investment cases are very mathematical. If investors have all the aforementioned information in an accurate form, then they can simply calculate the expected annualized return for the investment and gauge whether it is sufficient to warrant the investment.

To set the historical context, mergers and acquisitions (M&A) in the oil and gas industry in the southern and midwestern United States were quite common during the 1960s when domestic oil production was still in full swing, so this deal would not have been completely unusual in its context.[1] Certainly, there would have been other similar deals where precedence could be drawn and confidence gained in such transactions. In fact, Union Oil of California was no stranger to acquiring companies, having acquired Wooley Petroleum in 1959, and going on to merge in 1965 with Pure Oil Company in one of the largest mergers within the oil industry at that time.[2]

Coming back to the case of Texas National Petroleum, there were three outstanding classes of securities at the time the acquisition was announced. Research had to be done on the company disclosures, but such information would have been relatively easy for an investor to find. Buffett also includes the details in his discussion of the investment in his annual letter to clients.

First, there were bonds outstanding that had a coupon payment at an annualized rate of 6.5 percent of the face value of the bond. These bonds could be redeemed by the company for a value of $104.25, which was the plan at the close of this acquisition. Also, in April 1963 when the deal was announced, this was a precoupon date, so an investor would have likely expected to receive a coupon payment during the time of the workout. In total $6.5 million of these bonds were outstanding. Second, there was common stock; 3.7 million shares were outstanding, and the estimated price they were to fetch in the deal was $7.42 per share. Forty percent of this was owned by inside investors, with the balance being held by outside investors. Third, there were 650,000 warrants outstanding, which gave holders the option to purchase the common stock at $3.50 per share. This means that at the estimated deal price of $7.42 for the common share, the warrants had an estimated value of $3.92 in the deal.

Unlike most merger deals today, no exact closing date of the merger was formally announced, as far as I was able to determine, so it is not known when the acquisition was to be completed. To get an approximate time of the estimated completion date, however, two sources of information seem sensible to check into. The first source is disclosures from the parties involved, i.e., information given by either Texas National Petroleum or Union Oil of California. The other source is inferring from other similar deals at the time. Regarding the former, the management of Texas National Petroleum did provide some information. In his letter to shareholders Buffett discusses a conversation with the management of Texas Petroleum in which Buffett Partnership Limited pushed for a completion of the deal by August or September of 1963. If the end of September was the projected time for the completion of the deal, this would have meant that Buffett considered making the investment five months after the April announcement.

Although investors would normally seek to understand a business's inherent quality, in this case, inherent quality would only be relevant if the deal fell through and investors became holders of the company on a stand-alone basis. A fundamental assessment of the business would sensibly have involved understanding the quality of the oil or ore assets. As this was clearly not the focal point of the investment case, it is sensible to go straight to the valuation of the deal. After the announcement, the prices for the three categories of securities would have been approximately as follows:[3]

(a) For the 6.5 percent bonds, the price was $98.78, slightly below the face value of $100.

(b) For the common stock, the price was $6.69 ($0.74 or about 11 percent under the offer price).[4]

(c) For the warrants, the price was $3.19, at a similar discount to the common stock.

If one assumes a five-month period until the deal closes and perhaps another month until payment is made, a six-month total for the investment period, then the estimated returns based on the offer price estimates would be:

(a) For the bonds, an investor would receive coupon payments that would be adjusted to an annualized return of 6.5 percent. If one assumes that the deal takes six months to complete, then the coupon payment would amount to $3.25 in total. In addition to this, an investor would expect a gain of $5.47 ($104.25–$98.78). Hence the total absolute return would be a gain of $8.72. As a percentage of the purchase price this would be about nine percent or 18 percent annualized. This looks fairly attractive, so if an investor is quite certain about the deal going through, that investor would likely buy the bonds.

(b and c) For the common equity and the warrants that convert into equity, the calculation is simple. If one expects to make about 11 percent, which is the spread between the offer price and the prevailing price, in six months one would expect a return of 22 percent annualized. This would be a very attractive return. If the deal closes faster than expected, one would earn an even better rate of return. This is also true if the offer price were raised. Conversely, if the deal took significantly longer to complete, the return would be poorer on an annualized basis.

Overall, the spread in the price of the offer and the current price certainly would have looked attractive. The only remaining issue to consider would have been the risk of the deal not materializing. To assess this risk, one might first consider the chance that shareholders, who had yet to pass the acquisition, would not approve the deal. As the management of Texas National Petroleum led this deal-making effort and itself owned 40 percent of the shares outstanding, one can quickly conclude that shareholder approval was fairly likely. In fact, as long as the deal price seemed even remotely fair, an investor could be quite certain that the deal would be approved as only another 10 percent of the remaining votes were necessary for approval. Buffett reached a similar conclusion on the risk of shareholder approval.

Furthermore, one can look at legal approvals and any antitrust issues that may be present. On these issues, it is not clear what the risk is, but the fact that many similar M&A deals were completed in the previous decade, where smaller oil exploration companies were consolidated by the larger ones, would suggest that this is a fairly straightforward case. Hence, while investors certainly would have checked with expert lawyers at the time, this did not appear to be a significant issue.

Regarding these concerns, Buffett did his research thoroughly; he gives us a full report on any potential legal risks as well as the progress of key legal developments.[5] Specifically, Buffett details that title searches and legal opinions on the deal had passed with few issues and that the only major hurdle was that a tax ruling was necessary related to the University of Southern California, which had nonprofit status and was the holder of some production payments at the time. While this was an additional hurdle that might have delayed some processes, Buffett judged it not to be a threat to the overall deal because USC had suggested that it was willing even to waive its eleemosynary status to help complete the deal.

In this case, the potential rewards were clear. It would have been difficult for an individual investor to accurately assess the risk of the deal the way that Buffett had. In fact, I would have turned to lawyers in the field and conducted primary research. For a small investment fund, this is doable as such funds generally have access to a network of specialists. The individual investor, however, would have to make an extra effort. In any case, if one could have been sure about the risks, as seemed to be the case for Buffett, one could have expected to profit handsomely from this special situation investment.

In Buffett's investment case, he ended up investing in all three classes of securities, amassing debentures with a total face value of $260K, 60,035 shares of common stock, and 83,200 warrants to purchase common stock. While the deal ended up taking a bit longer to complete than expected (payout for the bonds was in mid-November, with payouts for equities and warrants in installments in December and early the following year), the overall payoff was also slightly higher than originally calculated (about $7.59 per share rather than $7.42). In light of this, Buffett commented: "This illustrates the usual pattern: (1) the deals take longer than originally projected; and (2) the payouts tend to average a little better than estimates. With TNP it took a couple of extra months, and we received a couple of extra percent."

Buffett's overall annualized return was approximately 20 percent for the bonds and 22 percent for the stock and warrants.

To sum up, this was a case of a special situation investment, specifically a merger arbitrage opportunity. The spread would have suggested an absolute return in the high single digits for the bonds and approximately 10 percent for the equities. On an annualized basis, an investor would have expected approximately a 20 percent return on the investment. Nevertheless, the focus is on assessing the risk of the deal. While the aforementioned upside should be necessary to warrant an investment, it is the determination that the risks are low that allows an investor to have confidence in pursuing this investment. To minimize the risk, an investor either has an intrinsically good sense of the value of the assets and business underlying the deal or has confidence in very thorough primary research that should be done in all cases of merger arbitrage. Here, primary research could involve speaking to lawyers about the legal basis on which this deal may hinge, and it could also involve analyzing in detail previous merger cases that were similar. If one is willing to dig as deeply as Buffett dug in such a case, then the rewards should be there.

4

1964: American Express

In a way, American Express seems to be as high tech of a company as Warren Buffett gets. In the early 1960s, American Express represented the new. As the U.S. population discovered air travel, payment by travelers cheque became an increasingly common trend. At this time American Express was also pioneering the first plastic credit card. The main advantage of both forms of paperless payment was that they were authentic and did not require transacting by cash. Cash simply did not make sense when dealing in large sums of money or when traveling internationally. When merchants or suppliers received an American Express travelers cheque, they knew that the check was trustworthy. The other alternative for large sums of money or international payments at the time was a letter of credit, but this was significantly more cumbersome as it involved paperwork with a bank. In this way, American Express pioneered a superior product, but more on this later.

In 1963, American Express suffered a catastrophe in what came to be known as the Salad Oil Swindle. In November of that year it was discovered that one of its subsidiaries, a warehouse in Bayonne, New Jersey, had written receipts, based upon which loans were made to a company called Allied Crude Vegetable Oil Refining. This company, as it later turned out,

Figure 4.1.

was committing fraud. Allied went bankrupt, and the warehouse, when collecting the collateral, realized that the tanks that it had thought were filled with valuable salad oil were instead filled with seawater. With an estimated liability of up to $150 million, Allied and the American Express subsidiary filed for bankruptcy protection. Whether American Express, the parent company, was liable was uncertain. Nevertheless, fearing damage to American Express's reputation, CEO and President Howard Clark issued a statement that American Express felt morally bound to see that such liabilities were satisfied.[1]

The word on the street was that American Express could face insolvency. Its stock, which had been trading at $60 per share before the news, dropped to $35 per share by early 1964 amid much bad publicity.[2] One comment often made about American Express was that it faced "*unknown and potentially enormous liabilities.*" In addition to the bad publicity, American Express shareholders sued Howard Clark when he offered the creditors $60 million to settle claims, which the shareholders judged to be an unnecessary fulfillment of a moral obligation. In comparison to the book value of American Express at the time, which was $78 million, this seemed like a very large sum.

According to Lowenstein's account, Buffett, sensing potential opportunity beneath the scandal, carefully began his primary research. He spoke to customers and vendors in Omaha, including restaurants and restaurant customers, to see if their using habits had changed. He also went to banks and travel agencies, and he even spoke to competitors. Everywhere he went, the conclusion he drew was that the use of American Express travelers cheques and credit cards seemed to be steady despite the scandal. He surmised that American Express would continue operating as is, that reputational damage was not likely to be permanent, and that the brand seemed very strong and synonymous with the product. He also concluded that the company was unlikely to go insolvent.[3]

It is important to look at how an investor may have pictured American Express at the time. (See tables 4.1 through 4.3 for a reproduction of several key pages of the 1963 American Express annual report, including the consolidated financial statements.[4]) As we can see, in the section titled the *Ten Year Financial Summary,* on pages four and five of the report, American Express publishes a full ten-year history of its income financials. We notice immediately how strong a business American Express was in the decade preceding 1963.

From 1954 to 1963, American Express's revenues grew from $37 million to $100 million. Even more impressive, in no single year during this period did revenues decline from the previous year. The picture for income per share and total book value of the company mirrored that of the revenues; income per share grew from $1.05 to $2.52, and book value increased from $42 million to $79 million. Hence on a per annum (p.a.) compounded basis, revenues increased 12 percent p.a., and net earnings increased 10 percent p.a. in the previous nine years.

During the year ending December 31, 1963, American Express delivered net earnings of exactly $11.2 million ($2.52 per share for each of the 4.46 million shares outstanding) on revenues of $100.4 million. The profit before tax (it reported "income before United States and foreign income taxes") was at $16.0 million. With a simple calculation, this translates to an operating margin of about 16 percent and a net profit margin of about 11 percent, both metrics, suggesting nice profitability.

At first glance, based on just the financial numbers, American Express looked like it was running well on all cylinders and had been doing so for quite some time. To really understand a business, however, and to determine whether it is truly a quality business, one must look at more than just financials. To understand American Express's business and how it delivered such good financial results year after year, it is important to analyze the operating segments of the company and the competitive environment in which these sub-businesses were operating.

In its 1963 annual report, American Express discusses its operating segments in a fair level of detail. In total, the report details ten separate businesses. Unfortunately, American Express at the time did not break down the size and margins of each business areas. Still, from the order and depth of the discussion, one can clearly infer which businesses are the core businesses, and which the secondary businesses. From largest to smallest in scale, the businesses included travelers cheques, money orders, utility bills, travel, credit cards, commercial banking, foreign remittances, freight, Wells Fargo, Hertz, and warehousing.

Before I discuss the workings of the major businesses, it should be noted that with ten separate operating segments, American Express was not a simple business in the traditional sense of one business involved in one clear activity. Nevertheless, if we anlayze each business individually, we can be reassured that an inquisitive investor should understand both businesses because they are based on business models and people rather than complex technology.

The largest business, which is also discussed first in the report, was the travelers cheque business. American Express sold paper checks that customers who are to travel abroad could purchase at numerous locations before departure, and which would subsequently be accepted at both venues and banks abroad. These venues and banks would then exchange these checks for foreign currency. American Express collected cash and a small fee from customers, while in turn providing them with a network of international banks and venues where their finances would be accepted without question. To encourage more international merchants to accept this product, American Express paid a small commission to the merchants for accepting their travelers cheques.

At the time, the main alternative to American Express travelers cheques was a letter of credit from a bank. A customer, the same international traveler for example, would go to a bank and, using a combination of deposits, collateral, or previous relationship, would ask the bank to issue a letter of credit. The customer would then present this letter of credit to a foreign bank, which would either provide the customer with foreign currency or otherwise enable the customer to make payments while abroad.

The travelers cheque has several key advantages over the letter of credit. First, while travelers cheques were very simple to purchase at any American Express affiliate, the process of getting a letter of credit depended on the specific issuing bank and usually involved significant paperwork and took several days. Because it was less complex, American Express's solution usually also entailed fewer transaction costs. Compared to cash, travelers cheques could be easily replaced when stolen and hence offered an additional protection for travelers.

Table 4.1.
Ten-year financial summary (1954–1963)
($ in millions except per share data)

Summary of operations	1963	1962	1961	1960	1959	1958	1957	1956	1955	1954
Sales										
Income from operations	100.4	86.8	77.4	74.7	67.1	59.0	53.8	47.9	42.2	37.1
Profit on sales of securities	1.4	2.0	2.9	2.7	2.5	2.4	0.9	1.4	1.3	1.2
Operating expenses	85.9	76.8	69.1	65.9	60.0	52.9	46.6	42.0	37.3	33.1
Provision for U.S. and foreign income taxes	4.7	1.8	2.0	2.5	1.2	0.9	1.2	1.0	0.8	0.5
Net income	11.3	10.1	9.2	9.0	8.4	7.6	6.9	6.3	5.4	4.7
Net income per share	2.52	2.27	2.06	2.02	1.89	1.70	1.54	1.42	1.22	1.05
Dividends declared per share	1.40	1.25	1.20	1.20	1.05	1.00	0.95	0.83	0.64	0.60
Number of shareholders at year-end*	24,055	23,366	23,814	24,665	24,335	25,341	25,111	25,302	25,366	25,642
Cash and due from banks	266.6	187.3	169.2	155.6	124.6	124.7	141.1	149.0	131.2	125.6
Security investments	443.8	463.5	473.5	461.9	453.6	443.2	445.8	453.2	423.9	390.2
Loans and discounts	172.4	141.5	85.1	58.4	39.3	29.0	24.5	15.7	11.5	8.0
Total assets	1,020.2	915.2	876.5	787.8	732.7	680.1	667.6	700.1	629.3	621.0
Travelers cheques and letters of credit outstanding	470.1	421.1	386.4	365.5	358.7	337.5	320.3	304.4	282.8	259.6
Customers' deposits and credit balances	366.5	337.2	303.5	286.1	223.8	215.6	243.0	266.8	243.1	222.8
Shareholders' equity	78.7	68.4	63.8	60.1	56.4	53.0	49.9	47.2	44.3	41.7

Number of employees at year-end:										
Domestic	5,530	4,944	5,138	5,326	5,213	4,839	4,114	4,054	3,847	3,638
Overseas	5,424	5,333	5,107	4,927	4,770	4,609	4,698	4,657	4,580	4,397
Total	10,954**	10,277	10,245	10,253	9,983	9,448	8,812	8,711	8,427	8,035
Number of offices at year-end:										
Domestic offices	115	105	108	99	96	96	96	91	85	77
Overseas commercial offices	110	105	98	99	102	94	90	87	84	75
Overseas offices at military bases	177	179	173	181	186	183	213	208	203	197
Total	402	389	379	379	384	373	399	386	372	349
American Express correspondents	5,921	5,902	4,631	4,551	4,541	4,465	4,478	4,399	4,351	4,267
Other American Express selling outlets	75,738	70,471	69,338	67,614	67,736	66,280	64,271	66,436	64,457	63,294
American Express credit card service establishments	85,580	81,989	50,676	46,982	41,455	32,183	—	—	—	—

Source: American Express, *1963 Annual Report*, 4–5.
*All figures based on 4,461,058 $5 par value shares.
**Includes 601 employees of Wells Fargo.

Moreover, the benefits of travelers cheques were not just for its customers. According to American Express, issuing banks saw selling travelers cheques as a way to bring in new customers to cross-sell other products. In doing so, the banks took a small fee and lessened their burden of doing letter-of-credit work for smaller sums, which likely was a side business. For receiving banks, i.e., the banks that accepted a letter of credit or that cashed travelers cheques, there was also an important advantage of standardization. Because letters of credit were guaranteed by the issuing bank, the receiving bank had to individually assess the credit worthiness of the issuing institution. In contrast, American Express travelers cheques were always guaranteed by American Express, an institution that by this time had become well-known internationally. As a result, it was much easier to cash a travelers cheque than receive payment under the terms of a letter of credit.

While the advantages of travelers cheques were easy to understand, what quantitative evidence was there to support this? Looking specifically at American Express's ten-year financial summary in table 4.1, we can see that outstanding travelers cheques had increased to $470 million in 1963 from $260 million in 1954. Calculated on an annualized rate, outstanding travelers cheques had increased seven percent per annum over the previous ten years.

This information, along with the positive qualitative details given by American Express President and CEO, Howard Clark, in his annual report,[5] should have shown investors that the travelers cheque business was in the midst of a multi-year (in fact multi-decade) trend of replacing letters of credit for a significant part of that market. American Express, the market leader for travelers cheques, would be the main beneficiary of this development. In sum, then, American Express's travelers cheque business seemed like a wonderful business that was growing and had significant advantages over its peers.

The second business that is discussed in American Express's annual report is the money orders and utility bills business. The business had its roots in the 1880s, when to counter the U.S. Postal Service's introduction of money orders, American Express developed its own competing product. The purpose of the product was very simple: the safe delivery via courier or mail service of money. By 1963, the American Express money order was the largest selling commercial instrument of its kind in the United States. It was the only commercial money order to be sold in all fifty states.[6] Although by this time it was also a stagnant business, the business itself was on solid footing, providing a useful service for customers and functioning as a complement to travelers cheques.

The third business of American Express was its travel business. Selling steamship cruise tickets and organizing international travel excursions, the travel component of American Express was a business that had many local and international competitors, both large and small. As such, this seemed to be an execution business, with few barriers to entry. Here, results were mixed year by year, and success simply meant better execution than peers with moderate returns. The discussion of the 1963 annual report on this business indicates that 1963 marked a second year of reorganization in this business where establishing a more decentralized business model and a more prominent focus on better customer service would result in greater effectiveness.

The fourth business discussed, the credit card business, was an important driver of new growth by 1963, even though it was not yet a huge business at this time. Although first pioneered in the 1910s by Western Union and commercialized in its current form in the 1950s by Diners Club, American Express quickly became a leader in this segment with its strong network and brand. The first American Express credit card was launched jointly with Bank of America and the BankAmericard in 1958. Despite remarkable growth in customer uptake, operational troubles hampered this division's early profitability, but by 1963 this business had been profitable for two years.[7]

In its 1963 annual report, American Express reports total card membership increasing to over one million members for the first time.

As shown in figures 4.2 and 4.3, annual credit billings were growing even faster.

Based on a business model that charged both merchants (a percentage commission) as well as cardholders (an annual fee), the American Express credit card division had a sensible way to monetize its services. Moreover, given that the business model revolved around having a network of cardholders and merchants accepting the card, American Express had a natural advantage with the strong reputation of the American Express brand, especially in travel and international business. The BankAmericard, initially targeted at businessmen and wealthy individuals as a travel and entertainment card, quickly became a hit. In addition to providing its customers with the "cool factor" of having a reputable charge card, the BankAmericard facilitated easy payment for travelers and conferred numerous additional benefits such as travel insurance, which soon became a signature service

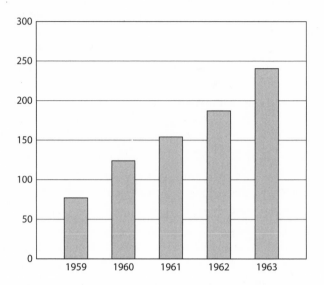

Figure 4.2.
Annual credit card billings. (American Express, *1963 Annual Report*, 13.)

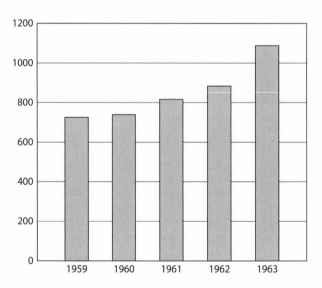

Figure 4.3.
Cardholders—year-end. *Source*: American Express, *1963 Annual Report*, 13.

for American Express cards. Merchants were willing to pay a commission for the opportunity to attract affluent customers who used the American Express credit card. Hence, there was clear customer value for both sides of the transaction.

If one considers this value and the absence of strong competitors, the value was likely significantly greater than what American Express was charging at the time, at least with respect to merchants. This would suggest some hidden pricing power. Because any competition would have to build a competing network as extensive as that of American Express to make it as valuable for cardholders and merchants, American Express had the clear advantage. All in all, investors would have seen very attractive prospects in this business in 1963.

Admittedly, it would have been difficult to foresee the development of MasterCard and Visa several decades later. The astute observer may have surmised that, unlike some of the safest products driven by network economics, in the case of the credit card, the cost for users was low enough that it did not preclude a user from having multiple cards.

The next five businesses for American Express were banking, foreign remittances, freight, Wells Fargo, and Hertz. I will discuss their key economics jointly as a group because they are smaller businesses that share some similarities.

Commercial banking as a business was not too different from a regular retail bank, taking deposits and making loans. The difference for American Express was that it had significant numbers of international branches, including branches on military bases. Foreign remittances provided commercial firms and individuals a safe and easy way of transferring funds across countries. The freight business was a freight forwarding and customs business similar to the freight forwarding businesses that operates currently in the United States. The next two businesses were Wells Fargo and Hertz. The former business was involved in transporting cash and valuables, much like today's armored transport businesses. The latter was a joint venture with the Hertz Corporation and a rental company for cars and trucks operating outside of the United States. American Express had a 49 percent stake in Hertz. Interestingly, both are familiar names today. In fact, Wells Fargo, the famous bank, was started by the founders of American Express, Henry Wells and William Fargo. Hertz, of course, remains one of the largest rental car companies in the world.

Still, looking at this group of five businesses, we must conclude that while obviously complementary to the main American Express businesses, they do not look like businesses where American Express would likely have had a particular competitive advantage over other established players of the time.

The last American Express business was its field warehousing business (the one hit by the salad oil scandal). The main activity of this unit was to provide authenticity receipts for inventory and other assets of customers so that these customers could use these assets for collateral in obtaining loans from banks and other financial institutions. The traditional business model for warehousing receipts involved public warehouses. In this business model a customer delivers its inventory into a public storage facility where it is held and monitored by a custodian. For products that require aging, such as tobacco and liquor, it is not unusual that they are financed and stored in public warehouses. However, in some cases it is not practical to transport inventory, such as when that inventory is bulky or difficult to transport. In such a scenario, a field warehouse may be established on the customer's or the borrower's grounds. In this field warehousing business that American Express was involved in, the field warehousing company would have had inspectors who established a control and supervision of inventory at the warehouse owned by the customer or borrower.

In the case of the Allied Crude Vegetable Oil Company, American Express had a touring inspector who monitored the inventory at Allied's Bayone, New Jersey storage tanks. American Express had hired some of Allied's own men as custodians. In this instance, the American Express's touring inspector did not take full physical inventory.

I will discuss the specific scandal and the nature and extent of issues later, but in terms of the overall business, the field warehousing business seems to have been a fairly simple, capital-light business where a company with a great reputation, such as American Express, would likely have an advantage over peers. The key risks here would involve the detailed legal terms of any contractual commitments that were made by American Express, specifically whether or not it would guarantee all collateral for which it had issued receipts.

Overall, American Express seemed like a great business with significant structural advantages in its core businesses. While some of the smaller business divisions like travel, Wells Fargo, and freight seem to have few fundamental advantages over peers, the most significant businesses, including the travelers cheque and the credit card businesses, were wonderful franchise-quality businesses that boasted long-term, sustainable growth.

To support this conclusion, we will take one more look at the income statement and balance sheets reported by American Express, shown in tables 4.2 and 4.3. The data in these tables suggest two additional insights that support this assessment.

Table 4.2.
Consolidated income statement (1963)

	1963	1962
Income:		
Income from operations	$100,418,244	$86,771,484
Profit on sales of securities	$1,435,903	$2,028,125
Total	$101,854,147	$88,799,609
Expenses and taxes:		
Salaries and wages	$41,308,088	$36,289,997
Cost of financial paper and other printing and stationery	$4,854,346	$4,168,274
Postage, telephone, telegraph, and cable	$3,605,062	$3,333,282
Travel, express, and other transportation costs	$2,995,345	$2,492,998
Property and equipment expenses	$7,602,788	$6,939,640
Advertising and literature	$5,700,052	$4,595,985
Other expenses	$14,920,469	$14,828,141
Taxes other than United States and foreign income taxes	$4,889,298	$4,200,086
Total	$85,875,448	$76,848,403
Income before United States and foreign income taxes	$15,978,699	$11,951,206
Provision for United States and foreign income taxes	$4,714,858	$1,820,263
Net income	$11,263,841	$10,130,943
Surplus at beginning of year	$46,051,152	$41,499,546
Surplus credits:		
Profit from special sales of securities—net of applicable taxes	$4,376,996	—
Excess of net assets over related investment at January 1, 1963 arising from consolidation of Wells Fargo & Company	$892,784	—
Total	$62,584,773	$51,630,489
Surplus charges:		
Dividends	$6,194,506	$5,537,114
Other charges—net	—	$42,223
Total	$6,194,506	$5,579,337
Surplus at end of year	$56,390,267	$46,051,152

Source: American Express, *1963 Annual Report*, 26.

Table 4.3.
Consolidated balance sheet (1963)

	1963	1962
Assets		
Cash and due from banks	$266,637,122	$187,306,540
Security investments—at cost		
U.S. government obligations	$141,208,249	$102,201,433
State and municipal obligations	$229,784,429	$225,241,401
Other bonds and obligations	$39,614,783	$92,676,747
Preferred stocks	$18,968,863	$19,451,610
Common stocks	$14,198,704	$23,908,432
Total security investments (current market valuation: 1963, $450,500,000; 1962, $479,010,000)	$443,775,028	$463,479,623
U.S. government depositary bonds	$35,000,000	$35,000,000
Loans and discounts	$172,410,264	$141,505,217
Accounts receivable and accrued interest (less reserves: 1963, $2,741,819; 1962, $1,714,232)	$51,660,293	$42,832,134
American Express company capital stock reacquired—at cost (1963, 33,340 shares; 1962, 37,700 shares)	$1,436,565	$1,627,535
Investments in subsidiary and affiliated companies not consolidated—at cost (equity in net assets: 1963, $4,096,000; 1962, $5,654,000)	$3,580,002	$4,791,987
Land, buildings, and equipment—at cost (less reserves: 1963, $11,927,151; 1962, $10,461,370)	$14,347,038	$12,669,124
Customers' acceptance liability	$18,873,203	$15,225,152
Other assets	$12,486,135	$10,741,415
Total	$1,020,205,650	$915,178,727
Liabilities		
Travelers cheques and travelers letters of credit	$470,126,789	$421,063,300
Customers' deposits and credit balances with the American Express Company, Incorporated	$366,490,835	$337,237,710
Deposit liability relating to U.S. government depositary bonds	$35,000,000	$35,000,000
Acceptances outstanding	$18,903,238	$15,690,404
Other liabilities	50,989,231	$37,830,871
Total	$941,510,093	$846,822,285
Shareholders' equity:		
Capital stock—authorized, 5,000,000 shares of $5 par value; issued 4,461,058 shares	$22,305,290	$22,305,290
Surplus	$56,390,267	$46,051,152
Total shareholders' equity	$78,695,557	$68,356,442
Total	$1,020,205,650	$915,178,727

Source: American Express, *1963 Annual Report*, 28–29.

In summary, we see several significant data points on the American Express balance sheet at the end of 1963. On the asset side, there are $267 million in cash and $444 million in investment securities (the vast majority of this sum was in U.S. government and state and municipal bonds), $35 million in U.S. government bonds (presumably held in custody for clients as there is a matching contra account in liabilities), $172 million in loans, $52 million in accounts receivables, and $14 million for PPE (reported as "Land, buildings and equipment—reported at cost"). Together, assets totaled $1.02 billion. On the liabilities side, there are outstanding travelers cheques of $470 million, customer deposits of $366 million, the contra liability for U.S. government bonds of $35 million matching that on the asset side, and several other smaller liabilities. Liabilities totaled $942 million. The resulting total shareholders' equity was $78 million.

First, one insight that can be derived from the balance sheet is that, in a way, American Express was very similar to a bank or an insurance company. With a business that inherently generates assets in the form of cash and investable securities as well as liabilities in the form of outstanding travelers cheques, American Express was creating a situation similar to the float of insurance companies (even when not considering the banking operations that it owned). This is reflected in the fact that, in 1963, American Express carried a total balance sheet more than ten times greater than its shareholders' equity. In fact, when the customer deposits and outstanding travelers cheques are tallied, American Express is effectively holding $837 million in value, which belongs to its customers. Like banks and insurance companies, it gains income from investing these assets into bonds, stocks, and loans.

Second, looking at the return on capital employed by the business, we see that American Express as a whole is very light on physical capital. When using the usual preferred metric of return on capital employed by dividing owner earnings[8] by capital employed[9] we can make a rough calculation. With only $14 million in land, buildings, and equipment, and a net working capital base that is effectively negative if one considers the float characteristics of having customer deposits and outstanding travelers cheques, the return on capital employed (ROCE) would be about 78 percent if we assume a net working capital of zero. If one fully considers the negative working capital, the total capital employed would be negative and the ROCE infinite. Net earnings for the year were $11.2 million. Note that net earnings is used in the calculation rather than the preferred metric of owner earnings because, without cash-flow statements at this time, owner earnings could not be meaningfully calculated. In any case, a 78 percent (or even higher) ROCE for normal businesses would be indicative of a very significant franchise value, which enables the business to generate returns far in excess of its cost of capital. It also means that the business has to reinvest very little additional capital to grow the business, which is beneficial because that cash can be used to pay shareholders or for acquisitions.

Howard Clark's letter to shareholders appears to support this view. In this letter, Clark explains that "in the four years ending December 31, 1963, with virtually no increase in the number of employees consolidated operating revenues have increased by almost 50%, pre-tax income from operations over 100%, and post-tax earnings from operations about 60%."

The astute investor may take issue with the use of the normal ROCE as a measure for performance of the business given the significant financial leverage inherent in the business. This concern is justified. If we look at financial performance based on return on equity (ROE), the more typical metric for financial firms, we arrive at a ROE of over 14 percent, which, while less impressive, is still significantly higher than the cost of capital and would also indicate a superior business.

Before I move on to the valuation of American Express, one other item that should be discussed—in any investment case—is the management. Here, what was known of Howard Clark, CEO and president of American Express, was that he joined American Express in 1960, three years prior to the time in question. Operationally, the two major efforts he had undertaken at American Express were fixing the credit card business and driving marketing efforts.

When Clark joined American Express the credit card division was losing money mainly because it had been overwhelmed in the back-office transaction processing of payments generated by the credit cards, which were quickly growing in number. Clark instituted immediate measures to lighten the burden on American Express, including introducing a requirement for cardholders to repay all debt within thirty days, establishing stricter guidelines for credit approval, and increasing fees for merchants and cardholders. On the marketing side, Clark increased the advertising budget annually, and he hired advertising agency Ogilvy, Benson, & Mather to develop American Express's first modern advertising campaign. Overall, Clark seemed a competent and decisive force when it came to fixing American Express's operational issues.[10]

In addition to addressing operational issues, Clark also promised to address the salad oil scandal, even though liability of the American Express parent company had not been established. In this sense, Clark appears to have been an individual of utmost personal integrity, a fact that Buffett surely respected.

Now that we have a fair idea of the business of American Express and who was running it, we turn to the purchase valuation that Buffett paid. Although Buffett does not give explicit details about his American Express purchase in his year-end 1964 partnership letter, American Express dropped to a price of around $35 per share during the time Buffett was making the purchase. If we then assume that Buffett bought his shares at an average price of $40 per share, as his purchase was significant and unlikely to have been made at a rock-bottom price, his purchase price would have looked like the following (at least at first glance). With 4.46 million shares outstanding, he would have valued American Express at a price-earnings multiple of 16× based on fiscal year 1963 net earnings of $11 million. On a trailing year EV/EBIT basis, Buffett would have paid a multiple of 8×, if we consider the cash and financial investments of American Express as well as its financial liabilities in its net financial debt calculation. Although one could argue against the true value of the investment assets, I believe that the aforementioned calculation is a conservative estimate because the investment assets were recorded at cost. If one is even more conservative and considers the net cash value of the company to be zero, the resulting EV/EBIT multiple would be 11×.

By Buffett's standards, this is not a cheap price by any means, even though the business had sold for what would have been a 24× price-to-earnings ratio (P/E) before the turmoil. This is somewhat perplexing. While acknowledging the superior quality of American Express, this is still a valuation that seems just a bit too high based on Buffett's usual criteria, and even more so because the liability that the company faced due to the Salad Oil Scandal was still unknown. The valuation remains key to understanding the purchase. Either Buffett was indeed willing to pay a high price for an outstanding business, or the valuation was not as high as it appears.

First, we must understand the liability of the scandal. The most detailed account of this liability comes from the management of American Express, who spends two pages of the 1963 annual report discussing this issue. Assuming one can believe management (who genuinely seems open about issues and trustworthy), the liability appears somewhat tenuous and capped at a bit under $100 million, significantly lower than the market estimates of $150 million. In the report, the company states that the amount of soy-bean oil for which American Express had written verification receipts totaled $82 million (this does not consider the worth of the high-quality seawater in the containers, which in fact also had some market value). In addition to this, another $15 million in delivery orders was being disputed. One-third of the $39 million of receipts for additional sunflower oil were found to be forged, so it appeared likely that American Express would not have any liability for this amount. While it is impossible to determine the extent of the final liabilities, based on the information it appears to have been between $20 and $80 million, with the high end reflective of manage-ment taking the moral high road and offering to pay for almost all liabilities that could be interpreted as American Express's mistake (this was man-agement's plan, as stated in the annual report). To put a rough figure on this, the real expected liability would be $60 million minus a potential tax shelter of $20 million (simply based on reduced earnings at a 34 percent corporate tax rate), or a net cash liability of $40 million.

If we look at the balance sheet, the intrinsic business of American Express generated so much gross cash that the company would certainly have had the cash to cover the liability (at the time, American Express had increased cash to over $250 million). It seems that the only way that they would have been unable to pay for this liabilities is if their customers stopped using their services. In this sense, it appears that Howard Clark's focus on maintaining the integrity of the company's reputation, even if it meant paying some unnecessary liabilitie, was justified. In terms of the impact on valuation, however, a $40 million cost would mean that for a $40 per share price investors would be purchasing the business for an even higher multiple, roughly 20× P/E and 11× EV/EBIT.

These are prices that Buffett almost certainly would not pay. So where is the missing link? After some further consideration, it seems that the operating earnings of American Express only tell part of the story. One key similarity American Express appeared to share with insurance companies was that the investment earnings arising from the float do not show up in the operating earnings. In fact, the float arising from travelers cheques seems to be one where American Express did not have to explicitly pay interest. In any case, if we look carefully at the comprehensive earnings in 1963,[11] it is clear that in addition to the $11 million in operating net earnings, American Express also earned a further $4.4 million after tax in additional realized investment gains, which are credited directly to share sharehold-ers' equity. This in fact had caused shareholders' equity to increase by about

$10 million, even though dividend payments in that year had totaled $6.4 million. This sum is in addition to approximately $1.0 million of returns on investments, which are reported within the $11 million total operating net income.

While $4.4 million in 1963 may be an unrepresentative extraordinary gain, directionally there should at least be more of this type of investment returns resulting from the float. If we assume that on average travelers cheques are outstanding for two months, and then take the 1963 year-end sum of outstanding travelers cheques of $470 million, one would expect a running float from travelers cheques of about $80 million. If one assumes a five percent return on assets, one would expect about $4 million to be generated from this float per annum. While this is a purely hypothetical example, and the portion of float that comes from the travelers cheque business, the credit card business (negative float), and the bank cannot be determined exactly, I suspect that, on the whole, the true intrinsic earnings power of the travelers cheque float was significant and additional to operating earnings.

If we were to take the $4.4 million after-tax additional income in 1963 as an example, an adjusted earnings, including both investment and operating earnings, would value American Express stock of $40 per share at a P/E multiple of 11.5× and an EV/EBIT of 6.5×. Adjusted for the scandal liability of $40 million, there is an adjusted P/E figure of 14.2× and an EV/EBIT of 8.5×. This seems much more reasonable in terms of valuation, and something that does make sense given the very good quality of the business.

In addition to the float, another argument that could be made was that the American Express credit card business, which fundamentally was a good quality business, was just recovering from operational issues. As previously mentioned, 1963 was only the second year of its profitability. Thus, one could assert that 1963 earnings were still understated given the hidden earnings power in the credit card business, which was surely just starting to be realized.

In the end, American Express was not a cheap purchase. It seems that Buffett focused on finding a truly great business with a structural competitive advantage and investing at a price that can be considered reasonable given the total picture. To get to this point, Buffett seemed to have benefited from his understanding of float as well as his understanding of how the structural advantages that American Express had in its core businesses would allow it to grow with high returns with limited additional capital. Buffett also conducted primary research that helped him assess if the scandal affected the core of the business. Here we should point out that the scandal involved an extraordinary liability in a small subsidiary of American Express that did not itself affect the core operations of the business.

Unlike Buffett's other early purchases, this was a cigar-butt[12] type of investment. Perhaps it was the subsequent success of this investment that helped inculcate Buffett's later preference for paying fair value for a really good business over paying a really good price for an average one.

5

1965: Berkshire Hathaway

By now, nearly everyone knows the name Berkshire Hathaway. But far fewer know about this company's early history or the state the company was in when Warren Buffett began the process of purchasing it in 1962.

The origins of Berkshire Hathaway were two New England textile manufacturing businesses dating back to the 1800s. Berkshire, formerly known as Berkshire Cotton Manufacturing Company, once spun as much as a quarter of the nation's fine cotton. Hathaway Manufacturing, named after its founder Horatio Hathaway, was also involved with numerous textile products before specializing in parachute material manufacturing during World War II. Subsequently, Hathaway became the largest maker of rayon suits. In 1955, the two companies merged, creating the combined entity Berkshire Hathaway.[1]

While Berkshire Hathaway was profitable during the postwar period, by the 1960s it was a shell of its former self. As Buffett comments in his annual letter to shareholders dated January 20, 1966 (the 1965 year-end annual letter), from an earnings figure before tax of $29.5 million in 1948, twelve mills, and 11,000 employees, the Berkshire Hathaway business had shrunk to marginal earnings, two mills, and 2,300 employees by 1965. Buffett attributed this to both the changing environment of the industry and a weak management that was unable to adapt to this change. Given these figures, an investor could

BERKSHIRE HATHAWAY INC.

Figure 5.1.

surmise that this business was in a structural decline. The apparent reason was that cheaper imports of fabrics were coming in from abroad.

Nevertheless, as far as the inherent quality of the business, I have to say that this case is not quite as obvious as most people think nowadays. With the benefit of hindsight, it is very easy to dismiss the failure of Buffett to recognize or adequately account for the structural decline of Berkshire Hathaway. This is made easier by the fact that Buffett admitted in interviews that the purchase of Berkshire Hathaway was a mistake. But at the time, the picture would have been less clear. First, Berkshire Hathaway's fabrics were sold to other clothing manufacturers as well as directly in retail channels in the form of curtains and other home furnishings. The latter, of course, were branded products.

As such, there certainly was the counterargument that Berkshire Hathaway was a premium segment product compared to the imports, and that while this might be a segment that was shrinking, there would still be a place for it. Moreover, as with any retail-related business, Berkshire Hathaway clearly was a business that could be influenced both positively and negatively by management decisions. One can see from Buffett's letter that although this business was poorly managed for many years prior to 1965, it had recently put in place new management led by Ken Chace, whom Buffett deemed an excellent manager. It is not difficult to imagine that several factors indicated a rebound in the Berkshire Hathaway business.

In fact, as we can see in table 5.1, the five-year financial summary published by Berkshire Hathaway[2] between 1962 and 1965, when Buffett made the bulk of his purchase into the company, the top line of the business would have appeared fairly stable—up one year and down another, rather than straight down. Keep in mind that by 1965 Buffett had already influenced a management change and put Ken Chace into the executive role, and Chace had already began to release value in a way reminiscent of Harry Boyle at Dempster Mill.

In any case, to summarize the business quality of Berkshire Hathaway from the viewpoint of an investor in 1965, it was clearly a business I would qualify as an "execution" business—one where execution is critical and one that does not have any inherent structural advantages over competitors.

Table 5.1.
Five-year financial summary (1961–1965)

Fiscal years →	1965	1964	1963	1962	1961
Sales	$49,300,685	$49,982,830	$40,590,679	$53,259,302	$47,722,281
Net earnings (loss) before charge (credit) equivalent to federal income taxes	$4,319,206	$175,586	($684,811)	($2,151,256)	($393,054)
Charge (credit) equivalent to federal income taxes	$2,040,000	$50,000	($280,000)	($1,140,000)	($240,000)
Net earnings (loss)	$2,279,206	$125,586	($404,811)	($1,011,256)	($153,054)
Net earnings (loss) per share of common stock outstanding	$2.24	$0.11	($0.25)	($0.63)	($0.09)
Cash dividends paid	—	—	—	$160,738	$1,205,535
Cash dividends paid per share	—	—	—	$0.10	$0.75
Additions to properties, plants, and equipment	$811,812	$288,608	$665,813	$3,454,069	$4,020,542
Working capital	$17,869,526	$14,502,068	$17,410,503	$16,473,783	$19,844,122
Working capital per share	$17.56	$12.75	$10.83	$10.25	$12.35
Stockholders' equity	$24,520,114	$22,138,753	$30,278,890	$32,463,701	$36,175,695
Stockholders' equity per share	$24.10	$19.46	$18.84	$20.20	$22.51
Common shares outstanding	$1,017,547	$1,137,778	$1,607,380	$1,607,380	$1,607,380

Source: Berkshire Hathaway, *1965 Annual Report*, 11.

Note: Net earnings (loss) and earnings (loss) per share of common stock for fiscal years ending 1961 through 1964 have been restated to give effect to a charge (credit) equivalent to federal income taxes. "Common shares outstanding" represents the total shares outstanding at the close of each fiscal year.

Still, it seemed to be a case where outstanding management may have worked something out. To a very astute investor, it would have been a very difficult case and likely much more positive than if one had just looked at the Berkshire business superficially in 1963 or 1964. However, the long-term risk of the business was there: revenues were in decline prior to 1960. A key question would have been to what degree the declines had been structurally driven rather than caused by poor management.

The second pillar of Buffett's investment was clearly the valuation of the business. Buffett had purchased the stock of Berkshire Hathaway between 1962 and 1965 and for a price between $7.60 and $15 per share (the average price was $14.86).[3] Regarding valuation, we must consider how an investor at the time might have valued the business. The income statement and the balance sheet from the Berkshire Hathaway October 2, 1965 year-end annual report are included in tables 5.2 and 5.3.[4] The Berkshire Hathaway

Table 5.2.
Consolidated statement of earnings and retained earnings (1964–1965)

Consolidated statement of earnings	1965	1964
Net sales	$49,300,685	$49,982,830
Cost of sales	$42,478,984	$47,382,337
Gross profit	$6,821,701	$2,600,493
Selling, general, and administrative expenses	$2,135,038	$2,072,822
Operating income	$4,686,663	$527,671
Other deductions, net	$127,348	$126,060
Idle plant expense	$240,109	$226,025
	$367,457	$352,085
Earnings before charge equivalent to federal income taxes	$4,319,206	$175,586
Charge equivalent to federal income taxes	$2,040,000	$50,000
Net earnings	$2,279,206	$125,586
Depreciation and amortization	$862,424	$1,101,147
Consolidated statement of retained earnings		
Balance at beginning of year	$19,417,576	$22,241,990
Net earnings for the year	$2,279,206	$125,586
Credit resulting from charge equivalent to federal income taxes	$2,040,000	$50,000
Retirement of treasury stock	($2,967,714)	—
Estimated loss on properties to be sold	($300,000)	(3,000,000)
Balance at end of year	($20,469,068)	($19,417,576)

Source: Berkshire Hathaway, *1965 Annual Report*, 8.

Table 5.3.
Consolidated balance sheet (1964–1965)

Assets	1965	1964
Current assets:		
Cash	$775,504	$920,089
Marketable securities (including $2,600,000 of short term certificates of deposit), at cost, approximate market	$2,900,000	—
Accounts receivable	$7,422,726	$7,450,564
(less allowance for doubtful accounts—1965—$280,302)		
Inventories	$10,277,178	$11,689,145
Prepaid insurance, taxes, and other expenses	$196,391	$190,563
Total current assets	$21,571,799	$20,250,361
Properties, plants, and equipment:		
Properties comprising land, buildings, machinery and equipment	$28,019,742	$33,635,553
Less accumulated depreciation and amortization	$19,593,163	$21,853,689
	$8,426,579	$11,781,864
Less estimated loss on properties to be sold	$1,809,132	$4,210,621
	$6,617,447	$7,571,243
Mortgage notes receivable and other assets	$33,141	$65,412
Total assets	$28,222,387	$27,887,046

Liabilities and stockholders' equity	1965	1964
Current liabilities:		
Notes payable—banks	—	$2,500,000
Accounts payable	$2,581,585	$2,096,726
Accrued wages and salaries	$296,256	$294,764
Accrued state and local taxes	$441,951	$365,112
Social security and withholding taxes payable	$382,481	$491,691
Total current liabilities	$3,702,273	$5,748,293
Stockholders' equity:		
Common stock ($5 par value) authorized 1,843,214 shares—issued 1,137,778 shares	$5,688,890	$8,036,900
Retained earnings	$20,469,068	$19,417,576
	$26,157,958	$27,454,476
Less common stock in treasury at cost—120,231 shares	$1,637,844	$5,315,723
	$24,520,114	$22,138,753
Total liabilities and stockholders' equity	$28,222,387	$27,887,046

Source: Berkshire Hathaway, 1965 Annual Report, 6–7.

2014 annual report included a reprint of the 1964 annual report; the interested reader might refer to this document.

Earnings Valuation

Assuming the stock price is at $14.06 per share, the average price at which Buffett accumulated his stake, the backward-looking EV/EBIT and price-to-earnings ratio (P/E) multiples would have appeared as the data shown in tables 5.4 and 5.5.[5]

We can see that, Berkshire Hathaway is a clear case where earnings instability at the operating level makes a fair assessment of multiples difficult. In fact, in the years immediately preceding 1964, Berkshire had made a negative EBIT. Still, an investor who had read the annual report in 1965 carefully, as Buffett surely did, would have realized that beneficial structural changes were occurring. As Ken Chace discusses in the section of the annual report titled "Review of Operations," in 1965 the United States Congress passed legislation that "provides for the extension of one-price cotton through July 31, 1970, which enable American textile mills to continue to purchase American cotton at the same Government established price at which it is sold to foreign countries." This was an extension of legislation first passed in 1964, which allowed U.S. mills to enjoy lower cotton costs at prices established by the government, and helped lower the cost of goods sold (COGS). If one puts together the effect of dramatically lower COGS, which is shown in the income statement in 1965, with the fact that the extension would guarantee some sort of fair pricing for cotton for the next five years, we can understand that this is very positive for Berkshire indeed. In light of this, if we assume a margin closer to that of 1965 and less of what appeared in 1964 and in prior years, the 2.4× *EV/EBIT* based on 1965 EBIT looks very low. Even if sustainable margins were only 7.5 percent rather than the 9.5 percent achieved in 1965, there would be an EV/EBIT multiple of 3.0× based on stagnant top line.

Table 5.4.
EV/EBIT multiples

EV/EBIT	1964 actual	1965 actual
Revenues	$50.0m	$49.3m
EBIT	$0.53m	$4.68m
EBIT margin	*1.1%*	*9.5%*
EV/EBIT	**21.3×**	**2.4×**

Table 5.5.
PER multiples

PER	1964 actual	1965 actual
EPS (as reported)	$0.11	$2.24
PER (as reported)	**134×**	**6.6×**
EPS (adjusted)	$0.15	$4.24
PER (adjusted)	**98×**	**3.5×**

In 1965, Ken Chace reported a net income and earnings per share (EPS) accounting for a tax rate of 47 percent. He did this to "prevent any misleading interpretation of future earnings when loss carryovers shall not be available." These taxes were not real costs during 1965 and 1964, and in fact, as Berkshire still had loss carryovers of about $5 million at the end of 1965, they would not be real costs for at least another year or two. As such, I have included as reported and adjusted figures for the PER in table 5.5, with adjusted being the PER based on the actual real net income for Berkshire during the year.

In PER terms there is a similar situation as with EV/EBIT—very volatile earnings. Based on the same logic as before, the PER based on 1965 figures looks fairly cheap, although less so than the EV/EBIT, as Berkshire had a net cash position of $3.7 million ($3.62 per share).

The other important point is that based on real earnings, which I will discuss in the next section on asset valuation, the cash generation of the business is significantly better than indicated by reported net earnings.

Asset Valuation

Net financial debt/cash items and net working capital items are summarized in Tables 5.6 and 5.7.

Table 5.6.
Net financial debt/cash items

	1964 actual	1965 actual	Change in $
Cash	$0.92m	$0.78m	−$0.14m
Marketable securities	$0	$2.90m	+$2.90m
Total financial debt	$2.50m	$0	−$2.50m
Net cash position	**−$1.58m**	**$3.68m**	**+$5.26m**
Per share	−$1.39	$3.62	+$5.01

Table 5.7.
Net working capital items

	1964 actual	1965 actual	Change in $
Accounts receivables	$7.45m	$7.42m	−$0.03m
Inventory	$11.69m	$10.28m	−$1.41m
Accounts payables	−$2.10m	−$2.58m	−$0.48m
Total NWC	**$17.04m**	**$15.12m**	**−$1.92m**

As we can see, even before the share price is compared to book value per share, in 1965 Berkshire Hathaway had a positive cash flow of over $5 million. With this cash, it paid off $2.5 million in debt and built a portfolio of marketable securities of $2.9 million. A portion of this cash generation came from the net working capital, which Ken Chance clearly improved, but a large part came from the cash earnings, which as mentioned was much greater than reported earnings because the "tax" cost was not a real cost.

But what is really astounding here is that a business whose entire market capitalization was approximately $11.3 million generated a positive cash amount of $5.3 million in one year. It means that if Berkshire had two more years like this, even when not fully considering the net cash already present, an investor would get the entire business for free. This realization makes this opportunity look far more appealing than if one only examined the business fundamentals or earnings.

Taking the share price of $14.69 we, one can see that based on the balance sheet dated October 2, 1965, Berkshire Hathaway was also trading at a significant discount to its book value. In fact, it was trading at an over 20 percent discount to the value of just its net working capital plus the net cash it had in the form of cash and marketable securities.

Table 5.8.
Book value items

	1964 actual	1965 actual	Change in $
NFD/NFC	−$1.58m	$3.68m	+$5.26m
NWC	$17.04m	$15.12m	−$1.92m
PPE incl. mortgage notes	$7.64m	$6.65m	−$0.99m
Other current assets	$0.19m	$0.20m	+$0.01m
Other liabilities	−$1.15m	−$1.12m	+$0.03m
Total shareholders' equity	**$22.14m**	**$24.53m**	**+$2.39m**
Per share	**$19.46**	**$24.11**	**$4.45**

Table 5.9.
P/B and P/(NWC + net cash)

	1964 actual	1965 actual
Share price (assumed)	$14.69	$14.69
Book value per share	$19.46	$24.11
P/B	**0.75×**	**0.60×**
NWC per share + net cash	$13.59	$18.48
P/(NWC + net cash)	**1.08×**	**0.79×**

As a last point, the PPE, which consisted of land, buildings, and machinery in the Berkshire business, has not been considered. This is because if we read the 1965 annual report carefully, we notice that on page five Ken Chace comments that a large part of the machinery at King Philip E. Division had been sold and that the remaining plant is to be disposed of during the coming year. While the sales would likely have been below their book value, they still would have been positive in terms of cash, indicating there was some value in here as well.

If we put all the information together, it seems quite clear what Buffett saw in the Berkshire Hathaway business. The combination of realizable value out of the book value with the very high cash generation of the business would make Berkshire Hathaway look very attractive to an analyst who examined the business in detail.

In his letters to shareholders dated November 1, 1965 and January 20, 1966, Buffett discusses the discount to book value for Berkshire Hathaway in some detail. He comments that net working capital (including net cash in my definition) alone was worth about $19 per share on December 31, 1965. He also comments that when calculating the fair value of BPL's Berkshire Hathaway stake, he had valued the business at "a price halfway between net current asset and book value . . . [with] current assets at 100 cents on the dollar and our fixed assets at 50 cents on the dollar." Basing the numbers from the balance sheet, this would imply that the fair value Buffett saw was around ½*($24.11) + ½*($18.48) = $ 21.30 per share. A share price of $14.69 would have implied a 31 percent discount to the fair value.

Clearly, this implies a margin of safety to asset values, and in a way this case is reminiscent of Dempster Mill and a Benjamin Graham type of net-net. However, it should be noted that in this case there is a clear indication that, especially in terms of cash earnings shown in 1965, the Berkshire

Hathaway business had a significant ability to realize value on top of the existing asset value.

In summary, Berkshire Hathaway seems to have been a combination of asset value play as well as the potential for cash generation of the business. In 1965, when Buffett made the bulk of his purchase, the business had undergone several positive changes. First, regulatory changes would have been seen as a positive at the time for all fabric mills. Second and more important, a new capable management had just taken control. While the business was clearly in a difficult market with risks, without the benefit of hindsight, it would have seemed to be one where good management may be able to do something. In fact, in 1965 Buffett commented that "while a Berkshire is hardly going to be as profitable as a Xerox, Fairchild Camera or National Video in a hypertensed market, it is a very comfortable sort of thing to own."[6] All things considered, it seems to me like a very sensible investment as a net-net type of investment at the time; it just was not one that worked out in the end.

With the benefit of hindsight, of course, the risks stemming from the market forces against American textile manufacturing would become too large for Berkshire to overcome by the 1980s. Buffett would later joke that in following the Graham perspective of investing in cigar butts, one tries to find a cigar butt for free that had one last puff in it, and Berkshire actually was a cigar butt that had no puffs left in it.[7] Still, it should be noted that while this investment is often identified as a "mistake" by Buffett, it likely did not actually lose money for Buffett in absolute terms. Given Berkshire Hathaway's profitability in 1965 and certainly quite a few more years in the 1960s and 1970s, one should remember that the shrinking business actually provided the capital that Buffett invested in many other businesses starting in 1967 with the purchase of National Indemnity.

The lessons to be learned from the Berkshire Hathaway investment seem to come from looking at the long-term numbers. One lesson is to be very wary of a business that has had a ten-year decline in revenues or gross margins, even if the last two or three years have been positive. Those last few years may simply be the work of an outstanding management team when structural issues that even the best management team cannot overcome make life as an investor in the business very difficult in the long term. An additional lesson also seems to be that for net-net investments, businesses are not meant to be held long term. Hence, perhaps, purchasing the business was not the big mistake, but not selling it or making it a control situation rather than having an exit strategy was. In the previous net-net investments discussed (Sanborn Maps and Dempster Mill), Buffett had clear exit options within a few years of investing in the businesses. This was not the case with Berkshire Hathaway.

The famed history of Berkshire had its beginning here, and Buffett would get attached to this company, even revising his investment objectives a few years later to include holding companies that may not always deliver the best returns but also to have an altruistic regard for its employees.

To digress for a moment, looking at today's business environment, there has been a similar structural attack in the retail sector in the last decade. But instead of foreign imports, this time the culprit is the Internet. As was the case with Borders, and to a lesser degree Barnes & Noble, the structural efficiency of the Internet model, apparent in companies such as Amazon, has wreaked havoc on the traditional business model of bricks and mortar book retailers. For Borders it has meant bankruptcy. Still, even the Internet has not affected all retail businesses in the same way. While its long-term success is still to be determined, Barnes & Noble's effort to add cafes in its bookstores is helping the business differentiate its business model as a lifestyle destination of reading. More impressively, WHSmith, the UK equivalent, through a strategy of shifting its mix of stores toward travel locations, such as airports and train stations, and adding convenience product categories, such as packed lunches, drinks, and snacks, has transformed its business from a book retailer to a convenience retailer over the last decade. While books and magazines still account for more than 50 percent of shelf space (and a significant portion of sales), it is enlightening to know that the average purchase now at WHSmith is under £5 (approximately $7), suggesting that most purchases are impulse purchases. While the store still faces significant risk because approximately half of its stores are at nontravel locations, at least on the group level WHSmith has not only slowed but in fact increased its operating margins with this strategy over the last several years.

While I do not know how this story will play out, it goes to show that sometimes measures can be taken to overcome a structural decline, but other times nothing can be done. A careful analyst must be able to understand whether a particular case or investment situation is predictable or not.

***

Reflections on Buffett's Partnership Years

Although I originally thought that Buffett focused primarily on cheap cigar-butt investments in his early partnership years, it is clear that, in reality, he was involved in many different types of investments. He neither invested exclusively in cheap Benjamin Graham–type cigar-butt opportunities nor did he focus only on great quality businesses. While Sanborn Maps and Dempster Mill were more of the former variety, American Express could only be categorized as the latter. In between, Buffett also invested in special situations, such as merger arbitrage in the case of Texas National Oil, and was willing to take control positions and catalyze change when he saw fit, as in the case of Dempster Mill. In fact, there is even a good indication that Buffett dabbled in long-short pair trades. In his annual letter to clients dated January 18, 1965, Buffett notes: "We have recently begun to implement a technique, which gives promise of very substantially reducing the risk from an overall change in valuation standards...[this was in reference to relatively undervalued companies]." While there was great diversity in the types of businesses in which Buffett invested in his partnership years, they shared some key commonalities. First, Buffett seemed to avoid situations where the business fundamentals were completely broken or deteriorating. Even in the cases of Sanborn Maps, Dempster Mill, and Berkshire, investments that were based primarily on the value of their assets rather than their earnings power (with the exception of Berkshire Hathaway where it was both), Buffett invested in companies when there was positive impetus in the business. Often, as in the case of Berkshire and Dempster Mill, there was a management change where a new capable manager replaced a poor previous management team in a business where execution mattered. In the three cases of Sanborn Maps, Dempster Mill, and Berkshire, Buffett also identified clear operational improvement opportunities, where a positive catalyst could be expected. Most important, in all the cases analyzed Buffett appeared to invest only in businesses that were still profitable. In the case of Dempster Mill, although the company was barely making a profit, it was still generating one. Buffett avoided companies that were quickly burning cash. I find this an important lesson because companies that trade below asset values, while not frequent, are not rare. However, many of these companies are burning cash, and it can be dangerous to be convinced of such turnaround stories, where if a turnaround does not happen, one loses one's whole investment. That risk is much lower with companies that are still profitable and have some positive impetus.

Second, Buffett conducted thorough primary research on each business he invested in. This research included a detailed understanding of how the businesses functioned fundamentally, which I would have suspected before examining these cases more closely. But it also included a thorough understanding of both the management and ownership structures to a level of detail that I found astounding. In the case of Sanborn Maps, Buffett knew the exact constellation of the board of managers, and even what their thinking was as pertained to Sanborn. In the case of Berkshire, Buffett knew intimately both the management team as well as the owners he was buying from.

Third, for businesses where there was more than one main business activity, most prominently in the example of American Express, Buffett clearly strived to understand the individual economics of the sub-businesses rather than viewing the business based on financials as a group. Because of this, he likely saw in the case of American Express a quickly growing credit card business that was only temporarily hampered by operational issues and that already showed clear signs of recovery and growth in 1963. He also likely saw that Dempster Mill was not simply a deteriorating windmill business. What this reveals is that investors should be careful not to focus only on financial metrics. Such metrics are reported for a group level and often are not as useful to an investor as understanding the core functions of businesses and how these functions might impact the financial developments of the company.

Allow me to draw an analogy between Buffett's research into his investments and the current investment universe in Europe. I recently visited a media company in the UK, the Daily Mail General Trust (DMGT). Although it was originally a newspaper company, namely the family-run Daily Mail group of newspapers, since the late 1990s DMGT has been accumulating a group of business-to-business (B2B) subscription-based businesses. As of fiscal year 2012, this set of B2B businesses now accounts for roughly 50 percent of revenues and over 70 percent of EBIT. The remaining 50 percent of revenues and about 30 percent EBIT still come from the original paper business, which for simplicity I will call the B2C (retail) business.[8]

Without looking too deeply at the fundamental business economics of the B2C business and the B2B business, what an investor would see in the last ten years based on group financials is stagnating revenues and profit margin. According to DMGT's group financials, it had revenue of GBP

1.96 billion and an EBIT of 192 million (EBIT margin of 9.8 percent) in FY 2001. In FY 2011A, the corresponding revenue was GBP 1.99 billion with an EBIT of 213.4 million (EBIT margin of 10.7 percent).

Based on the financials alone, an investor could easily conclude that the business had not changed much—that in aggregate it was stagnant. However, this is far from the truth. If an investor were to delve into the fundamental business economics of the two sub-businesses, that investor would see that the B2B business, for example, has much lighter capital intensity than the newspaper business and much higher operating margins. What this means is that the newspaper business is shrinking in size, and the B2B business is growing. The need for replacement capital expenditure is much lower than the level of depreciation that DMGT as a group charges, leading to much higher cash generation than ordinarily warranted by the stagnant level of earnings. In the total group figures the numbers are not necessarily easy to see due to layers of exceptional and restructuring costs related to winding down some of the newspaper businesses, but if one focuses on understanding the separate businesses and their inherent characteristics, I believe it is much easier to see. And in the end, the higher level of cash generation, which continues to increase, is critical because that is what an investor is paying for.

Overall, regarding Buffett's assessment of the DMGT case, I find that if an investor does not delve into sub-businesses like Buffett must have done, one will miss many aspects of an investment case that may be central to one's investment strategy.

Part II

The Middle Years (1968–1990)

Between 1968 and 1990, Warren Buffett moves away from his investment partnership and guides Berkshire Hathaway as his new investment vehicle. Increasingly, he invests in private companies and builds up his asset base in insurance, regional banks, and other *control assets* such as Nebraska Furniture Mart and See's Candies. Fundamentally, we also see Buffett gradually shift focus from investing in stocks that appeared cheap compared to their asset values to incorporating more qualitative factors when selecting his investments.

The economic context of the years between 1968 and 1990 was complex. The end of the 1960s was characterized by booming stock markets and few value opportunities. It was in fact because of this economic environment that Buffett closed his partnership in 1968. In 1969, the market finally broke into the first of a sequence of market crashes that continued for several years. The 1970s were tough years for the stock market, with the markets ending the decade with the S&P 500 at around the same level at which it had started. In the interim, there were two major economic recessions: one in 1974, which included one of the largest stock market crashes of recent times, and another in 1979. Inflation also became rampant in the late 1970s with interest rates shooting up to 15 percent by the end of the decade.

The 1980s was then the decade when inflation was brought under control through policies implemented by Paul Volker. Soon to follow were the proliferation of company debt and the rise of junk bonds and corporate takeovers. Large blue chip companies were not safe with business people like Ivan Boseky acting in financial markets. However, after a brief recession in 1982, a long period of economic prosperity and stability in the financial markets began, which lasted until 2000.

6

1967: National Indemnity Company

The story of National Indemnity brings back an old character from Warren Buffett's earlier career. The company's private owner, Jack Ringwalt, was the same Omaha businessman who had turned down the opportunity to invest $50,000 when Buffett first established his investment partnership. Ringwalt's business insured risks that were difficult to price, and his corporate mantra went along the lines of "There are no bad risks, only rates that are bad." According to those who knew him, Ringwalt had been very successful in his enterprise and was only willing to sell his business once every year or so, when he was feeling particularly frustrated about something. Through a mutual acquaintance, in early 1967 Buffett apparently got word that Ringwalt was in one of these moods. The story, as told by Alice Schroeder, was that Buffett was looking for a business that could counteract the poor returns of Berkshire Hathaway and wanted to invest some of the cash flow from Berkshire into a steadier company. National Indemnity was a perfect fit, and after a short meeting and a firm handshake, Buffett—despite valuing the company at $35 a share—offered Ringwalt $50 a share for the business.[1]

Clearly, Buffett saw something promising in this fundamental business. Established in 1941, National Indemnity initially wrote liability insurance on taxis. The company focused on writing specialty insurance. Prior to 1967, the business had become broader in scope and was closer

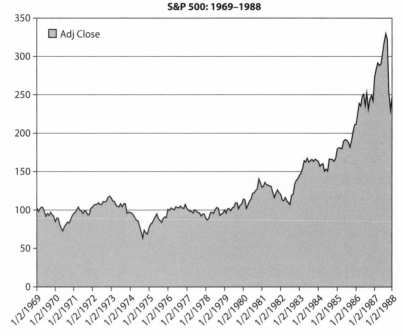

S&P 500: 1969–1988

Figure 6.1.

to a more general fire and casualty insurance operator. What really set National Indemnity apart was Ringwalt's business philosophy. National Indemnity was based on the founding principle that there was a proper rate for every legitimate risk and that the focus of the insurer was to always make the correct assessment and walk away with an underwriting profit. Unlike typical car insurers at the time, the company was willing to insure risks such as casualty for long-haul trucks, taxis, and rental cars. Also unlike its peers, National Indemnity did not chase revenues when they would not be profitable at the underwriting level. This capital discipline was another key element of good management at National Indemnity.

Discussing his purchase of the business in his 1968 annual letter to shareholders, Buffett gushes about Ringwalt's management: "Everything was as advertised or better." While some insurance companies were managed to grow as large as possible, National Indemnity was managed conservatively, with profit as an aim.

As a private company, the individual small investor would not have had access to the detailed financials of National Indemnity. An investor could, however, see the big picture: the company had grown from a four-person operation to a much larger business, and one that was writing insurance profitably. However, an investor like Buffett who was in a position to buy the whole company would most likely have had access to the company's financial information, some of which we can access from various sources including Buffett's letters to shareholders. In 1967, National Indemnity had a net income of $1.6 million on $16.8 million in premiums earned. In 1968, its first year as a Berkshire subsidiary, National Indemnity had increased its net income to $2.2 million on $20.0 million in premiums earned.[2] To any potential investor, the company at the very least would have seemed like a growing company that had solid profit margins.

Buffett clearly valued the inherent quality of the business, and in March 1967 he paid $8.6 million for National Indemnity (along with National Fire & Marine, an affiliated company). Based on the net earnings of the business of $1.6 million, the $8.6 million purchase price reflects a price-to-earning ratio multiple of 5.4×. At face value, even assuming natural lumpiness in underwriting earnings, this seems downright cheap for any well-run business. In a 1969 letter to partners of his investment partnership Buffett commented that the business generated a return on capital employed of approximately 20 percent—meaning that it likely had some structural advantages—which makes the price seem even more attractive.[3]

But perhaps even more important, a look at the assets of the business reveals that Buffett was also getting something meaningful that the earnings of the business did not show. At the time, National Indemnity together with National Fire & Marine had a bond portfolio worth more than $24.7 million and a stock portfolio worth $7.2 million—a management portfolio in excess of $30 million.[4] That was three times more than the $8.6 million Buffett spent. Although the company certainly also had liabilities as an insurer, meaning this amount could not be simply returned to shareholders, it appears that Buffett had recognized this key quality in the business—the ability to raise capital and use this capital to invest in stocks. I will discuss this aspect of *float* in more detail in chapter 17, but in very simple terms: The insurance business receives premiums as soon as customers buy policies, and it faces liabilities some time in the future when policyholders make claims. While insurance companies will reserve some of the premiums received for claims on a yearly basis, the rest of the cash received will be available to be invested. This money that the insurance company holds but does not own is called the *float*, and Buffett was able to invest and make earnings on this amount.

Soon after buying his stakes in National Insurance, Buffett started investing the float successfully. After two years of investing in the portfolio of National Indemnity (including National Fire & Marine Insurance Company) the portfolio value increased from $32 million to $42 million. This was the start of a career-long fascination with the insurance business, which Buffett continues to use for float and investments.

7

1972: See's Candies

In 1972, the president of Blue Chip Stamp, a Berkshire Hathaway subsidiary, contacted Warren Buffett to let him know that See's Candies was for sale. The California company—founded in Pasadena in 1921 by Charles See and his mother Mary See—had always been run by the See family, but the latest owner, Harry See, was interested in selling the business so he could focus on his Napa Valley vineyard. Robert Flaherty, an investment advisor to Blue Chip stamps, introduced the deal to Blue Chip president Bill Ramsey, who in turn made the call to Buffett.

Buffett was immediately interested—and not only because his wife, Susie, was crazy about the candy. See's was well-known throughout the state and had a long-standing reputation for quality; when many other candy stores diluted their recipes during the sugar-rationing period of World War II, See's maintained its recipe and simply sold its candy until it sold out. With its potential for continued strong operations, See's was notably different from some of the businesses that Buffett had invested in previously. This was not a cigar-butt type of investment, but rather a high-quality business that held the promise of long-term success. And although Buffett had invested in high-quality growth businesses before, notably American Express, the See's Candies acquisition was reflective of Buffett's inclination toward such businesses and also performing them as private transactions.

Because See's Candies was a private company, its financial information would not have been readily accessible to potential private investors. Had they been able to access it, here are the numbers they would have seen: In 1972, the business had revenues of $31.3 million and profits after-tax of $2.1 million (which, based on the normal 48 percent corporate tax rate at the time, would have meant a pretax profit of approximately $4 million). The business had net tangible assets of $8 million. Operationally, the company had 167 stores open at the end of that year and sold 17 million pounds of candy during the year.[1]

These numbers gave a return on tangible capital (ROTCE)[2] of 26 percent. For a business that actually produces a good and does not have an inherently asset-light business model, this ROTCE indicates a very high-quality business able to compound returns at a rate significantly higher than its cost of capital. The question for potential investors at the time would then have been: Is this impressive after-tax return of greater than 25 percent sustainable? In other words, is this a business that can consistently generate better returns than a comparable business with the same assets? Anecdotally, from Berkshire's letter to shareholders, See's Candies had a very strong brand especially in the western United States, where it had a dominant market share. It also enjoyed a network of owned stores with dedicated personnel rather than franchisees.[3] It operated in an industry with little technological risk and it appeared to have a history of consistent financial performance. All in all, to a potential investor, the company would likely have seemed able to maintain its competitive edge and continue generating a 25 percent (or greater) rate of return on tangible capital.

The second trait I would have looked for as a potential investor would have been the company's ability to grow. Usually, value investors do not want to pay for this growth, but in this case an essential part of the valuation was the company's compounding ability—hence, an understanding of growth was necessary. This is so because even if a business has a very high ROTCE, if it is not growing, it will not benefit from having to invest less than peers in growth. To assess growth for a product-driven company, I would normally have looked at its historical track record of growing volume or prices. Since See's operates with directly owned stores (DOS) as its major distribution channel, I would also want to look at like-for-like data per store and the growth in store numbers. While pre-1972 numbers are not available, one can assume, given the consistency of the business, that the post-1972 years serve as a good substitute for what these pre-1972 numbers probably looked like. Those results are summarized in table 7.1.

Table 7.1.

Operating statistics, See's Candies (1972–1976)

		1976	1975	1974	1973	1972
Revenues	$	56,333,000	50,492,000	41,248,000	35,050,000	31,337,000
NOPAT	$	5,569,000	5,132,000	3,021,000	1,940,000	2,083,000
Candy sold	Lbs.	20,553,000	19,134,000	17,883,000	17,813,000	16,954,000
Directly owned stores (DOS)	#	173	172	170	169	167
Revenue per DOS	$	325,624	293,558	242,635	205,396	187,647

Source: Table 7.1 is reconstructed from data presented on page 6 of Warren Buffett's letter to Berkshire Hathaway shareholders dated February 25, 1985.

As table 7.1 shows, in every metric from revenues to operating profits to per store sales (except one off-year) See's consistently shows growth. In the years between 1972 and 1976, net operating profit after taxes (NOPAT) averaged 16 percent per annum.

Thus, it seems clear that See's was a company with both high ROTCE and the potential for continued growth. After considering how a potential contemporary investor may have viewed the business fundamentally, one must next consider the valuation of See's Candies and the price that Buffett paid for it.

Buffett paid $25 million for the entire company;[4] knowing the afore-mentioned earnings figures, one can calculate a P/E multiple of 11.9× and an EV/EBIT multiple of 6.3×. Unlike some of his previous purchases, such as Berkshire Hathaway, this was not cheap in the traditional sense of an extremely low multiple (5× or below). Much more like the American Express case, Buffett paid a fair value for the business. Unlike a business purchased at a P/E ratio below 5×, See's Candies, at 11.9 times earnings, would have a *margin of safety* only if the business had a significantly better internal rate of compounding than its competitors. In other words, for a business without growth, a ten to twelve times earnings multiple might be a fair value, but would not provide a margin of safety. And for a business that does have growth but is unable to grow without incurring a cost in additional capital much less than the value of the growth, the value of the growth would be limited. To have a margin of safety, the business must have both growth and a high ROTCE. Thus it seems that Buffett here assumed and paid for at least some growth.

To understand how growth is "priced into" Buffett's purchasing price, let me give an example. To decide the price at which an investor is will-ing to purchase a stock, a value investor might calculate the value of the business based on its current earnings and then require a *margin of safety* of 30 percent. But if this value investor, instead of requiring a margin of safety based on current earnings, is willing to pay full price for current earnings, one can ask another question: how much growth is required to still satisfy a margin of safety of 30 percent? In other words, what growth in earnings is required to make the intrinsic value of a business worth 43 percent[5] more than a business with the same current earnings, but with zero growth? Mathematically, the case is fairly straightforward. One can use See's Candies's $2.1 million earnings in 1972 as a basis. If one does not pay for growth at all and thinks a fair PER multiple to pay for such a busi-ness is 10 times and one requires a 30 percent margin of safety, one would be willing to pay \$14.7 million for the business. In this example, the fair value of the business would be \$21 million and \$14.7 million would reflect a discount of 30 percent to that fair value. Now assume that an investor were willing to pay the full \$21 million fair value of the business; what percentage growth per year is required to still provide the 30 percent margin of safety? To achieve this, the growing business needs to have an intrinsic value of 143 percent of \$21 million, which is \$30 million. Using the simple perpetuity formula[6]—present value = C / (r − g)—one can calculate the required growth in earnings to achieve a \$30 million fair value.[7] The specific math is: PV = fair value = 30.0 = C/(r − g) = (2.1)/(0.1 − g) → (0.1 − g) = 2.1/30.0 → 0.1 = 0.07 + g → g = 0.03. It might come as a shock, but the required growth mathematically indeed is only three percent per annum in earnings to get to a fair value of See's Candies at \$30 million.

In the real world, things are slightly more complicated—but not much more. First, to achieve this 30 percent margin of safety requires three percent earnings growth into perpetuity; in reality, few businesses can be assumed to grow ad infinitum. However, because of the 10 percent discount rate, the value of growth in dollars is highest for the first few years, so that a business that grows for ten years would certainly capture the vast majority of the value of growth, even if the growth does not continue forever. Second, the aforementioned would be for a business that just grew three percent per annum without needing any costs to achieve this growth; this is also not true for a business like See's Candies. For instance, See's Candies has a ROTCE of about 25 percent, so if the business grows three percent, it will require roughly one-quarter of that amount to finance the growth (if one assumes the capital intensity for the marginal new business is the same as for the overall business). Because of the requirement of growth capital, for a business like See's Candies, roughly a four percent growth rate rather than a three percent growth rate is required to achieve a 30 percent margin of safety.

Overall, even with these few complexities, two insights are critical. First, if an investor can have a fair amount of certainty about future growth in earnings, even if it is not a high rate but only four or five percent per year, the value of this could be very significant, in fact, as significant as taking a discount of 30 percent when buying a business that is not growing its earnings. Second, given that Buffett paid 11.9× PER for See's Candies, one can infer that he likely saw and paid for a growth of approximately five percent per year in this business. He must have assumed that this growth would last quite a few years if he ordinarily would only have paid 7× PER (10× PER with 30 percent margin of safety) for a similar business not considering any growth.

Going back to the overall analysis of the business quality of See's Candies, it seems clear that it fulfilled the criteria of high ROTCE and growth. Buffett seemed to both understand this and be flexible enough to pay an otherwise full price when not considering growth when he had the chance in early 1972. In fact, in his March 1984 annual letter to shareholders, Buffett goes on to tie together his apparent view regarding See's Candies's future prospects to the intrinsic operations: See's Candies is worth more than its book value suggests. It is a brand, it is a product which is able to sell above its cost of production, and it has pricing power into the future.

This investment opportunity was a private transaction, so it would not have been readily accessible for a private investor. Nevertheless, it seems to be a good example of Buffett's focus during this period on businesses that had the ability to grow consistently with relatively limited additional capital.

In the end, See's Candies would become one of Buffett's very best investments. By 2010, See's Candies earned a pretax income of $82 million on sales of $383 million. The assets on the books at year-end 2010 were $40 million, meaning that only $32 million additional capital had to be put into this business since 1972. At the same P/E ratio of 11.9 times and assuming the now more prevalent corporate tax rate of 30 percent, the value of the firm as of last year would be $683 million. This is a more than twenty-five times increase over the original purchase price even without considering the cash that had been distributed in the interim.

8

1973: The *Washington Post*

The *Washington Post* newspaper was founded in 1877 by Stilson Hutchins. The paper was bought and sold to several private owners in the ensuing decades, including John McLean, who also owned the *Cincinnati Enquirer*. After being mismanaged by McLean's son, the *Washington Post* found itself in insolvency by the 1930s.

In 1933, the company was purchased out of bankruptcy by Eugene Meyer, whose son-in-law, Philip Graham, and later his daughter, Katharine Graham, played major roles in the paper's history. The Washington Post Company became a publically listed company in 1971. When the Chairman, Fritz Beebe, died unexpectedly in 1973, Katharine Graham became the first female chairman of a Fortune 500 company.

It was during this timeframe (1972–1973) that Warren Buffett began accumulating shares in the company. By late 1973, Buffett had accumulated an ownership of about 10 percent.[1]

The annual reports of the Washington Post Company for the years ending 1971 and 1972 represent the information a potential investor would have had about the company, immediately before Buffett purchased into it. I have included the four pages of consolidated financial statements at the end of the chapter.

Figure 8.1.

First, we must examine the businesses. The Washington Post Company had three major business divisions.[2] I have summarized in table 8.1 the relative importance of each division to the overall company based on their financials for 1972.

As we can see, at the time the newspaper division was clearly still the most significant division of the business, accounting for approximately half

Table 8.1.
Overview of business segments (1972)

Business segment	Revenues (mio)	% total revenue	% total EBIT	EBIT margin
Newspaper publishing	**$99.8**	46%	47%	10.2%
Magazine and book publishing	**$93.8**	43%	26%	6.0%
Broadcasting	**$24.3**	11%	27%	24.4%
Total	**$217.9**	100%	100%	10%

Source: The Washington Post Company, *1972 Annual Report*, 2.

of total company earnings. However, the other two divisions were certainly financially relevant.

Reading the annual report more closely, one quickly realizes that it is more informative than most reports, full of discussions of operational metrics that matter. To me it indicates a management team that was focused and knew what it was doing.

The report starts with John S. Prescott's discussion of the newspaper business. Specifically, he details a structural change that occurred in the market that year when the *Washington Daily News* ceased publication in July 1972. For an investor interested in the company, this is an extremely significant event. Foremost, it removed one out of three daily papers in the D.C. market, which automatically forced customers who still wanted to receive a paper to turn to one of the remaining two papers. In addition, a duopoly is a much preferred situation for a company to be in than an oligopoly with three players—at least from my own experience observing competitive dynamics. Usually competitive action is much more rational, resulting in fewer price wars and higher margins.

As for operational metrics, the factual data are overwhelmingly positive. Lines of advertising increased by 6.5 million—an increase of nearly nine percent based on prior year total lines of about 73 million. Quoting market share, this represented 63 percent of all advertising lines placed in metropolitan papers in its area. Circulation had increased by 6,000 for the daily paper (an increase of about one percent) and by 15,000 for the Sunday edition (an increase of about two percent). While these numbers are not astounding as percentages, the report points out that they are significantly more than the numbers posted by its main remaining competitor, the *Star-News*. This implies that the *Washington Post* was gaining market share. Prescott goes on to reference a market study conducted by an independent agency, W.R. Simmons & Associates, that determined that three out of five—or about 60 percent—of all adults in the *Washington Post's* market read the *Post*. He goes on to calibrate this number compared to other newspapers with leading market positions in the country. I find this exercise very compelling; not only does John Prescott show that the Washington Post Company is indeed a great franchise, but he also demonstrates that he is a manager who steers by key metrics and is attuned to his competition. In sum, the core newspaper business of the Washington Post Company clearly was a great business.

The second business division discussed is the magazine and book publishing division. Its primary asset was *Newsweek* magazine, which at the time ranked fourth among all magazines in advertising revenue. Osborn Elliott, the divisional head, says that 1972 was a record year for *Newsweek*. Revenues rose eight percent year-on-year, and this was accompanied by a circulation growth of 125,000 per week (about five percent) from 2,600,000 per week to 2,750,000 per week. As is seen elsewhere in the report, an independent third-party source is cited when presenting these data; in this case, it was the Publishers Information Bureau.

Operationally, 1972 marked the year when the veteran *Newsweek* management team, which had been very successful during the sixties, resumed management responsibility of the paper. This strengthening of the divisional management included Elliott himself taking over the editorship, while Gibson McCabe and Robert Campbell were placed to lead operations and publishing, respectively. Their focus on providing content that their readers valued resulted in *Newsweek* winning 11 major journalism awards during the year, including the American Bar Association Gavel, the G.M. Leob Award, and the Overseas Press Club Award. Along with a final discussion on the opportunity that lay ahead for *Newsweek* in terms of continued expansion abroad, the *Newsweek* business, like the *Post*, seemed to be churning on all cylinders.

The last business within the Washington Post Company was the *Post–Newsweek* Stations (broadcasting). Larry Israel, who was responsible for this division, had less specific market share data and third-party accolades to present. Nevertheless, again one receives a very positive picture of the business. Israel speaks about one successfully completed acquisition (of WTIC-TV, Hartford, Connecticut) but focuses the discussion on the excellence of the stations' local area generation of media content.

However, in this division there was also some negative news among all the positives. There were two competitive challenges to license renewals for two of the division's TV stations (WJXT-TV in Jacksonville and WPLG-TV in Miami). Israel tried thoughtfully to dismiss the real risk of this challenge by citing that both previous examples of such challenges and the legal principles involved in judging such cases pointed toward a positive resolution for the group. Had I been I an investor, unaware of the inner workings of broadcasting regulation, I would not have been completely convinced by this explanation. This would be an area where I would have to assess the risk.

Aside from this potential structural issue, we can quantify the success of the division by looking at the divisional numbers on page two of the 1972 annual report. The broadcasting division in 1972 increased its revenues to $24.3 million from $20.8 million year-on-year (an increase of 17 percent) and its reported operating income to $5.9 million from $3.8 million year-on-year (an increase of 55 percent). This is an astounding financial performance for a business one might otherwise consider relatively stable with the same set of TV channels and radio stations. Although one large acquisition of WTIC-TV was discussed, this was being finalized in January 2013, so I am assuming that since no other acquisition was discussed in the 1972 divisional review of broadcasting the aforementioned divisional financial growth is mostly if not entirely organic.

When synthesizing the performance at the overall group level, the total operational performance seems so positive that, as a contemporary investor, I would frankly have had a hard time believing it. If it were not for the very factual and independent market data presented in the newspaper and magazine divisions, I would indeed be feeling very suspicious that the management was being overly optimistic in their reporting and would check this by turning to the hard numbers.

The first item of note is the 10-year review of the *Washington Post* presented on pages 22 and 23 of the annual report. In every one of the years, the revenue figures increased from the previous year. Over the total 10-year period, revenues increased to $217.8 million from $85.5 million, which comes to a figure of about 11 percent per annum. On the reported operating income, the picture is a bit more volatile, though also realistic because not every single year is a positive. Here, if we take the 10 years in total, operating income grew to $21.8 million from $9.4 million. The corresponding annual rate of growth is about 10 percent, slightly behind the top line growth. Although this means that margins have not increased despite the obvious gain in scale from a growing business, I would not see this as negative. If one of my concerns was that 1972 was a year of peak margins (operating margin grew to 10 percent from 7.9 percent in 1971) I would be reassured to see that during the 10-year period, operating margin varied between 7.8 percent and 12.2 percent, placing the 10 percent margin in 1972 right in the middle of the range. This means that if there is a capable management in place—and there are some indications in the report that this is the case—there is potential for a margin increase with higher operational efficiency. In fact, because the business in 1972 had even more scale than in 1968, it could be reasonably argued that the potential margin under a good management should be even higher than the 12.2% achieved in 1968.

Turning to the financial review and financial statements of the *Washington Post*, two items require further scrutiny and would be areas of concern for me as a potential investor. First, there is the section on retirement accounts. Like other media companies at the time, The *Washington Post* had defined benefit retirement liabilities to its employees. This, which is still a large issue especially with European companies, creates uncertainty and could result in repeated demands on cash if not carefully managed. On page 14 of the annual report, the reader is told that in general "the accrued costs and liabilities of these plans are fully funded." But later in the section, there is one set of plans associated with the newspaper dealer incentive plans that is unfunded and whose costs are charged directly to current expenses. The expense under this set of plans was $3.6 million in 1972. This is not completely insignificant, but overall, without further inspection, the retirement plans seem to be a contained issue.

Second, there are capital stock and stock options, which are discussed on page 16 of the 1972 annual report. Here we see that in 1971, along with the initial public offering, the company adopted a stock option plan, for which 365,000 shares of common stock were reserved, out of which 279,650 were subject to options outstanding and 64,175 were available to be allocated at a later date. Although there were already options outstanding prior to 1971 and there were also two classes of common shares to complicate things further, to simplify we should look only at the 279,650 options outstanding at the end of 1972, and when they became exercisable.

As defined by the Association of British Insurers (ABI),[3] general good practice is not to allocate more than 10 percent of share capital in 10 years, that is, one percent per year. Although the figure between 1972 and 1975 exceeds this general rule of thumb, which would make me a bit wary as a potential investor, it is not unusual to give a few more options with an IPO, which is the case here. What is reassuring is that the IPO price was $25.18 per share,[4] and the average option price is struck at about $26.00 per share,

Table 8.2.
Analysis of stock options (1972)

Date exercisable	No. of shares	Avg. option price	Effect of dilution (% of outstanding shares)*
1972 EOY	65.625	$26	1.4%
1973 EOY	71.300	$26	1.5%
1974 EOY	69.800	$26	1.4%
1975 EOY	69.050	$26	1.4%
...	...	...	...
1960 EOY	3.875	$26	0.1%
Total	**214.025**	**~$26 per share**	**5.8%**

*Calculation is based on using the weighted average number of common shares outstanding in 1972 or 4,806,802.

slightly higher than the IPO price and around or above the market price at the time. So overall, these observations would ease my concerns.

Finally, I turn to the financial statements, which can be found on pages 17 to 21 of the 1972 annual report. To assess the quality of the overall Washington Post business, an investor could calculate the returns on tangible capital employed (ROTCE) because this is a proxy for the ability of the business to generate returns above the cost of comparable businesses.

Table 8.3.
Analysis of total capital employed (1972)

Category	Capital employed (mio)	As a % of revenues
PPE	$46.2	21.2%
Intangibles excluding goodwill	$0*	0.0%
Inventories	$3.8	1.7%
Accounts receivable	$25.8	11.6%
Accounts payable	−$19.4	−8.9%
Total capital employed (TCE)	**$56.4**	**25.6%**

*Based on The *Washington Post*'s definition of its balance sheet item "Goodwill and other intangibles" as "the excess of acquiring subsidiary companies over the related fair values of tangible assets at the dates of acquisition" on page 14, I have assumed all goodwill and other intangibles to be goodwill and none to be intangible assets that should be amortized.

If we take net operating profit after tax (NOPAT) but before exceptional items of $10 million as the basis for the calculation of ROTCE, we come to a ROTCE of 17.9 percent based on a total capital employed (TCE) of $55.8 million. This indicates a fairly good business with the ability to compound returns internally with growth. Because the business grew at 11 percent per annum in the last 10 years, we can be fairly certain that it is a good compounder.

Finally, coming to the valuation of the business, a sensible assessment would be to look at the conventional valuation metrics of EV/EBIT and PER. On page three of Buffett's 1975 year-end annual letter to Berkshire Hathaway shareholders, Buffett describes Berkshire's "largest equity investment [at the time] is 467,150 shares of Washington Post 'B' stock with a cost of $10.6 million." Calculating the per share price basis, Buffett paid roughly $22.69 per share for the stock. Note that the 467,150 shares would have represented approximately 10 percent of the total common shares outstanding of The Washington Post at the time. From other accounts of the stock price movement, one knows that while the Washington Post stock was first quoted on the stock exchange after going public at about $26 per share, it had fallen to as low as $16 per share during 1973.[5] Although this is based on third-party accounts of what was happening in the stock market at the time, I believe that the share price drop was a result of both macroeconomic concerns and bad press for the *Washington Post*. The bad press related to the *Post's* investigation into the Watergate scandal that led to President Richard Nixon's resignation and the presumably Nixon-led challenges to the *Post's* television licenses mentioned earlier. In fact, alluding to this situation is the following quote from Beebe and Graham on page five of the 1972 *Washington Post* annual report: "There is nothing surprising in the adversary relationship between government and the press. It is as old as the Republic. Yet for those of us in the news business, the intense hostility evident during the recent past has been disquieting."

Looking at the stock price at $22.69 per share, the average price at which Buffett accumulated his stake, the backward looking EV/EBIT and PER multiples would have appeared as listed in tables 8.4. and 8.5.[6] Note that this price would have been approximately 40 percent above the 52-week low price of the share in 1973.

At a last full year EV/EBIT of 5.3×, a good quality business like the *Washington Post* would seem very cheap by today's standards. However, this is a bit misleading. Looking at the income statement of the *Washington Post*, we note that the total tax rate paid in 1971 and 1972 by the company amounted to 50.2 percent and 49.5 percent respectively. This compares

Table 8.4.

EV/EBIT	1971 actual	1972 actual
Revenues	$192.7m	$217.8m
EBIT	$15.2m	$21.8m
EBIT Margin	*7.9%*	*10.0%*
EV/EBIT	7.7×	5.3×

quite unfavorably with the approximate 30 percent total tax rate that most companies pay today. In fact, as we see in table 8.5, this was a result of the prevailing federal corporate tax policy at the time.

In effect, the higher tax rate in 1973 means that for the same amount of EBIT, a shareholder would get less in cash earnings compared to someone who owned the business today. If we were to adjust for this factor, a comparable EV/EBIT at today's 30 percent tax rate would be 7.5×. When I say comparable, I specifically mean an EV/EBIT figure based on an EBIT that would have resulted in a comparable NOPAT to what the *Washington Post* made in 1973. The EV/EBIT of 7.5× is still cheap for such a good business that is growing, but not extraordinarily so.

Looking at the PER, we also see a moderate valuation.

Note that I have used adjusted EPS, which does not include extraordinary items or special credits, which is reported on page 17 of the annual report under the consolidated income statement. I have done so to make a valuation judgement based only on income generated from the business. At a 10.9× 1972 fiscal year PER, again, the *Washington Post* looks fairly cheap given its high-quality business and growth at a high ROTCE (compounding ability).

To summarize the valuation, the *Washington Post* seems to be a case where Buffett paid a decent multiple for a great growing business with an inherent ability to compound. By earnings power standards, based on the information an investor had at the beginning of 1973, it would not have looked like rock-bottom valuation. That said, it is certainly true that when

Table 8.5.

PER	1971 actual	1972 actual
EPS (adjusted)	$1.52	$2.08
PER	14.9×	10.9×

Table 8.6.
Historical corporate top tax rate and bracket (1909–2010)

Year	Top tax rate (%)	Top tax bracket ($)	Year	Top tax rate (%)	Top tax bracket ($)	Year	Top tax rate (%)	Top tax bracket ($)
1909	1		1943	40	50,000	1977	48	50,000
1910	1		1944	40	50,000	1978	48	50,000
1911	1		1945	40	50,000	1979	46	100,000
1912	1		1946	38	50,000	1980	46	100,000
1913	1		1947	38	50,000	1981	46	100,000
1914	1		1948	38	50,000	1982	46	100,000
1915	1		1949	38	50,000	1983	46	100,000
1916	2		1950	42	25,000	1984	46	1,405,000
1917	6		1951	51	25,000	1985	46	1,405,000
1918	12		1952	52	25,000	1986	46	1,405,000
1919	10		1953	52	25,000	1987	40	1,405,000
1920	10		1954	52	25,000	1988	34	335,000
1921	10		1955	52	25,000	1989	34	335,000
1922	12.50		1956	52	25,000	1990	34	335,000
1923	12.50		1957	52	25,000	1991	34	335,000
1924	12.50		1958	52	25,000	1992	34	18,333,333
1925	13		1959	52	25,000	1993	35	18,333,333
1926	13.50		1960	52	25,000	1994	35	18,333,333
1927	13.50		1961	52	25,000	1995	35	18,333,333
1928	12		1962	52	25,000	1996	35	18,333,333
1929	11		1963	52	25,000	1997	35	18,333,333
1930	12		1964	50	25,000	1998	35	18,333,333
1931	12		1965	48	25,000	1999	35	18,333,333
1932	13.75		1966	48	25,000	2000	35	18,333,333
1933	13.75		1967	48	25,000	2001	35	18,333,333
1934	13.75		1968	52.8	25,000	2002	35	18,333,333
1935	13.75		1969	52.8	25,000	2003	35	18,333,333
1936	15	40,000	1970	49.2	25,000	2004	35	18,333,333
1937	15	40,000	1971	48	25,000	2005	35	18,333,333
1938	19	25,000	1972	48	25,000	2006	35	18,333,333
1939	19	25,000	1973	48	25,000	2007	35	18,333,333
1940	24	38,566	1974	48	25,000	2008	35	18,333,333
1941	31	38,462	1975	48	50,000	2009	35	18,333,333
1942	40	50,000	1976	48	50,000	2010	35	18,333,333

Source: Office of Tax Policy Research, *1909–2001: World Tax Database*. http://www.wtdb.org/
index.html. Accessed October 17, 2002. 2002–2010: Internal Revenue Service, Instructions for
Form 1120.

Buffett began buying, it was at a lower price than his average, and he continued buying and was intent on accumulating a 10 percent stake of the company, which is fundamentally much more difficult than if a small investor acquires a small amount of stock.

There are two learning points I draw here. First, it seems that the *Washington Post*, like American Express, was a very high-quality business, with a historical 10-year track record of growth and ability to generate a superior ROTCE. In this case, the business was selling at a cheap price, but not ridiculously so. Second, given all the detailed circulation and competitive data given in the annual reports, there was clearly a very high quality of information available to the investor who looked carefully.

The lifelong friendship between Buffett and Graham developed from this point on. Buffett became a director of the *Washington Post* in the fall of 1974 and over time became a trusted advisor to Graham, instilling in her the conservatism in capital allocation that would make her a CEO who rarely overspent on acquisitions, but who also at times missed development opportunities that might have been stellar. The largest impact Buffett had on Graham, however, was instilling a shareholder-friendly mindset and a focus on operating the business efficiently. By 1985 operating profit margin had increased to 19 percent from 10 percent in 1974. The Washington Post also had used its excess cash to retire almost 40 percent of total shares in the interim. Net earnings grew seven times over, but earnings per share grew by a factor of ten.[7]

Table 8.7.
Income statement (1971–1972)

	1972	1971
Operating revenues		
Advertising	$166,100,000	$147,633,000
Circulation	$47,421,000	$42,397,000
Other	$4,323,000	$2,719,000
Total operating revenues	$217,844,000	$192,749,000
Costs and expenses		
Operating	$146,644,000	$133,869,000
Selling, general, and administrative	$46,254,000	$41,250,000
Depreciation and amortization	$3,140,000	$2,436,000
Total costs and expenses	$196,038,000	$177,555,000
Income from operations	$21,806,000	$15,194,000
Other income/deductions		
Other income (incl. interest of $804,000 and $845,000)	$1,143,000	$1,091,000
Other deductions (incl. interest of $2,484,000 and $2,774,000)	−$3,240,000	−$3,275,000
Equity in earnings of affiliates	$512,000	$509,000
Total other income/deductions	−$1,585,000	−$1,675,000
Income before income taxes, extraordinary items, and special credits	$20,221,000	$13,519,000
Income taxes		
Currently payable	$7,485,000	$5,698,000
Deferred	$2,721,000	$1,037,000
Total income taxes	$10,206,000	$6,735,000
Income before extraordinary items and special credit	$10,015,000	$6,784,000
Extraordinary items	−$283,000	$387,000
Special credit*	—	$4,586,000
Net income	$9,732,000	$11,757,000
Earnings per common share and common equivalent share		
Income before extraordinary items and special credit	$2.08	$1.52
Extraordinary items	$0.06	$0.09
Special credit	—	$1.04
Net income	$2.02	$2.65

Source: Washington Post, *1972 Annual Report*, 17.

*Cumulative effect on years prior to 1971 of changes in accounting methods for magazine subscription procurement and book promotion costs.

Table 8.8.
Balance sheet (January and December 1972)

Assets	Dec. 1972	Jan. 1972
Current assets		
Cash and time deposits	$10,215,000	$10,268,000
Commercial promissory notes at cost which approximates market value	$19,635,000	$15,224,000
Accounts receivable, less estimated returns, doubtful accounts and allowances of $2,663,000 and $2,342,000	$25,195,000	$19,992,000
Inventories at lower of average cost or market	$3,801,000	$4,641,000
Prepaid expenses and other	$2,908,000	$2,012,000
	$61,754,000	**$52,137,000**
Investments in affiliates		
Bowaters Mersey Paper Company Limited	$8,649,000	$8,834,000
Other	$2,679,000	$1,736,000
	$11,328,000	**$10,570,000**
Plant assets, at cost		
Buildings	$30,185,000	$16,258,000
Machinery, equipment, and fixtures	$34,412,000	$25,549,000
Leasehold improvements	$2,473,000	$2,378,000
	$67,070,000	**$44,185,000**
Less accumulated depreciation and amortization	($27,625,000)	($25,796,000)
	$39,445,000	**$18,389,000**
Land	$6,403,000	$6,403,000
Construction in progress	$323,000	$16,323,000
	$46,171,000	**$41,115,000**
Goodwill and other intangibles	$36,860,000	$37,517,000
Deferred charges and other assets	$4,918,000	$4,353,000
	$161,031,000	**$145,692,000**
Liabilities and shareholders' equity		
Current liabilities		
Accounts payable and accrued expenses	$19,437,000	$17,368,000
Federal and state income taxes	$3,142,000	$735,000
Contributions due to employee benefit trust funds	$1,316,000	$837,000
Current portion of long-term debt	$1,734,000	$797,000
	$25,629,000	**$19,737,000**
Other liabilities	$5,529,000	$5,467,000
Long-term debt	$35,436,000	$38,033,000
Deferred subscription income less related magazine subscription procurement costs of $11,998,000 and $10,496,000	$8,973,000	$7,900,000
Deferred income taxes	$6,077,000	$3,891,000
Minority interest in subsidiary company	$356,000	$313,000
Shareholders' equity		
Preferred stock, $1 par value, authorized 1,000,000 shares		
Common stock:		
Class A common stock, $1 par value, authorized 1,000,000 shares; 763,440 shares issued and outstanding	763,000	763,000
Class B common stock, $1 par value, authorized 10,000,000 shares; 4,304,040 shares issued; 3,982,888 and 3,993,257 shares outstanding	4,304,000	4,304,000
Capital in excess of pay value	$10,149,000	$10,079,000
Retained earnings	$68,835,000	$60,052,000
Less: cost of 321,152 and 310,783 shares of Class B common stock held in treasury	($5,020,000)	($4,847,000)
Total shareholders' equity	**$79,031,000**	**$70,351,000**
	$161,031,000	**$145,692,000**

Source: Washington Post, *1972 Annual Report*, 18–19.

Table 8.9.
Cash flow (1971–1972)

Fiscal year	1972	1971
Financial resources were provided by		
Operations		
Net income	$9,732,000	$11,757,000
Less: portion of 1971 special credit not affecting working capital	—	($4,300,000)
	$9,732,000	**$7,457,000**
Depreciation and amortization of plant assets	$3,140,000	$2,436,000
Amortization of deferred film costs	$1,661,000	$1,306,000
Income tax timing differences	$2,186,000	$808,000
Sale of Art News goodwill	$650,000	—
Other	$386,000	$296,000
	$17,755,000	**$12,303,000**
Increase in long-term debt	—	$8,222,000
Increase in deferred subscription income	$2,575,000	$875,000
Proceeds from issuance of Class B common stock		
Stock options	$161,000	$929,000
Public offering and sales to employees	—	$15,025,000
Newsweek employees saving plan trust	—	$58,000
Other	$375,000	$118,000
	$20,866,000	**$37,530,000**
Financial resources were used for purchases of		
Plant assets	$8,820,000	$13,748,000
Television film rights	$2,232,000	$1,449,000
Treasury stock	$307,000	$530,000
Reduction of long-term debt	$2,597,000	$10,061,000
Increase in deferred magazine subscription procurement costs	$1,502,000	$1,128,000
Dividends on common stock	$949,000	$871,000
Increase in other investments	$700,000	—
Other	$34,000	$319,000
	$17,141,000	$28,106,000
Net increase in working capital	**$3,725,000**	**$9,424,000**
Changes in composition of working capital		
Increase (decrease) in current assets		
Cash and time deposits	($53,000)	$1,231,000
Commercial and promissory notes	$4,411,000	$3,815,000
Accounts receivable	$5,203,000	$99,000
Inventories	($840,000)	$922,000
Prepaid expenses and other	$896,000	$348,000
	$9,617,000	**$6,415,000**
(Increase) decrease in current liabilities		
Accounts payable and accrued expenses	($2,069,000)	($1,980,000)
Dividends payable	—	$200,000
Federal and state income taxes	($2,407,000)	$1,116,000
Contributions due to employee benefit trust funds	($479,000)	1,157,000
Current portion of long-term debt	($937,000)	$2,516,000
	($5,592,000)	$3,009,000
Net increase in working capital	**$3,725,000**	**$9,424,000**

Source: Washington Post, 1972 Annual Report, 20.

9

1976: GEICO (Government Employees Insurance Company)

Warren Buffett's investment in the automotive insurer GEICO spans several decades and includes many twists and turns. He learned of GEICO during his time at Columbia Business School when his professor and mentor, Benjamin Graham, sat on the board of the company. Buffett began researching GEICO out of curiosity, leading to the much-cited anecdote of a young Buffett visiting GEICO's headquarters on a Saturday morning when the premises were empty except for a janitor and an investment officer named Lorimer Davidson. Davidson later became CEO, and Buffett eventually became owner of the entire company.

Buffett first invested in GEICO immediately after this memorable visit, quickly recognizing the strength of its business model. Unlike its contemporaries, GEICO sold directly to customers rather than through insurance agents—so instead of incurring the usual 30 percent of revenues in underwriting costs, its costs were only about 13 percent of revenues. GEICO was able to pass some of this savings on to its customers in the form of cheaper insurance prices. Moreover, GEICO, which stands for Government Employees Insurance Company, catered to a select customer base that was, on average, lower risk. In 1951 GEICO was trading at $42 per share, or roughly eight times its recent earnings. Noting the high level of growth, the competitive costs, and the superior customer base, Buffett—still a

Reprinted from

The COMMERCIAL and FINANCIAL CHRONICLE

Thursday, December 6, 1951

The Security I Like Best

WARREN E. BUFFETT
Buffett-Falk & Co., Omaha, Nebr.

Government Employees Insurance Co.

Full employment, boom time profits and record dividend payments do not set the stage for depressed security prices. Most industries have been riding this wave of prosperity during the past five years with few ripples to disturb the tide.

Warren E. Buffett

The auto insurance business has not shared in the boom. After the staggering losses of the immediate postwar period, the situation began to right itself in 1949. In 1950, stock casualty companies again took it on the chin with underwriting experience the second worst in 15 years. The recent earnings reports of casualty companies, particularly those with the bulk of writings in auto lines, have diverted bull market enthusiasm from their stocks. On the basis of normal earning power and asset factors, many of these stocks appear undervalued.

The nature of the industry is such as to ease cyclical bumps. Auto insurance is regarded as a necessity by the majority of purchasers. Contracts must be renewed yearly at rates based upon experience. The lag of rates behind costs, although detrimental in a period of rising prices as has characterized the 1945-1951 period, should prove beneficial if deflationary forces should be set in action.

Other industry advantages include lack of inventory, collection, labor and raw material problems. The hazard of product obsolescence and related equipment obsolescence is also absent.

Government Employees Insurance Corporation was organized in the mid-30's to provide complete auto insurance on a nationwide basis to an eligible class including: (1) Federal, State and municipal government employees; (2) active and reserve commissioned officers and the first three pay grades of non-commissioned officers of the Armed Forces; (3) veterans who were eligible when on active duty; (4) former policyholders; (5) faculty members of universities, colleges and schools; (6) government contractor employees engaged in defense work exclusively, and (7) stockholders.

The company has no agents or branch offices. As a result, policyholders receive standard auto insurance policies at premium discounts running as high as 30% off manual rates. Claims are handled promptly through approximately 500 representatives throughout the country.

The term "growth company" has been applied with abandon during the past few years to companies whose sales increases represented little more than inflation of prices and general easing of business competition. GEICO qualifies as a legitimate growth company based upon the following record:

Year—	Premiums Written	Policyholders
1936....	$103,696.31	3,754
1940....	768,057.86	25,514
1945....	1,638,562.09	51,697
1950....	8,016,975.79	143,944

Of course the investor of today does not profit from yesterday's growth. In GEICO's case, there is reason to believe the major portion of growth lies ahead. Prior to 1950, the company was only licensed in 15 of 50 jurisdictions including D. C. and Hawaii. At the beginning of the year there were less than 3,000 policyholders in New York State. Yet 25% saved on an insurance bill of $125 in New York should look bigger to the prospect than the 25% saved on the $50 rate in more sparsely settled regions.

As cost competition increases in importance during times of recession, GEICO's rate attraction should become even more effective in diverting business from the brother-in-law. With insurance rates moving higher due to inflation, the 25% spread in rates becomes wider in terms of dollars and cents.

There is no pressure from agents to accept questionable applicants or renew poor risks. In States where the rate structure is inadequate, new promotion may be halted.

Probably the biggest attraction of GEICO is the profit margin advantage it enjoys. The ratio of underwriting profit to premiums earned in 1949 was 27.5% for GEICO as compared to 6.7% for the 135 stock casualty and surety companies summarized by Best's. As experience turned for the worse in 1950, Best's aggregate's profit margin dropped to

3.0% and GEICO's dropped to 18.0%. GEICO does not write all casualty lines; however, bodily injury and property damage, both important lines for GEICO, were among the least profitable lines. GEICO also does a large amount of collision writing, which was a profitable line in 1950.

During the first half of 1951, practically all insurers operated in the red on casualty lines with bodily injury and property damage among the most unprofitable. Whereas GEICO's profit margin was cut to slightly above 9%, Massachusett's Bonding & Insurance showed a 16% loss, New Amsterdam Casualty an 8% loss, Standard Accident Insurance a 9% loss, etc.

Because of the rapid growth of GEICO, cash dividends have had to remain low. Stock dividends and a 25-for-1 split increased the outstanding shares from 3,000 on June 1, 1948, to 250,000 on Nov. 10, 1951. Valuable rights to subscribe to stock of affiliated companies have also been issued.

Benjamin Graham has been Chairman of the Board since his investment trust acquired and distributed a large block of the stock in 1948. Leo Goodwin, who has guided GEICO's growth since inception, is the able President. At the end of 1950, the 10 members of the Board of Directors owned approximately one-third of the outstanding stock.

Earnings in 1950 amounted to $3.92 as contrasted to $4.71 on the smaller amount of business in 1949. These figures include no allowance for the increase in the unearned premium reserve which was substantial in both years. Earnings in 1951 will be lower than 1950, but the wave of rate increases during the past summer should evidence themselves in 1952 earnings. Investment income quadrupled between 1947 and 1950, reflecting the growth of the company's assets.

At the present price of about eight times the earnings of 1950, a poor year for the industry, it appears that no price is being paid for the tremendous growth potential of the company.

This is part of a continuous forum appearing in the "Chronicle," in which each week, a different group of experts in the investment and advisory field from all sections of the country participate and give their reasons for favoring a particular security.

Figure 9.1.
Source: Berkshire Hathaway, *2005 Annual Report*, 24.

student—put three-quarters of his money in this one investment. He sold this stake a year later for a 50 percent profit.[1]

In the *Commercial and Financial Chronicle* dated December 6, 1951, Buffett wrote a brokerage note speaking of GEICO as "The Security I Like Best." The note—reprinted in the 2005 Berkshire Hathaway annual report—demonstrates that even at just 21 years of age, Buffett already understood many keys to successful investment research. He did not look at GEICO by itself, but calibrated it with the development of the overall car insurance sector it was operating in. He also looked deeply at specific operating metrics of GEICO. Realizing that the high growth many insurance companies claimed was merely a function of increasing prices due to inflation, Buffett broke out the growth in policyholders from the growth due to higher prices, thereby legitimizing GEICO's true growth;[2] GEICO had increased policyholders from approximately 26,000 in 1940 to 144,000 in 1950.

In 1976 Buffett returned his attention to GEICO. While it had grown significantly during the 1950s and 1960s, expanding its customer base and its pricing model, by 1976 it was in serious trouble. CEO Norm Gidden's focus on growth had led to years of poor underwriting decisions, and claims costs were spiraling out of control. By mid-1976, GEICO was on the verge of bankruptcy, and the share price had dropped to $2 per share from as high as $61 several years earlier. Strapped for cash, the company cut its dividend and desperately needed an injection of cash to continue as a business. As the situation worsened, Gidden was fired, and Sam Butler, a lawyer from Cravath, Swain, & Moore who at the time was the chairman of the board, took over as temporary CEO.[3] To most potential investors at the time, the situation would have seemed to be in free fall. At the annual shareholders meeting that year at the Washington Statler Hilton, a mob of angry investors grilled and booed management.[4]

Clearly, Buffett had a different take on GEICO than the multitude of investors who had given up on the company. As the financials of GEICO reveal, the company indeed had some positives. Buffett knew from his prior experience (and as he recounted frequently in hindsight) that GEICO still had a unique position in the insurance industry. It insured a safe set of public employees and other low-risk customers and had built a good reputation within this market segment over the years. Also, unlike most of its larger peers, it sold its insurance directly instead of through agents, and its significant savings on distribution costs gave it a structural cost advantage. Based on this, the business had consistently grown policy numbers and underwriting profit in the 1950s and 1960s.

But there were many negatives. The business reported a loss of $190 million in underwriting for the year 1975, and—as Buffett attested—it was clear that the business was far underreserved for claims.[5] With $25 million in book capital, it would not have taken much to put the business's survival at risk. The negatives of GEICO in 1976 are not often discussed now, but these would have seemed very significant to a potential investor at the time. First, an insurance business with a $190 million underwriting loss and only $25 million in equity capital was almost certainly in breach of regulatory capital requirements. It was no surprise that insurance commissioners from numerous states, including Washington, D.C.'s Max Wallach, were poised to declare GEICO bankrupt.[6] The risk that GEICO would be forced to stop operating was very real.

Moreover, a potential investor would have found it impossible to determine the actual scope of underreserving. The very nature of automotive insurance is that losses can be incurred many years into the future—for example, an injured individual who requires lifelong care. Hence, once an insurer is known to have set incorrectly low reserves, the extent of its error is very difficult to pinpoint. Much of the security of the business depends on the trust that management has been conservative, and once that trust is breached, it is very difficult to find footing. Considering these obvious negatives, GEICO would have been a heavy lift for any potential investor.

GEICO's luck began to turn in May 1976, when Jack Byrne, a self-made insurance prodigy who had turned around Travelers Group, was recruited and appointed CEO, replacing the temporarily appointed Butler. Byrne, who had been disgruntled at having been passed over for the job of CEO at Travelers, would soon show his brilliance as an insurance executive. Indeed, he was a major reason for Buffett's renewed interest in the company.

While Buffett understood that there were similarities to the American Express situation, GEICO, unlike American Express, was not strong enough to recover without help. What he needed to know, then, was whether there was management in place that would be able to pull off the turnaround and if the issues relating to having enough capital—both to satisfy regulatory requirements and to correct the issue of underreserving—could be resolved. On management, Buffett needed to know Jack Byrne. On capital, he had to understand the regulatory mandates for additional capital, how those could be met, and whether other insurance companies or banks would be willing to provide additional capital.

To assess Jack Byrne, Buffett scheduled a meeting through Katherine Graham and Lorimer Davidson. The key question "was whether Byrne

really was cool, unflappable, and professional . . . a leader and a pro-
moter . . . [able] to solve [GEICO's] problem . . . [and] make that sale to
all the constituencies."[7] The meeting was more than reassuring. Buffett was
so impressed with Byrne that he started purchasing shares the very next
morning.[8] Buffett later said that he believed in Jack and thought he was the
right man in every way to get GEICO back on track.

As far as the need for capital, Buffett knew he would be able to play
a role. He went to see Wallach, the D.C. insurance regulator, and personally negotiated the deadlines and the stringency of the regulatory capital
requirements set for GEICO. Moreover, Buffett significantly increased his
own investment in the company, thereby giving a vote of confidence from
a well-respected investor at this critical juncture. Although it was still an
extremely difficult time to raise capital, Salomon Inc. (and specifically
John Gutfreund, the influential executive at Salomon) ultimately agreed to
underwrite a $76 million convertible stock offering for the company. Other
reinsurance companies soon came forward to provide reinsurance, and the
stock that had traded at $2 per share jumped to $8 per share.

Valuation

There were approximately 26.6 million shares of GEICO outstanding. The
$190 million net loss in 1975 represented a loss of $7.14 per share. In this
$7.14, investment income had been roughly $1 per share, while underwriting
loss was roughly minus $8 per share. The combined ratio (when including
reserve additions) on the roughly $900 million premiums written would
have been an abysmal 124 percent. Although any valuation multiples based
on these negative earnings would be nonsensible (the historical PER and
EV/EBIT multiples for GEICO were negative), what Buffett likely calculated was what would happen if Jack Bryne was able to stop the bleeding
and save some of the GEICO business. One can use a back-of-the-envelope
scenario to estimate this: The scope of GEICO's business is cut in half—
written premiums go from $900 million to $450 million—but the combined ratio becomes 95 percent, a respectable but not unreasonable level.
In this case, the underwriting loss would become an underwriting profit
of approximately $22.5 million—a bit less than $1 per share in underwriting earnings. Assuming that, on average, half of a year's premium would be
held as float to be invested at the prevailing interest rate of around seven
percent,[9] one would expect a further investment income of a bit more than

$0.50 per share. In this scenario, the steady-state earnings of GEICO before tax would be around $1.50, with an after-tax figure of around $0.75 (the prevailing corporate rate was 48 percent). If one assumes that a fair PER multiple for this business would be 10×, the fair value of GEICO under this scenario would be $7.50 per share. Of course if the investor of the *float* were to get more than seven percent per annum (i.e., if Buffett were to get a return of 20 percent per annum), the business would have been worth much more than $7.50 per share. Likewise, if the premiums written did not stay at the reduced $450 million level but were able to grow again under Bryne's leadership, the business would also have been worth significantly more.[10]

Whatever the calculations here, Buffett clearly saw an opportunity. He paid $3.18 per share for the 1.3 million shares of GEICO common equity he bought in 1976.[11] At that price, even under the assumption of GEICO's business being cut in half, Buffett would, incredibly, have had a *margin of safety* of over 50 percent. Buffett clearly did believe in Jack Bryne and GEICO's inherent business quality, but he was also buying the business dirt cheap— cheap enough to compensate for what potential investors would have rightly seen as real business risks.

The rest of GEICO's story was a fairy tale; Jack Byrne did everything right. He instituted proper underwriting standards and cut unprofitable business. A notable example of this is the story of Byrne walking into the office of James Sheeran, the New Jersey insurance commissioner, and— after unsuccessfully asking to raise rates in New Jersey—throwing GEICO's state license on the table and firing two thousand New Jersey employees and terminating thirty thousand policyholders that very afternoon. GEICO quickly emerged as a leaner but also a healthier business. By 1977, GEICO returned to profitability. In the states it still operated in, GEICO was able raise its premiums by an average of 38 percent.[12] By 1979, GEICO made pretax profits of $220 million—an unimaginable figure just three years earlier.

With the turnaround going well, Buffett continued to accumulate shares of GEICO. In 1977, Berkshire owned 1,986,953 convertible preferred shares as well as 1,294,308 common shares of GEICO, then valued at $33.5 million. In 1979, the shareholder letter showed that Berkshire owned 5,730,114 shares in total. By 1980, GEICO had become the largest noncontrolled holding of Berkshire, representing 7.2 million shares. In 1981, over half of the gain in Berkshire's net worth resulted from GEICO's performance. By 1990 Berkshire owned 48 percent of the company.

In 1995 Berkshire's investment went the *control* route when Buffett completed the purchase of 100 percent of the company, paying $2.3 billion for the approximately 50 percent that Berkshire did not own. While Buffett pointed out that Berkshire paid a steep price for the half of GEICO it did not own, the move was in line with his strategy of paying fair prices for good businesses. Buffett believed that GEICO still had the same structural advantages he first saw in 1951: selling directly, to better customers, at lower costs. As had been the case since Jack Byrne joined, GEICO was focused on building long-term relationships with its policyholders and benefiting from higher margins as the customer profile became more mature.

Overall, the investment case of GEICO was an amazing story spanning five decades. Buffett first invested in the company as a solid quality business selling at a reasonable valuation while he was still a student. In the 1970s, Buffett then bought the company as a turnaround situation where there were clear risks, but he was comfortable with an excellent manager in a business he still believed had a structural advantage in its industry. In the late years, GEICO then became a control situation. Buffett at this time paid a fair valuation for a business that continued to grow and perform operationally year after year. What ties the whole investment experience together is Buffett's lifelong devotion to following a high-quality business over a truly impressive time period and acting when there was an opportunity.

10

1977: The *Buffalo Evening News*

The *Buffalo Evening News* was first brought up as an investment idea by Vincent Manno, a newspaper broker shortly before Christmas 1976 at a dinner party organized by *Newsweek*. Although Manno intended to present the newspaper as an acquisition target for the *Washington Post*, Warren Buffett, a close friend of Katharine Graham, was at the party and also heard about the deal. When Graham decided that the paper was not a good fit for the *Washington Post*, Buffett decided to invest in the newspaper himself for Berkshire Hathaway.

The *Buffalo Evening News* was being sold by the estate of the late Kate Robinson Butler (Mrs. Edward H. Butler, Jr.). Founded in 1873 by Edward Hubert Butler, Sr., it was originally a Sunday-only newspaper. Over the years it transitioned to an opposite schedule and was released daily Monday through Saturday. By 1977, it had become one of only two major newspapers in Buffalo; the other newspaper was the *Buffalo Courier-Express*. With both papers under family ownership, it was widely known that a gentlemen's agreement between the families had resulted in the *Evening News* being exclusively an afternoon newspaper, while the *Courier-Express* maintained morning editions seven days a week, including an important Sunday edition.

The two papers shared the Buffalo, New York market, and while Buffalo was neither a large city nor one with a promising economic outlook, it nevertheless had a fantastically loyal newspaper readership with a higher percentage of local household subscriptions than any other big city in the country.[1] In this market, the *Evening News* enjoyed a higher readership circulation during the week—268,000 compared to the *Courier-Express*'s 123,000.[2] Key to this success was the strong brand name of the *Evening News* and its long history in the city. Still, the *Evening News* was not particularly profitable; in 1976, it had a total operating profit of $1.7 million, which represented an operating profit margin of approximately four percent.[3]

The lack of an *Evening News* Sunday edition clearly hobbled the paper. By the 1970s, it was one of the few newspapers in the country to take the old-fashioned approach of having no Sunday release. This was a major source of missed revenue because Sunday was when many families had the most time to read—a fact not lost on advertisers, who would pay a premium to run ads in the Sunday edition. Without this key component, the paper feared that it would soon start losing market share to the *Courier-Express*. Another fundamental concern was that the *Evening News* operated in a market that was strongly unionized.[4] Looking past these negatives, however, the *Evening News* was a high-quality business. It had a strong repeat customer base of loyal readers and advertisers due to its strong name recognition and circulation during the week.

Because the *Evening News* was a private company, a potential investor would only have had a few clues on which to base a financial assessment. According to a solicitation letter sent to advertisers in May 1977, of the 471,515 households located in the relevant Buffalo area, the *Evening News* daily edition covered 58 percent, and its Saturday edition covered 61 percent, compared to 24 percent of the households covered by the weekday *Courier-Express* and 53 percent covered by the Sunday *Courier-Express*.[5] So it was known that the *Evening News* was the leading paper in the city and had a circulation in the hundreds of thousands. General knowledge of the newspaper business would help a potential investor better understand the opportunity. If well run, a newspaper business was a fantastic business both in terms of return on capital and profit margins. The *Washington Post* in 1977, for example, made an after-tax return on tangible capital of 43 percent and had an operating profit margin of 16 percent.[6] As Buffett and other potential investors would have known, a newspaper business is a relatively cap-ital-light business; printing equipment and some facilities are needed, but the key resource of a newspaper is the quality of its editorial team and its brand among readers and advertisers. These factors are what determine profitability, and that of the *Buffalo Evening News* seemed significantly lower than what it should have been given its strong posi-tion in the market.

Before turning to the valuation of the *Evening News*, another key aspect to consider is the management situation at the newspaper, which was in flux in 1977. Kate Robinson Butler had run the paper until her death in 1974, when Henry Z. Urban was appointed by the Butler estate as the new publisher. Investors would have realized that Urban's short tenure opened up the opportunity for significant changes to the team.

In 1977, Buffett purchased the entire business for $32.5 million. This was a significant investment for him (through his investment vehicle Berkshire Hathaway); his estimated net worth at the time was only about $70 million.[7] In terms of valuation, this represented a very high mul-tiple (EV/EBIT of 19) based on the *Evening News*'s $1.7 million operating income in 1976. Buffett likely saw three upsides in making this purchase. First, he saw a business he liked and understood. Buffett had by this time accumulated plenty of knowledge about media companies, and he knew the demographics that would make a newspaper business a good one, in particular through his involvement with the *Washington Post*. He likely thought that the readership of the *Evening News* in Buffalo and its reputa-tion fit this picture. Second, he saw a business where significant improve-ments were possible. Noting a low profit margin, obvious opulence in the offices, and high salaries in comparison with peers, Buffett likely saw many opportunities to improve the net income figures. And of course, there was the lack of a Sunday edition. With the *Courier-Express* barely profitable,[8] publishing on Sunday could make the *Evening News* the only major newspaper in Buffalo. Third, Buffett knew that he could bring in new management talent to run the business, and he had individuals in his personal network, including Stan Lipsey (former head of Buffett's news-paper, the *Omaha Sun*), who were ideal candidates for this task. As Buf-fett noted later in his 1977 letter to shareholders,[9] publisher Henry Urban and editor Murray Light were people he and Charlie Munger admired. But they also knew that there were others, like Lipsey, who could help transform the business.

Despite these opportunities, the road to success was not easy. First, there were legal issues. Immediately after Buffett's purchase of the *Evening News* a Sunday edition launched, with a free introductory offer to its regular weekday customers. Fearing for its livelihood, the *Courier-Express* brought a lawsuit against the *Evening News* on grounds of monopolistic behavior. The case was presided over by Judge Charles L. Brieant, Jr. in U.S. District Court in Buffalo, New York, and the initial verdict was against the *Evening News,* limiting its ability to promote its Sunday edition aggressively. But in 1979, the U.S. Court of Appeals in New York reversed the earlier decision, allowing the *Evening News* more freedom in competing aggressively against the *Courier-Express.* This competition became an all-out war, and both newspapers lost money for the next few years. By 1982, total accumulated losses for the *Evening News* amounted to $12.5 million since 1977. Then in September 1982, the *Courier-Express* shut down. In the *Evening News*'s first year as a monopoly, the paper—now renamed the *Buffalo News*—made $19 million in pretax profits.[10]

In the following years, business went from good to great. In 1986, the *Buffalo News* made a pretax profit of $35 million, more than the total purchase price of the business paid by Buffett nine years earlier. In the Berkshire Hathaway letter to shareholders of that year, Buffett reported, "The *Buffalo News* has the highest weekday penetration rate (the percentage of households in the paper's primary marketing area purchasing it each day) among any of the top 50 papers in the country. Our Sunday penetration, where we are also number one, is even more impressive. It now has a penetration ratio of 83 percent and sells about 100,000 copies more each Sunday than did the *Courier-Express* ten years ago."

Although the investment clearly worked out for Buffett, it would not have been an easy decision for a potential investor considering investing in the *Evening News* in 1977. The competition the newspaper faced was significant, and at the time the paper had limited profitability. An investment for the price that Buffett paid would have meant paying a very high multiple on the earnings at the time—banking on the assumption that the future profitability of the newspaper would be significantly more than its past profitability.

A key insight to Buffett's decision to invest in the *Evening News* seemed to be exactly this conviction about the positive future prospects of the newspaper. With an extensive understanding of how newspaper businesses worked, he seemed comfortable in making the call that the stronger newspaper in a two-paper city with the demographics of Buffalo would eventually win at the expense of the weaker one. Ultimately, Buffett clearly believed that the profitability of the *Evening News* could be improved significantly with just a few operational changes, and he must also have seen a significant chance that the *Evening News* would become the monopoly paper in Buffalo.

11

1983: Nebraska Furniture Mart

The history of the Nebraska Furniture Mart starts with the history of its founder, Rose Blumkin. A Jewish immigrant and one of eight children, she was born in a small village in Russia near Minsk on December 3, 1893. In 1917, she followed her husband of four years, Isadore Blumkin, to the United States. Blumkin, who came to be known as "Mrs. B," came from a modest background and never received a formal education. What she had instead were guts, determination, and an iron will to succeed. In 1919, she helped her husband open a second-hand clothing store, which ran relatively successfully for the next decade. But when the Depression hit, and her customers had little money, Blumkin came up with a proposition that fit the times—dressing a man from head to toe for $5. She distributed 10,000 flyers, and through her ingenuity drove sales when most of her competitors were shutting their doors.[1] In 1937, with $500 of savings, she opened the Nebraska Furniture Mart in a basement room across the street from her husband's clothing store.[2] Blumkin was 44 years old at the time.

For the first few years, business was not always easy. At one point, Blumkin even sold the furniture in her own home to make good on her payments to suppliers. When her children came home to find their beds missing and their living room completely devoid of furniture, she told

Figure 11.1.
Updated logo for the iconic Omaha store
Source: *http://www.nfm.com.*

them, "Don't worry, I'll buy you better beds. We'll have another kitchen table. But I owe this person money, and that's what's most important."[3] Blumkin made good on her promise to her children, as she did with all her promises to pay suppliers.

The concept behind Nebraska Furniture Mart was simple: Buy quality items that customers wanted and sell them cheaper than anyone else. When competitors balked at her low prices and put pressure on local suppliers to boycott her, Blumkin simply went to other cities—Chicago, Kansas City, New York, wherever she could—to buy the products that her customers demanded.[4] With her relentless focus on bringing the best value to her customer, she turned Nebraska Furniture Mart into a beloved local establishment. By the mid-1970s it had become so dominant in Omaha that numerous retail chains refused to put stores in the city because they did not want to compete against her.[5]

The story has it that on a summer day in 1983 Warren Buffett walked into Mrs. B's store and, after only a short conversation and a firm handshake, agreed to buy 90 percent of Mrs. B's business for $60 million.[6] Blumkin, who was 90 years old at the time and who had been thinking about the future of her business, decided this proposition made sense for her business and her family. In the spirit of two fair parties with nothing to hide, the deal was quickly finalized. Mrs. B remained chairwoman of the business and stayed on the sales floor seven days a week, as she wished, and her son Louie Blumkin maintained his longtime role as president of the business.[7] In his 1983 annual letter, Buffett called his acquisition of a majority interest in the Nebraska Furniture Mart and "the association with Rose Blumkin and her family" the high point of his year.

What would potential investors considering the business at the time have seen? Without access to the financials of the private business, they would still likely have been able to find out the history of the celebrated business. They would also know some key facts: that the Nebraska Furniture Mart was a single store in central Omaha, selling a full range of home furnishings from sofas to kitchens to appliances. With an estimated 200,000 square feet of floor space and $100 million in sales, it was by far the largest furniture locale in the area. As Buffett commented, "No other home furnishings store in the country comes close to that volume. That single store sold more furniture, carpets, and appliances than do all Omaha competitors combined."[8] Nebraska Furniture Mart certainly had local brand recognition and a local scale advantage— whether it was in advertising (posting in The *Omaha World-Herald*) or in purchasing (buying kitchen cabinets from local suppliers). While the store would not have purchasing advantages over some national store chains when sourcing from national suppliers like General Electric or Whirlpool, Nebraska Furniture Mart still had a major advantage in having the largest single store—it had the widest selection of products, so when a potential customer in the area wanted to furnish a home, they were more likely to find what they wanted there than anywhere else. Locally, Nebraska Furniture Mart was a giant fish in a small pond.

Potential investors also could have determined the store's customer interface: it bought directly from suppliers and sold directly to its customers, adding only a small markup from wholesale prices. Here several aspects are important to understand. First, Nebraska Furniture Mart practiced what today would be known as the discounter concept. Like Aldi, Lidl, or Walmart, the business focused on getting its customers the best value proposition based on price, passing its cost savings to the customer in the form of lower prices. Like-for-like, customers actually got the best value, and a virtuous circle ensued of low prices leading to more customers, leading to greater scale and cost savings, leading to even lower prices for customers. Blumkin was practicing this concept before Walmart or Aldi were successful in doing so on a national and international level.

Moreover, Nebraska Furniture Mart also had a cost advantage. Because Blumkin disliked having debt and generally paid cash for everything, Nebraska Furniture Mart's overhead expenses were at "ratios competitors don't even dream about," according to Buffett. It had neither interest payments nor operating leases to weight it down. In fact, in a later interview, Blumkin revealed that store expenses were just $7 million annually in 1983, meaning overhead costs, incredibly, were only seven percent of revenue, which were $100 million.[9] For comparison's sake, 1983 selling, general, and administrative costs for Walmart—itself a lean operation—were 19.8 percent of revenue, not including another one percent of revenue in interest payments and leases.[10] So even compared to Walmart's overhead expenses, those for Nebraska Furniture Mart were merely one-third as a percentage of revenue. The impressive low-cost basis was one more obvious reason why Nebraska Furniture Mart was able to sell much cheaper than competitors and still be more profitable.

Finally, even without having the usual financial statements of a public company, it was obvious that Nebraska Furniture Mart had impeccable operating metrics. The $100 million revenue on 200,000 square feet of retail space meant sales of $500 per square foot. Nebraska Furniture Mart handily bests Walmart here as well. With sales of $3.37 billion and reported a total retail square footage in their around 550 stores of 25.825 million square feet in 1983[11] had sales per square foot of only $130.

In sum, even though potential investors would not have had full financial information, Nebraska Furniture Mart would still have looked like an extremely well-run business with a few distinct local advantages. It was a simple business that had advantages in brand name and local scale, and—most important—was run by an impossible-to-match Rose Blumkin.

Valuation

Buffett offered $60 million for 90 percent of the business. He also offered an option for key members of the Blumkin family to buy back 10 percent of the equity for $5 million, which was subsequently exercised, so the final price for Berkshire was $55 million for 80 percent of Nebraska Furniture Mart. This valued 100 percent of Nebraska Furniture Mart at $68.75 million. Pretax earnings in 1983 were approximately $15 million,[12] suggesting an after-tax profit of $8.1 million.[13] For the 1984 fiscal year, the exact earnings of Nebraska Furniture Mart from Berkshire's annual report are available: pretax earnings were $14.5 million, and after-tax earnings were $7.4 million. In addition to the earnings power of the business, the business had cash on hand as well as significant value in the inventory of goods it held. Although a potential investor would not have known the exact figure, because most assets were paid for and the business had no debt, a rough estimate could probably have been made without difficulty. A later audit showed that the balance sheet value of the business was $85 million.[14] Table 11.1 summarizes the valuation multiples.

No matter how one looks at these figures, the price paid for Nebraska Furniture Mart was extremely reasonable. Buffett paid less than nine times

Table 11.1.
Valuation multiples

	1983 estimated/actual
Net income	$8.1 million
PER	**8.5×**
EBIT	$15.0 million
EV/EBIT*	**4.3×**
P/B	0.80×

*Assumption of $5 million net cash figure.

after-tax earnings and less than five times EV/EBIT, which was especially cheap as Nebraska Furniture Mart almost surely had net cash.[15] The valuation was especially attractive considering that the business had grown from nothing to $100 million revenue, and there were no signs that this growth would stop.[16] Moreover, in addition to the downright cheap earnings-based valuation, the whole business valuation had downside protection in the form of the assets of the store and inventory. Blumkin had realized the value of her inventory many times in the past, so there would be no reason to believe that it would not be possible again if it were necessary. In the unlikely case that the business were to become loss-making, Buffett could sell the assets and still realize a gain (as he had done earlier with Dempster Mill). From a valuation perspective, this was a dream acquisition.

Without even doing a formal audit on receivables or inventory, Buffett wrote a check to Mrs. B, knowing that she was good for her word. Looking at the business and the price, I would not be surprised if a potential investor with this opportunity would have done the same. Nebraska Furniture Mart was a superbly run business that depended on good execution, but it had also built important structural advantages over time. For a price that seemed to greatly undervalue the business's inherent ability to generate cash earnings and that would also have been fully covered by just its net asset value, it was a great buy (even by Buffett's lofty standards). From Buffett's perspective, however, this seemed foremost to be an investment in people—Mrs. B and her family. Nebraska Furniture Mart was exceptional because of how Mrs. B had made it so, and to ensure that her family would continue to have a part in running this business as they had done for decades, Buffett made sure that the family retained a 20 percent stake in the business.

After the purchase by Buffett, Nebraska Furniture Mart continued to grow and be very successful. By 1986, revenues had increased to $132 million, and pretax earnings had increased to $18 million.[17] Buffett would remark that "Nebraska Furniture Mart appeared to be doing just about all of the business available in the Greater Omaha Area . . . [while other] competitors come and go (mostly go)." By the late 1980s, a dispute about how to run the business developed between Mrs. B and her grandsons, who had succeeded her son Louis in running the Nebraska Furniture Mart operation. It escalated to the point of Mrs. B, at age 95, opening a competing carpet store across the street from Nebraska Furniture Mart in 1989. But the family, with some help from Buffett, soon reconciled. There was no lasting damage to Nebraska Furniture Mart, and the business continued its incredible performance into the next decade. Mrs. B lived to an equally incredible age of 104, spending her last weeks in close touch with the business that she had built from nothing more than an American dream.

12

1985: Capital Cities/ABC

Warren Buffett's first investment in Capital Cities came in 1977, when he invested $10.9 million at an after-tax earnings multiple of approximately 10 times. In his annual letter that year, he goes on to praise both the quality of Capital Cities's business as well as its management, led by Tom Murphy.[1]

However, the significant part of Buffett's investment in Capital Cities came in 1985, in the aftermath of the purchase of ABC by Capital Cities through a friendly takeover. My analysis of the investment focuses on this time period.

As background: Facing threats of corporate raiders, ABC asked Tom Murphy, the CEO of Capital Cities, to consider a merger. Corporate raiders were not uncommon at the time, and ABC was popular. It was one of the three major American television networks (CBS and NBC being the other two). By the mid-1980s, Buffett had also built a mentoring relationship with Murphy, and so it came as no surprise that, when Buffett recommended Murphy to find a "gorilla" investor to further protect the joint company from corporate raiders, Murphy recommended that Buffett himself become this investor.

The deal was announced on March 18, 1985. Buffett, whose investment is detailed later in this chapter, had a part in the transaction. Berkshire Hathaway was to contribute approximately $517 million in cash for three million shares of new equity in the combined entity. The transaction was completed January 3, 1986.

The annual report of Capital Cities/ABC year-end 1985 provides valuable insight into its fundamental business. The financial information is detailed for both the calendar years 1985 and 1984, and a potential investor would have had access to this information. On page three, there is a segmental breakdown of the combined Capital Cities and ABC business, which is calculated excluding the discontinued operations that had to be sold to fulfill the regulatory requirements of the merger. I have summarized the breakdown of revenues as well as operating margins in the different Capital Cities and ABC divisions in table 12.1. Note that for segmental margins, I have allocated group selling, general, and administrative costs to divisions based on divisional revenues. I have also included the financial statements of both the aforementioned Capital Cities/ABC 1985 annual report as well those from the 1984 ABC annual report at the end of the chapter.

As we can see, even though Capital Cities was acquiring ABC, ABC was the larger business based on 1984 year-end figures, both in terms of revenues (about 80 percent) and EBIT (about 59 percent) of the overall group. However, we can also see that the Capital Cities businesses were higher-margin businesses.

To analyze the business divisions of both Capital Cities and ABC and what would result after the merger, detailed information is presented in the operational discussions in the 1985 annual report. Starting with Capital

Table 12.1.
Overview of operating segments (1984)

Business segment	Revenues	% total revenue	EBIT	% total EBIT	EBIT margin
Cap cities					
Broadcasting	$271.8m	6%	$138.7m	21%	52%
Publishing	$591.6m	14%	$126.4m	20%	21%
Cable TV	$76.3m	1%	$2.3m	0%	11%
ABC					
Broadcasting	$3304.3m	71%	$392.3m	61%	13%
Publishing	$316.2m	7%	$30.8m	5%	11%
Other	$64.3m	1%	−$45.3m	−7%	−69%
Total	**$4623.5m**	**100%**	**$645.3m**	**100%**	**14%**

Cities's broadcasting business in 1985, the business consisted of a number of fairly prominent TV stations and radio stations across the United States. Out of this, three TV stations and five radio stations were to be divested from the Capital Cities side. A similar number of required divestitures also had to be made from the ABC side. The business that was to result from the merger is detailed on pages eight and nine of the annual report. It would include eight TV stations that together had an estimated total outreach[2] to about 24.4 percent of the country's TV audience. The FCC had a regulatory requirement that any television company could at a maximum reach 25 percent of total ADI television homes, so the combined Capital Cities/ABC TV stations would be just below the regulatory maximum. This indicated that Capital Cities/ABC would have the maximum scale and penetration advantage allowed by law. Even more impressive, all of the remaining eight TV stations were, judged by the rankings of their respective news programs, ranked number one or number two in their markets, all of which were major metropolitan U.S. cities. This suggested that the TV assets of the combined Capital Cities/ABC entity would be even better than the individual networks of the two predecessors and thus constitute a truly superb set of assets with major draw of viewership and advertisers.

On the radio stations front, the picture looked similarly strong from a fundamental perspective. At the beginning of 1986, Capital Cities/ABC owned 17 radio stations, seven of which occupied strong roles in the top 10 metropolitan areas in the United States. Although FCC regulation at the time[3] required the company to divest some of its radio assets, it had a very strong portfolio and would likely keep the best combination of assets possible under the regulation.

The publishing business of Capital Cities was a very diverse mix of traditional publishing businesses. This included specialty publications like *Institutional Investor,* an electronic database, and a large number of newspapers. The individual newspapers and magazines are discussed at length in the operational review. The main point that arises, however, is that the business was one that grew in circulation and advertising revenues, and included leading publications in niche market segments. To sum up this point, Figure 12.1 illustrates the development of Capital Cities's publishing business over the previous 10 years, which is detailed on pages 12 and 13 in the operational business review.

Clearly, the annual compounded growth rate for the publishing business had been an impressive 20 percent-plus both in terms of revenues and operating earnings.

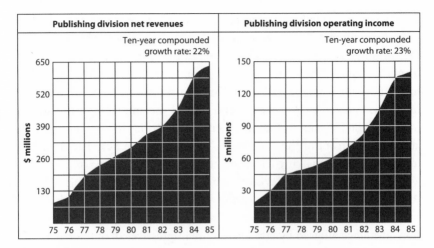

Figure 12.1.
Publishing division—development of revenues and income (1975–1985).

The last business from the original Capital Cities group was the cable television business. In note 11 of the Notes to Consolidated Finance Statements, which is the segmental data, we can see that the cable business first became positive income (going through breakeven) in 1982, and had been growing both revenues and operating profit like the other business units. Still, with $5 million in annual operating income, it was by far the smallest of the three Capital Cities divisions.

Taking a look at the financial statement of Capital Cities, one can calculate based on the 1984 year-end balance sheet what the return on tangible capital (ROTCE) of the overall Capital Cities business was.

The tangible capital base is calculated as $923 million. However, this includes an amount of $482 million (a bit more than half of the total TCE),

Table 12.2.

Category	Amount in $	As a % of revenues
PPE	$317.9m	31.1%
Intangibles excluding goodwill	$481.5m	47.2%
Inventories	$9.8m	1.0%
Accounts receivables	$145.4m	14.2%
Accounts payables	−$31.6m	−3.1%
Total capital employed (TCE)	**$923.0m**	**90.4%**

which are intangible assets such as broadcasting licenses, network affiliation contracts, and publishing franchises. Although strictly speaking, these
assets are not goodwill, I would tend to agree with the management that
their amortization is theoretically incorrect as their value does not tend
to be consumed over time. I have included the note of the management,
which is note 8 of the notes to the consolidated financial statements, to
further clarify this asset.

A conservative but fair adjustment—to consider only 25 percent of the
total intangible assets in calculating the total capital employed base—would
result in figures as follows:

Intangible Assets*

The broadcasting and substantially all publishing intangible assets represent
broadcasting licenses, network affiliation contracts and effective economic publishing franchises, all of which may be characterized as scarce assets, with very
long and productive lives. Such assets have historically increased in value with the
passage of time. In accordance with *Accounting Principles Board Opinion No. 17*,
those intangible assets acquired subsequent to 1970 are being amortized over periods of up to 40 years, even though in the opinion of Management, there has been
no diminution of value of the properties. Cable television intangible assets principally represent amounts related to individual cable television franchises. Such
franchise intangibles are amortized over the remaining lives of the franchises;
other cable television intangible assets are amortized over 40 years. At December
31, 1985, the Company's intangible assets were as follows (000s omitted):

Table 12.3.

	Total	Broadcasting	Cable television	Publishing
Intangible assets not subject to amortization	$123,815	$103,099	—	$20,716
Intangible assets required to be amortized	438,700	54,877	120,769	263,054
	562,515	157,976	120,769	283,770
Accumulated amortization	81,003	4,398	30,817	45,788
	$481,512	$153,578	$89,952	237,982

*Note 8 from Capital Cities/ABC 1985 Annual Report.

Table 12.4.

Category	Amount in $	As a % of revenues
PPE	$317.9m	31.1%
Intangibles excluding goodwill	$120.4m	11.8%
Inventories	$9.8m	1.0%
Accounts receivables	$145.4m	14.2%
Accounts payables	−$31.6m	−3.1%
Total capital employed (TCE)	**$561.9m**	**55.0%**

For the after-tax earnings, I use NOPAT based on EBITA (excluding amortization of intangibles) and then adjusted for a prevailing tax rate, which is about 50 percent in 1984. I agree with the management's viewpoint that these intangibles are for the most part not consumed over time. The costs of maintaining these franchises and licenses are already included in the P&L, and thus should not be considered additional expenses that are capitalized as an asset and then consumed over time. Based on this, the NOPAT in 1984, based on pro forma figures is:

Table 12.5.

Reported operating income	$277.5m
Add-back of amortization	+$19.7m
EBITA	$297.2m
Adjustment for tax (50%)	−$148.6m
NOPAT	**$148.6m**

Based on these figures the ROTCE is $148.6m/$561.9m = 26.4 percent. This number is based on the after-tax earnings for assuming an unleveraged business.

This is a very healthy return indicating a business that is a good inherent compounder of capital given its double-digit growth (see details in the 10-year financial summary on pages 20 and 21 in the Capital Cities/ABC annual report for year-end 1985).

Switching over to the ABC business, ABC's largest division was also their broadcasting division. Besides the aforementioned television stations and radio stations, the largest part of ABC's broadcasting division was the

ABC television network. This was the distribution and sales arm responsible for delivering the content produced by ABC Entertainment, ABC News, and ABC Sports with a reach of 99 percent of the nation's 84.9 million television homes at the time in 1984.

Delivering such prominent TV shows as *Dynasty* in entertainment ("ranked as the most watched series many weeks [in 1984]") and *20/20* in news, ABC claimed on page two of its annual report to be "the world's largest advertising medium for the eighth consecutive year." Whether this was a clear case of dominance or not, it is certain that ABC was one of the three largest broadcasting networks along with NBC and CBS. With it came advantages of scale and bargaining power with content providers and advertisers.

In 1984, ABC had the very unique position of having the rights to cover both the 1984 Winter Olympics in Sarajevo, Yugoslavia as well as the 1984 Summer Olympics in Los Angeles. The effect of higher advertising coverage on revenues and income was obvious. Although ABC's revenues had increased by 11 percent between 1982 and 1983, this figure accelerated to 27 percent between 1983 and 1984. Likewise, the operating earnings increased seven percent between 1982 and 1983 and 18 percent between 1983 and 1984. As such, there was a level of "exceptional" profits and earnings, which one should note would not have been expected in 1985 without any Olympic events.

Given that the broadcasting division was by far the dominant business of ABC at the time, as a potential investor I would likely have looked at its other two divisions at a more basic level. The publishing business was an aggregation of several magazine and niche periodicals as well as a book publishing business, which fundamentally was similar to the publishing business of Capital Cities. However, with an 11 percent operating margin, it seemed significantly less well managed or advantaged compared to Capital Cities's publishing division, which has an operating margin of 21 percent. The last division designated as "other" in the Overview of Operating Segments in table 12.1 includes a set of cable businesses, with ownership of ESPN and a motion pictures studio. Fundamentally, cable television would have seemed a decent quality business as it usually involves recurring subscriptions, but this division was unprofitable at the time.

Looking at the overall financials of the ABC business, one can calculate the following ROTCE based on its 1984 annual report:

Table 12.6.

Category	Amount in $	As a % of revenues
PPE	$563.2m	15.2%
Program rights, production costs*	$409.9m	11.1%
Inventories	$24.8m	0.7%
Accounts receivables	$422.5m	11.4%
Prepaid expenses	$136.3m	−3.7%
Accounts payables	−$31.6m	−0.9%
Accrued program costs	−$213.7m	−5.8%
Accrued compensation	−$81.1m	−2.2%
Total capital employed (TCE)	**$957.7m**	**25.8%**

*ABC makes a distinction between program rights that are for production of programming and other intangible assets like those related to a brand. The former are considered an asset, while the latter have been excluded (the same as Capital Cities had done).

The NOPAT calculation is as follows:

Table 12.7.

Reported operating income	$368.8m
Add-back of amortization	+$5.8m
Add-back of interest	+$5.8m
EBITA	$380.4m
Adjustment for tax (47%)	−$178.8m
NOPAT	**$201.6m**

Based on these figures, the ROTCE is 21.1 percent. This is somewhat lower than at Capital Cities, but still over 20 percent, again indicating a good business. This is consistent with an understanding of ABC as one of the leading television networks in the United States with successful TV, radio station, and publishing businesses.

Although it is clear and detailed in the 1985 annual report that some parts of the businesses were to be divested between 1985 and 1986, the core combined entity of Capital Cities/ABC would become a very good-quality business. This entailed that it would certainly be as good of an inherently compounding business, with growth and high ROTCE, as the two original parts.

Turning now to valuation, according to page two (as marked) of the Capital Cities/ABC 1985 annual report, the merger incorporated an investment of $517 million for three million new shares of common stock of the combined Cap Cities/ABC company. This suggests that Buffett paid $172.5 per share. This is consistent with the information given on page 18 of the Berkshire Hathaway annual letter to clients dated March 4, 1986 (1985 year-end). The shares would come into effect at the completion of the merger.

According to the annual report, at year-end 1985 13.08 million shares of Capital Cities were already outstanding. As part of the merger, another $100 million in warrants would be issued, which would give the right of holders to acquire up to 2.9 million shares at a price of $250, i.e., it was out of the money when issued, but would be dilutive once the share price of Capital Cities/ABC went above $250 per share. Hence upon the completion of the merger, a shareholder of the company could be expected to face an outstanding share count of common shares of approximately 16 million shares with dilutive options, further increasing share count to about 19 million shares in the case the stock price went above $250 per share. The 16 million shares were simple enough to handle; any earnings figures would simply be divided by the 16 million shares rather than 13 million shares postmerger.

The cost of the warrants would have been another story. As the value of options is inherently uncertain, there would have been many ways to account for the options. The typical way to handle stock options these days would be to use the Black-Scholes formula in calculating the value of the outstanding options and including it as a liability. Because this method makes use of various assumptions like the beta of a stock, which I find questionable, and was certainly less prevalent as an accepted method at the time, I would not have preferred this method. As there was a market transaction involving these options, a second method for calculating the value of the options would have been attributing the price directly of about $34.48 per warrant, i.e., $100 million for the entire 2.9 million shares. A third method, and the most conservative, would have been to see the full effect of the maximum dilution; in this case, it would be if all warrants were exercised and the share count increased to 19 million shares. In that case, one would have added the additional capital paid in to net cash, which would be $250 × 2.9 million or $725 million, but then would have had to consider the effect of dilution to 19 million outstanding shares. In reality, of course, the actual cost of the options would be based on the share price developments. If the share price never exceeded $250 per share, the options would be worthless. Alternatively, if the share price increased to $1,000 per share, the options would be very valuable.

To start, I assume as a base case that there are 16 million shares outstanding and the cost of the warrants is a liability worth $100 million, not yet considered in the balance sheet. Given the information detailed in the annual report, I come to the following calculation of enterprise value (EV):

Table 12.8.

Share price	$172.50
Number of shares outstanding	16.1m
Market capitalization	$2777.3m
Net financial debt (including cost of options)*	$2027.9m
EV	**$4805.2m**

*Note that for the net financial debt, I calculated the figure based on the balance sheet dated December 31, 1985 plus the additional debt that was to be assumed to finance the merger. The calculation includes $768.8m in cash and short-term investments, minus $714.2m in outstanding debt, minus $250m in used cash, minus $1,375 in additional debt, minus $357.5m in commercial paper. As at the end of 1984, ABC itself did not have significant debt, and I assumed that the merger would not have included any additional assumption of debt not already covered by the previously mentioned financing.

The second part of the valuation involves the earnings. As Capital Cities/ABC was to divest a somewhat significant part of its combined business in the merger, the postmerger operating earnings and net earnings would presumably be less than the pro forma figures based on 1984 fiscal year earnings of the Capital Cities and ABC businesses. That figure, as presented previously in table 12.1, was $645.3 million for operating earnings. Moreover, there would be adjustments based on amortization of intangibles and interest to get to EBITA, a metric that reflects the unleveraged earnings power of a business. The EBITA figure for fiscal year 1985 would have been $677.6 million.

Because the exact amount of divestitures necessary would be unknown, I would have approximated that 26 percent of EBITA of the ABC business or about $100 million of EBITA would have been divested postmerger, consistent in the timeframe with how the EV was calculated. This assumption is based on the statement in the 1985 annual report that $920 million in cash would be raised through the divestitures premerger (information one would roughly have known as an investor premerger). The amount represents 26 percent of the total acquisition price of ABC, which was $3.52 billion. Given this assumption that the divestitures made by Capital Cities/ABC are at the same multiples as the overall business, the resulting EBITA would have been $577.6 million. Adjusting for the interest payments and in calculating the EBTA, one would have needed to consider the additional debt load on the new business. If I assumed that the average cost of debt is 10 percent (which given the terms of the outstanding debt seems roughly accurate), the interest cost of the $2027 million net debt would be approximately $200 million. Adjusting for this, the EBTA would be 377.6 million. Assuming a 49 percent tax rate for the overall group (fiscal year 1984 tax rate was 50 percent for Capital Cities and 47 percent for ABC), the adjusted net earnings figure would be $192.6 million. On a per share basis (counting 16.1 million shares outstanding), the figure is $12.0 per share. I use this as the figure for EPS adjusted.

Looking at the EV/EBITA, one sees the following:

Table 12.9.

EV/EBITA	1984 pro forma
EBIT	$577.6m
EBIT margin	14%
EV/EBITA	8.3×

Based on the EV/EBITA figures, Capital Cities/ABC would have appeared somewhat undervalued, but not tremendously so. On the positive side, the Capital Cities/ABC business was certainly a quality business and one that could compound due to its high ROTCE and 10 percent-plus per annum growth rate. On the negative side, a 8.3× EV/EBITA when the tax rate is almost 50 percent is not a very low multiple.

Looking at the PER, one sees the following:

Table 12.10.

PER	1984 pro forma
EPS (adjusted)	$12.00
PER	14.4×

This is consistent with the assessment of EV/EBITA, that for an inherently great business, Buffett seems to be paying a reasonable but not cheap multiple. One could argue that the resulting business is better than the sum of the parts, and that there are synergies, which I did not consider. This is by choice, as I generally do not want to value things that may be possible but are not there yet. On the negative side, it could also be argued that the year 1984 obviously includes the Olympic effect for ABC and overstates somewhat the inherent earnings power of the company. This is also true, and we should keep this in mind when looking at the 14.4× PER.

Given the fair but not cheap multiples paid, Buffett's rationale for purchasing Capital Cities/ABC seems to be because the resulting Capital Cities/ABC business would be a great quality business. Both individual businesses had long histories of high steady growth with a high return on tangible capital. Moreover, the fundamental scale and leadership economics that made the two businesses successful would only increase as a result of the merger. Buffett already knew the managerial competence of Tom Murphy, the CEO of Capital Cities, who was to lead the merged company. In speaking about Murphy in his annual letter to Berkshire Hathaway shareholders dated March 4, 1986, Buffett states, "I have been on record for many years about the management of Cap Cities: I think it is the best of any publicly-owned company in the country." In numbers, according to a story recounted by Alice Schroeder in her book, *The Snowball*, Charlie Munger wrote to Buffett that Murphy had been able to compound the intrinsic value of Capital Cities since 1958 (for 25 years) at 23 percent per annum.[4]

In sum, Capital Cities/ABC was a case where Buffett had confidence in the inherent quality of the business and management to a degree where he paid a fair valuation. He did this when he was presented with the opportunity to purchase a large block of shares at a price of $175.25 per share. As an interesting final fact, he did not seem to care about the share price movement previous to his acquisition because the range of the share price of Capital Cities in 1984 was between $123.5 and $174.5, indicating that Buffett paid near the 52-week high of the year.[5]

Table 12.11.

Consolidated income statement (Capital Cities/ABC, Inc. 1983–1985)

Year ended Dec. 31
($ in thousands except per share data)

	1985	1984	1983
Net revenues	1,020,880	939,722	762,295
Costs and expenses			
Direct operating expenses	428,992	388,110	311,788
Selling, general, and administrative	256,687	232,383	189,870
Depreciation	37,990	34,084	28,099
Amortization of intangible assets	19,710	17,633	12,174
Total costs and expenses	743,379	672,210	541,931
Operating income	277,501	267,512	220,364
Other income/expense			
Interest expense	−22,738	−27,161	−14,633
Interest income	19,033	27,352	16,418
Miscellaneous, net	3,026	1,090	2,355
Total other income/expense	−679	1,281	4,140
Income before income taxes	276,822	268,793	224,504
Income taxes			
Federal	117,700	116,000	95,800
State and local	16,900	17,600	14,000
Total income taxes	134,600	133,600	109,800
Income before extraordinary gain	142,222	135,193	114,704
Extraordinary gain, net of taxes	—	7,585	—
NET INCOME	142,222	142,778	114,074
Income per share			
Before extraordinary gain	10.87	10.40	8.53
Extraordinary gain	—	0.58	—
Net income	10.87	10.98	8.53
Average shares outstanding	13,080	13,000	13,455

Source: Capital Cities/ABC, Inc., *1985 Annual Report*, 22.

Table 12.12.
Cash-flow statement (Capital Cities/ABC, Inc. 1983–1985)

Year ended Dec. 31
($ in thousands except per share data)

	1985	1984	1983
Cash provided			
Operations			
Income before extraordinary gain	142,222	135,193	114,704
Depreciation	37,990	34,084	28,099
Amortization of intangible assets	19,710	17,633	12,174
Other, net	23,374	9,690	14,386
Total cash from operations	223,296	196,000	169,363
Less capital expenditures for operations	75,384	53,866	44,418
Available cash flow from operations	147,912	142,734	124,945
Proceeds from issuance of long-term debt	493,329	4,500	197,250
Common stock sold under employee stock plans	15,662	15,127	12,559
Disposition of interest in operating properties	7,222	5,000	3,200
Long-term debt issued or assumed on acquisitions	—	13,565	5,277
Proceeds from sale of investment in stock, net of taxes	—	17,769	—
TOTAL CASH PROVIDED	664,125	198,695	343,231
Cash applied			
Acquisitions of operating property	51,109	146,843	22,016
Acquisition of stock purchase options	53,000	—	—
Purchase of common stock for treasury	484	46,135	43,619
Changes in other working capital items	3,960	1,747	13,320
Reduction of long-term debt	7,872	16,030	32,766
Dividends	2,595	2,570	2,656
Other, net	12,645	20,851	−2,558
TOTAL CASH APPLIED	131,665	234.176	111,819
Increase/decrease in cash and investments	532,460	−35,481	231,412
Cash and cash investments			
Beginning of period	236,399	271,880	40,468
End of period	768,859	236,399	271,880

Source: Capital Cities/ABC, Inc., *1985 Annual Report*, 23.

Table 12.13.

Consolidated balance sheet (Capital Cities/ABC, Inc. 1984–1985)

Year ended Dec. 31

($ in thousands except per share data)

Assets	1985	1984
Current assets		
Cash	8,031	7,737
Short-term cash investments	760,828	228,662
Accounts and notes receivable*	145,382	134,224
Inventories	9,791	10,744
Film contract rights	14,637	11,912
Stock purchase options	53,000	—
Other current assets	14,726	9,149
Total current assets	1,006,395	402,428
Property, plant, and equipment, at cost		
Land	22,726	21,941
Buildings	77,419	74,716
Broadcasting, printing, cable television, and other equipment	418,347	343,750
Total property, plant, and equipment	518,492	440,407
Less accumulated depreciation	200,596	166,014
Property, plant, and equipment, net	317,896	274,393
Intangible assets**	481,512	477,537
Other assets	79,128	53,814
TOTAL ASSETS	1,884,931	1,208,172
Liabilities and stockholders' equity		
Current liabilities		
Accounts payable	31,663	32,433
Accrued compensation	30,041	28,838
Accrued interest	21,601	3,608
Accrued expenses and other current liabilities	46,232	36,328
Film contracts	15,342	14,252
Taxes on income	24,446	38,094
Long-term debt due within one year	6,084	7,890
Total current liabilities	175,409	161,443
Deferred compensation	29,897	22,495
Deferred income taxes	41,144	25,537
Unearned subscription revenue	22,258	21,285
Other liabilities	18,546	13,424
Long-term debt due after one year	708,214	215,105
Total liabilities	995,468	459,289
Minority interest	203	14,428
Stockholders' equity:		
Preferred stock	—	—
Common stock, $1 par value (80 million shares authorized)	15,394	15,394
Additional paid in capital	37,844	26,111
Retained earnings	997,227	857,600
Total	1,050,465	899,105
Less common stock in treasury, at cost***	161,205	164,650
Total stockholders' equity	889,260	734,455
TOTAL LIABILITIES AND STOCKHOLDERS' EQUITY	1,884,931	1,208,172

Source: Capital Cities/ABC, Inc., *1985 Annual Report,* 24–25.

*Less allowance for doubtful accounts of $6,745 in 1985 and $7,369 in 1984.

**Net of accumulated amortization of $81,003 in 1985 and $61,497 in 1984.

***2,395,831 shares in 1985 and 2,526,305 shares in 1984.

Table 12.14.

Consolidated income statement and statement of retained earnings
(ABC, Inc. 1982–1984)

Year ended Dec. 31
($ in thousands except per share data)

Statement of consolidated income

	1984	1983	1982
Revenues			
Broadcasting	3,304,430	2,614,274	2,341,860
Publishing	316,249	279,858	255,429
Video enterprises	54,424	13,376	14,950
Motion pictures, scenic attractions, and other	27,883	32,629	28,514
Interest income	4,727	8,712	23,775
Total revenues	3,707,713	2,948,849	2,664,528
Expenses			
Operating expenses and cost of sales	2,596,832	2,006,949	1,792,977
Selling, general, and administrative	677,201	576,256	532,704
Depreciation and amortization of property and equipment	58,998	53,193	44,895
Interest	5,844	143	1,120
Total expenses	3,338,875	2,636,541	2,371,696
Earnings from operations before income taxes and minority interest	368,838	312,308	292,832
Provision for income taxes	−174,175	−152,474	−132,805
Minority interest	669	—	—
Net earnings	195,332	159,834	160,027
Per share earnings	6.71	5.45	5.54

Statement of consolidated retained earnings

	1984	**1983**	**1982**
Balance at beginning of year	1,012,228	899,060	785,250
Retained earnings of pooled company	—	125	—
Net earnings	195,332	159,834	160,027
Cash dividends on common stock ($1.60 per share)	−46,619	−46,791	−46,217
Balance at end of year	1,160,941	1,012,228	899,060

Source: American Broadcasting Companies Inc., *1984 Annual Report*, 53.

Table 12.15.
Consolidated balance sheet (ABC, Inc. 1982–1984)
($ in thousands except per share data)

Assets	1984	1983	1982
Current assets			
Cash and cash equivalents	154,480	52,336	66,474
Receivables less allowances of $32,957 in 1984, $25,309 in 1983, and $23,619 in 1982	422,532	368,958	359,558
Program rights, production costs, and advances less amortization	409,940	543,099	383,362
Inventory of merchandise and supplies, at the lower cost (principally on the first-in-first-out basis) or market	24,861	24,315	24,190
Prepaid expenses	136,293	119,989	110,917
Total current assets	1,148,106	1,108,697	944,501
Property and equipment			
Land and improvements	40,551	36,880	36,536
Buildings and improvements	322,901	269,880	228,896
Operating equipment	448,926	423,827	369,073
Leaseholds and improvements	39,701	60,897	40,656
Total property, plant, and equipment	852,079	791,484	675,161
Less accumulated depreciation and amortization	288,805	267,927	221,035
Property, plant, and equipment, net	563,274	523,557	454,126
Other assets			
Intangibles, at cost, less amortization	247,680	66,316	69,828
Program rights, noncurrent	309,210	300,359	379,865
Deferred charges	19,535	7,646	11,116
Other	47,577	83,963	62,856
Total other assets	624,002	458,284	523,665
TOTAL ASSETS	2,335,382	2,090,538	1,922,292
Liabilities and stockholders' equity			
Current liabilities			
Accounts payable	73,175	64,291	50,651
Accrued program costs	213,658	176,120	193,893
Accrued compensation	81,068	63,457	52,082
Federal income taxes	47,218	35,126	28,055
State, local, and other taxes payable	28,276	26,870	19,610
Accrued interest	6,218	6,234	4,773
Other accrued expenses	122,725	94,829	80,925
Long-term payable within one year	22,288	9,756	9,208
Total current liabilities	594,626	476,683	439,197
Long-term liabilities			
Long-term debt	116,650	147,923	152,577
Program rights	107,620	146,156	152,306
Capital leases	23,807	23,083	23,176
Other	62,591	50,260	34,982
Total long-term liabilities	310,668	367,422	363,041
Deferred income	33,038	32,422	22,099
Total liabilities	938,332	876,527	824,337
Minority interest	44,746	—	—
Stockholders' equity:			
Common stock, par value $1 per share, authorized 50 million shares	29,398	29,405	29,072
Capital in excess of par value	179,729	174,813	172,280
Retained earnings	1,160,941	1,012,228	899,060
Total	1,370,068	1,216,446	1,100,412
Less common stock in treasury, at cost	17,764	2,435	2,457
Total stockholders' equity	1,352,304	1,214,011	1,097,955
TOTAL LIABILITIES AND STOCKHOLDERS' EQUITY	2,335,382	2,090,538	1,922,292

Source: American Broadcasting Companies Inc., *1984 Annual Report*, 54–55.

13

1987: Salomon Inc.—Preferred Stock Investments

Warren Buffett's dalliance with Salomon started a decade before his investment in the company. Salomon had played a key role in the turnaround of GEICO, and John Gutfreund—then an executive and later Salomon's CEO—had helped secure the financing that made GEICO's turnaround possible. As described in Buffett's letter to shareholders,[1] it was through this experience that Buffett had come to trust Gutfreund as a competent and fearless executive.

In September 1987, Salomon received notice that Ronald Perelman, one of the takeover kings who took over Revlon in 1985, was in discussions to acquire a major stake in Salomon. Given management concerns with a potential hostile takeover, CEO Gutfreund needed capital to prevent a South African investor from selling a 12 to 14 percent stake of the company to Perelman. After several revisions of offers, Buffett, acting as a white knight, agreed to invest in Salomon to keep Perelman out.

The Buffett deal was announced in late September 1987 and entailed a $700 million investment for convertible preferred stock in Salomon with a dividend of nine percent per year. The shares also carried the option of being converted to common stock at $38 per share after a three-year holding period. If not converted, the preferred shares were to be redeemed over a five-year period beginning in 1995. Buffett, it was said, told Gutfreund

1986 Annual Report

SALOMON INC

Figure 13.1.
Source: Salomon Inc., *1986 Annual Report*.

that he would be happy to buy "$700 million of Salomon preferred stock, as long as it made fifteen percent." The conversion feature was struck so that an expected profit was 15 percent.[2] As an investment, the convertible preferred shares could be seen as either a fixed-income product with an upside kicker, or as an investment into a company's equity with a solid downside protection in the form of an almost guaranteed fixed-income stream.

Putting aside, for a moment, the sensational news of hostile takeover offers and investments by white knight investors, how did Salomon look purely from the investment perspective in 1987? Taking a look at the 1986 annual report—the most recent that would have been available to investors at the time—the segmental reporting shows that the business at the time was divided into three main operating segments.

Securities, as shown here, was by far the largest operating segment. In the first part of the annual report, John Gutfreund discussed the business developments during the year and reveals that the securities segment was composed of numerous national entities in addition to the main U.S. business, including Salomon Brothers International Limited, based in London; Salomon Brothers AG, based in Frankfurt; and Salomon Brothers Asia Limited, in Tokyo. In terms of business activity, the report states that Salomon Securities focused on a combination of core investment banking activities like debt and equity underwriting along with trading/market making and research. The report notes that in 1986, Salomon managed or comanaged 764 corporate issues worth in excess of $100 billion in the U.S. capital markets. A total of 617 were U.S. corporate debt issues worth $86.2 billion, reflecting Salomon's expertise in debt. A large portion of the remainder was related to equity issues, an area in which Salomon claimed to be gaining leadership.

In the report, Salomon emphasizes its expertise in market making and transaction handling, describing its execution of the largest trade in

Table 13.1.
Overview of operating segments (1987)

Operating segment	Revenues	EBT	Assets
Securities	$6341 million	$787 million	$72 billion
Commercial finance	$190 million	$173 million	$2.5 billion
Commodities	$258 million	$52 million	$3.5 billion
General corporate		−$219 million	$0.8 billion
Consolidated	**$6789 million**	**$793 million**	**$78.2 billion**

the history of the New York Stock Exchange—a 48.8 million share block trade of Navistar International Corporation, which totaled $488 million. Gutfreund also discusses the firm's research capabilities, which were being strengthened internationally to focus on Japanese companies, in Tokyo, and on European equities, in London.

All in all, the annual report portrays the business as transaction based, with its reputation, people, and relationships as its key assets. As a potential investor in 1987, I would have concluded that Salomon was a well-run and global business, but nevertheless one without many structural advantages over its peers on Wall Street.

Salomon's second and third businesses, both much smaller, are covered in less detail in the report. Commercial finance is described in the report as a business making short-term loans to mostly European and Asian clients including corporations, banks, governments, and financial institutions. Comparing 1986 with 1985, one sees that pretax earnings in this business declined by a small amount, from $182 million to $173 million.

The last business was called Phibro Energy. As the report details, Phibro Energy had actual refinery plants with a total refining capacity of more than 200,000 barrels per day. In fact, it operated as a full-spectrum oil refiner with the ability to serve a wide range of customer requests from crude oil to finished products. In addition to refining, Phibro also had a commodity trading business that conducted hedging, brokerage, and general trading of oil as well as nonoil commodities. The report reveals a severe contraction in the energy business from the year before, with pretax earnings dropping from $119 million in 1985 to $33 million in 1986. Gutfreund comments, however, that sequentially the fourth quarter showed some improvement over the third quarter and that he hoped that this business was on its way toward recovery.

Assessing the inherent business quality of the commercial finance and energy trading businesses, a potential investor would likely have considered them similar to the securities business. Commercial finance and energy trading had some advantage due to having larger networks than most peers, but to a large degree, their performance was based on good execution rather than structural advantages.

One must now look at Salomon's financial statements. According to the selected financial data reproduced in table 13.2, Salomon increased its revenues five years in a row, from $2.9 billion in 1982 to $6.8 billion in 1986. This growth in size is matched by the growth in total assets carried by Salomon, which increased from $40 billion in 1982 to $78 billion in 1986.

On the earnings front, however, there was much more volatility. While 1982 and 1983 were fairly good years, with net earnings margins above 11 percent and 15 percent, respectively, 1984 was a down year with a net earnings margin of only five percent. Return on equity (ROE) is another important metric to consider when assessing financial institutions; for this metric, Salomon earned greater than 20 percent in 1982 and 1983, but less than 10 percent in 1984. In 1986, the ROE was 16 percent. Given that the interest rate for 10-year government bonds was roughly seven to eight percent during that time, a 16 percent ROE is a fairly good performance.

Another metric useful for assessing financial businesses is return on assets (ROA). However, the balance sheet figures make it clear that many of Salomon's assets were held in inventory for selling or passing on in investment banking transactions. Specifically, out of a total of $78.2 billion of Salomon assets, $42.5 billion related to bonds, equities, and commodities classified as inventories, and another $18.8 billion related to securities purchased under agreements to resell. Hence, ROA is not as helpful, as most of the assets held by Salomon were not expected to generate an investment return for the company. (I will discuss the ROA metric as well as ROE in more detail later when discussing Buffett's investment in Wells Fargo.) In the

Table 13.2.
Five-year financial summary (1982–1986)
($ in millions except per share data)

Summary of operations	1986	1985	1984	1983	1982
Revenues	6.789	5.701	4.039	3.123	2.947
Net earnings	516	557	212	470	337
Primary earnings per share	3.45	3.78	1.48	3.35	2.48
Fully diluted earnings per share	3.32	3.60	1.41	3.10	2.26
Total assets	78.164	88.601	58.370	42.017	39.669
Long-term debt	1.245	917	680	711	780
Stockholders' equity	3.454	2.954	2.406	2.240	1.769
Cash dividends per share	0.64	0.54	0.54	0.52	0.47
Stockholders' equity per share	22.72	19.93	16.62	15.73	12.84
Return on average stockholders' equity (%)	16.1	20.8	9.1	23.5	21.2

Source: Salomon Inc., *1986 Annual Report*, 1.

Note: Revenues prior to 1986 have been restated to include commodity transactions on a gross profit basis. The 1984 earnings and return on average stockholders' equity are after deducting special items amounting to $224 million after taxes ($1.55 and $1.45, respectively, for primary and fully diluted earnings per share), resulting primarily from a write-off of oil and gas properties and a restructuring of the nonenergy commodities business.

case of Salomon, the main takeaway is that the business seemed to be fore-most a people and transactional business. Net property, plant, and equip-ment account for only $311 million in total, and it is clear that the great profitability generated by the company is a result of the work its people have done. Once again, the report suggests that Salomon is a well-run business, but one that is heavily dependent on the skill of its business execution.

In terms of valuation, one can see from the Salomon annual report that Salomon's stock ranged from $38 to $44 per share in the fourth quarter of 1986. By mid-1987, it was clear that the year would be a poor one for financial institutions in general. Salomon's closing price on September 25, 1987—the Friday before Buffett's purchase announcement—was $32 per share.[3] While there was obviously much volatility around the stock price (and in fact, like all other U.S. stocks, Salomon became significantly cheaper in October 1987 during Black Monday), the share price a potential investor would have seen in the first three quarters of 1987 would have roughly ranged between $30 and $40 per share.

Based on the $38 per share conversion feature of Buffett's investment in Salomon, the valuation would have been as follows:

Table 13.3.
Calculation of market capitalization

Share price	$38.00
Number of shares outstanding*	156.3 million
Market capitalization	**$5,939 million**

*Based on average number of shares outstanding for diluted earnings per share 1986, reported on page 38 of Salomon's *1986 Annual Report*.

Since Salomon Inc. is a financial institution, the price/earnings ratio (PER) and price to book ratio (P/B) are crucial in assessing the value of the company. Enterprise value to earnings before interest and tax (EV/EBIT) is less relevant due to the inherent nature of financial debt and interest in this business.

Table 13.4.

PER	1986	1985
Share price	$38.00	$38.00
EPS as reported	$3.32	$3.60
PER	**11.4×**	**10.5×**

Based on the historical 1986 net earnings, Salomon was trading at an 11.4 times multiple of net earnings. For a well-run business—but again, one with few inherent structural advantages—I would have found this to be a reasonably good value were I looking to invest at the time. If one considers a price of $30 per share, the PER based on 1986 full-year earnings would have been 9.0×. This would have been a very good value, if the ROE of 16 percent achieved in 1986 was representative of the business.

In P/B terms, the market capitalization was $5.9 billion based on the $38 share price. Given that the sharaeholders' equity totaled $3.5 billion, the P/B for Salomon would have been 1.7×. Again, for a business that earns a 16 percent ROE, this is a fair price. A P/B of 1.4×, corresponding to a $30 share price, would of course have been more appealing.

In contemplating both the PER and P/B valuation, I would have considered the historical growth of Salomon, which had been significant on the revenue level but had been much less impressive on the earnings per share level. Along with the seemingly difficult business environment, I thus would have factored in only limited growth in assessing the fair valuation of Salomon. Given all this, had I been faced with investing in 1987, I would have been hesitant to invest at a $38 per share price but would possibly have invested at a $30 per share price. Note that in this hypothetical case, I am referring to the common equity of the company.

It seems to me that Buffett must have considered this investment foremost for its fixed income properties as preferred shares and only taken the equity potential for a well-run business in the framework of the convertible feature of those preferred shares. Looking for clues in Berkshire's letter to shareholders, it seems that Buffett does indeed think of the Salomon investment first as a bond-like product, saying, "From most standpoints, this commitment fits into the medium-term, fixed-income securities category. In addition, we have an interesting conversion possibility."[4]

This investment in Salomon reflected a wider trend by Buffett of investing in companies through (convertible) preferred shares. This approach differed not only from the industry norm, but also from Buffett's historical investments in common shares that defined his investing style up to this point. In his 1989 letter to shareholders, Buffett pointed out that although the convertible preferred shares did not match the returns possible when investing in businesses with wonderful economic prospects unappreciated by the market, he still expected these investments to achieve good returns above fixed-income portfolios. Moreover, these investments were in line with Buffett's mentor

Benjamin Graham's idea that "A true investment must have two qualities—some degree of safety of principal and a satisfactory rate of return."[5]

 Subsequent to Buffett's investment, the Salomon investment case unfolded as a fascinating story of ups and downs. First came the stock market crash in October 1987, shortly after Buffett's announcement to purchase Salomon. As first, Buffett had no significant cause for concern regarding his investment in Salomon. While the preferred shares seemed less likely to be converted through the equity conversion feature as stock prices plummeted, the fixed-income position would continue to guarantee a healthy dividend payout of nine percent per year. However, in the ensuing years, turmoil followed unexpectedly. In August 1991, Salomon announced that the company had violated U.S. Treasury rules regarding bond auctions and, as a result, top management resigned. What began as a submission of false bids by one rogue employee, Paul Mozer, ballooned into a cover-up by the management—up to and including Gutfreund. The situation became so dire that, at one point, the Treasury Department threatened to remove Salomon from its role as a primary dealer for government bonds. The saga is detailed in numerous books, including *Nightmare on Wall Street* by Martin Mayer, but the gist is that Salomon came very close to going under due to the pressures from the scandal. Several years later, Buffett took control of the company as interim chairman and restructured the entire business with integrity as the number one principle. In the end, Salomon was fined $290 million, and Gutfreund left the company. In 1997, the Travelers Group purchased the entirety of Salomon Brothers for $9 billion, and Buffett, after spending nine months running Salomon in 1991 and 1992, left to return to his normal responsibilities at Berkshire Hathaway. In 1998, Travelers Group merged with Citicorp to form Citigroup, an entity that still exists and includes what was the Salomon business.

Financially, the Salomon investment had been a huge hassle but was ultimately profitable for Berkshire. In addition to receiving the steady nine percent dividend until conversion, Buffett was able to exercise the conversion feature. Overall, this was perhaps a case where Buffett's initial analysis, while probably sound, did not play out as expected. However, his deal structuring and his subsequent ability to influence the situation ultimately mitigated any financial losses he would have to suffer.

Table 13.5.
Statement of earnings (1984–1986)
($ in millions except per share data)

Three years ended Dec. 31, 1986	1986	1985	1984
Revenues[a]	6,789	5,701	4,039
Interest expense	−4,484	−3,622	−2,504
Selling, administrative, and general expenses	−1,512	−1,132	−875
Special items[b]	—	−4	−400
Earnings before income taxes	793	943	260
Taxes on income	−277	−386	−48
NET EARNINGS	516	557	212
Per share of common stock:			
Primary earnings[c]	3.45	3.78	1.48
Fully diluted earnings[d]	3.32	3.60	1.41
Cash dividends	0.64	0.54	0.54
Average number of shares outstanding (in thousands):			
For primary earnings per share	149,529	147,205	143,479
For fully diluted earnings per share	156,349	155,853	154,745

Source: Salomon Inc., *1986 Annual Report*, 38.

[a]Revenues prior to 1986 have been restated to include commodity transactions on a gross profit basis.

[b]Special items in 1986 include costs of $54 million relating to a restructuring of the nonenergy commodities business and a gain of $50 million upon termination of a retirement plan. In 1984, special items result primarily from a $307 million write-off of oil and gas properties and costs associated with a restructuring of the nonenergy commodities business.

[c]Based on average number of common shares outstanding, applied to net earnings.

[d]Based on average pro-forma number of common shares outstanding, assuming full conversion of convertible securities and exercise of dilutive stock options, applied to net earnings plus the after-tax effect of interest on convertible securities (1986—$4 million; 1985—$5 million; 1984—$7 million).

Table 13.6.
Balance sheet (1985–1986)
($ in millions except per share data)

Dec. 31, 1986 and 1985	1986	1985
Assets		
Cash	1.224	931
Inventories—		
Securities owned—		
U.S. government and federal agencies	25,611	30,253
Bankers' acceptances, certificates of deposit, and commercial paper	2,628	3,494
Corporate debt	7,768	8,110
Mortgages	3,008	5,360
Equities, municipal debt, and other	2,309	1,932
total securities	41.324	49.149
Commodities	1.138	631
Securities purchased under agreements to resell	18.797	22.424
Loans and receivables	10.972	11.343
Net property, plant, and equipment	311	140
Assets securing collateralized mortgage obligations	3.586	3.333
Other assets	812	650
TOTAL ASSETS	78.164	88.601
Liabilities and stockholders' equity		
Liabilities		
Securities sold under repurchase agreements	31.140	37.959
Short-term borrowings:		
Banks	7.469	8.844
Commercial paper	3.993	4.294
Securities sold but not yet purchased:		
U.S. government and federal agencies	15.397	18.543
Corporate debt	1.218	685
Equities, municipal debt, and other	314	400
Total securities sold but not yet repurchased	16.929	19.628
Payables and accruals	10.360	10.683
Collateralized mortgage obligations	3.574	3.322
Long-term debt	1.245	917
Total liabilities	74.710	85.647
Stockholders' equity		
Preferred stock, without par value: authorized—5,000,000 shares; none issued	—	—
Common stock, par value $1 per share: authorized—250,000,000 shares; issued, 1986—152,512,432 share	153	149
1985—149,061,380 shares		
Additional paid-in capital	264	211
Retained earnings	3.055	2.635
Cumulative translation adjustments	−11	−29
Common stock held in treasury, at cost:		
1986—485,108 shares	−7	−12
1985—856,588 shares		
Total stockholders' equity	3.454	2.954
Total liabilities and stockholders' equity	78.164	88.601

Source: Salomon Inc., *1986 Annual Report,* 36–37.

14

1988: Coca-Cola

In the fall of 1988, Roberto Goizueta and Donald Keough, the chairman and president, respectively, of Coca-Cola, noticed that someone was buying large numbers of shares in the company. As it later turned out, that man was Warren Buffett. The stock had fallen about 25 percent from its pre-1987 Black Monday crash high, and Buffett was accumulating what he could. By spring of 1989, Buffett had acquired approximately seven percent of the company, at an average price of around $42 per share.[1] The joke was that this was for Buffett, a huge fan of Cherry Coke, the ultimate example of putting one's money where one's mouth was.

To a potential investor in 1988, Coca-Cola would have been a familiar name. It was a company with a fascinating history that had some notable recent developments. Originating in the 1880s as a patented medicine drink, the company had become a national icon by the 1940s. Coca-Cola was listed as a public company on the stock exchange in 1919 and by the 1980s was a well-entrenched international company. According to Coca-Cola's 1985 annual report, 62 percent of soft drink sales by volume were sold outside of the United States that year.

The 1970s and 1980s were also the decades when Coca-Cola fought the most striking part of the "Cola-Wars" with Pepsi. In 1975, Pepsi introduced the "Pepsi Challenge," in which it carried out blind taste tests between Coca-Cola

THE COCA-COLA COMPANY ANNUAL REPORT 1988

Figure 14.1.

and Pepsi-Cola at malls across the United States. Leveraging on the preference in such tests for more sugary drinks, Pepsi continuously came out ahead in the challenge with the majority of participants. By the 1980s, this advertising victory had tarnished Coca-Cola's image and had also led Pepsi to gain market share from Coke. The battle culminated in 1985 with the introduction of "New Coke"—a fairly radical reformulation of the original Coca-Cola that outperformed both Coke and Pepsi in blind taste tests. A likely reason was that New Coke was much sweeter than its predecessor; this, however, was ironic, as Coke had previously campaigned to differentiate its product as being less sweet than Pepsi. While the early acceptance of New Coke was fair, a large minority of very vocal customers quickly began to demand the return of the Old Coke. In a case that has become a standard lesson in marketing textbooks today, the ingrained image of Old Coke was so strong that—regardless of the taste of the New Coke in blind taste tests—there was an undeniable demand for a return of the original product. By July 10, 1985, Old Coke—rebranded as "Coca-Cola Classic"—was back on store shelves. By December 1985, it was said that Coca-Cola Classic was outselling both New Coke and Pepsi. Public opinion seemed to be that while the introduction of New Coke was clearly a marketing misstep, Coke's brand was strong enough to carry it through.[2]

This was the context of the company when Buffett invested in it in 1988. Two other facts would likely have been relevant to an investor at the time: In 1982, Coca-Cola had introduced Diet Coke, and in 1985, it had introduced Cherry Coke. Diet Coke was certainly a product that had been developing into its own powerhouse by 1988.

Of the public documents available to investors at the time, the most informative would have been the 1987 annual report, the latest full year report for someone looking at the company in 1988. On page six, Roberto Goizuetta, chairman and CEO, contends that the primary business of Coca-Cola was sales of soft drinks, which accounted for 95 percent of operating income. The structure of the overall business of Coca-Cola at the time is summarized in table 14.1.

As we can see, the vast bulk of Coca-Cola's operating profitability comes from the soft drinks division. Potential investors in the company would likely have focused their analysis on this division.

Table 14.1.
Overview of operating segments

Segment	Revenues	% total revenue	Operating margin	Comments
Soft drinks	$6229m	82%	23.0%	Coke, Diet Coke, Cherry Coke
Foods	$1414m	18%	7.3%	Minute Maid juices
Equity investments	Not consolidated	N/A	N/A	Stakes in bottling subsidiaries and Columbia Pictures
Total	$7658m	100%	17.8%	Figures include SG&A costs

Source: The figures were assembled from assorted financial information from the Coca-Cola Company's 1987 Annual Report.

Starting on page eight of the annual report, management describes its core soft drinks business as a business where Coca-Cola focuses on (1) selling soft drink syrups and concentrates to bottlers and fountain customers and (2) building a brand under the Coca-Cola franchise that facilitates the purchase of end-consumers. Management also gives clear operating metrics for 1987: six percent growth in volume overall. Given that the segmental revenue growth in soft drinks was 10 percent,[3] we can infer that there was also an average price increase of four percent in 1987. A business that is able to achieve both increased unit sales and higher prices has wonderful business economics, and it is not surprising that Coca-Cola's soft drinks division achieved a 21 percent increase in operating income in 1987, as reported in the same discussion.

In addition to information showing Coke's ability to sell more and at higher prices, the management team provides a breakdown of volume developments on a country-by-country basis (see figure 14.2 for information from page eight of the 1987 annual report).

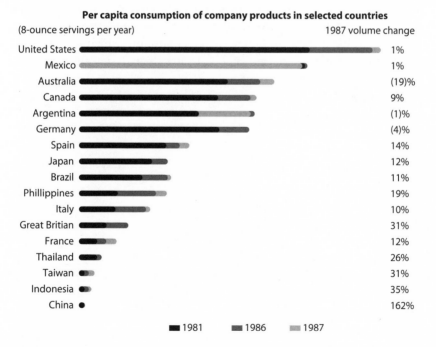

Per capita consumption of company products in selected countries

(8-ounce servings per year)		1987 volume change
United States		1%
Mexico		1%
Australia		(19)%
Canada		9%
Argentina		(1)%
Germany		(4)%
Spain		14%
Japan		12%
Brazil		11%
Phillippines		19%
Italy		10%
Great Britian		31%
France		12%
Thailand		26%
Taiwan		31%
Indonesia		35%
China		162%

■ 1981   ▩ 1986   ▨ 1987

Figure 14.2.
Worldwide consumption of Coca-Cola.

This figure alone would have made it easy for the potential investor at the time to understand the significant growth of Coca-Cola's international markets. The inference is clear: People outside of the United States in 1987 consumed significantly less Coke compared to their U.S. counterparts, and there was huge scope for further increases. This is evidenced by the numbers, which show double-digit volume increases in many of the countries with lower absolute consumption of Coke—Spain, Japan, Brazil, and China. The potential of these markets would not have been lost on the astute investor of the time.

In table 14.2, I show the numbers for the soft drinks division between 1985 and 1987[4] and modeled what those numbers would have looked like between 1987 and 1990 if one assumes that the domestic and international revenue growth between 1985 and 1987 continued to 1990. Note that I am modeling no margin increase from the 1987 level. I believe these projections to be very conservative because any such business with a distribution network and ability to raise prices has inherent scales that would lead to higher margins with higher volumes.

As one can see, even without the benefit of higher margins, which should have been the case, the core soft drinks business of Coca-Cola, would have grown EBIT by about 20 percent per annum over the next few years due to the growth of the international business, which was already the dominant business and growing at greater than 20 percent based on

Table 14.2.
Numbers for the soft drinks division (1985–1987)

Soft drinks								
Revenue	1985	1986	1987	Growth 1985–1987	1988E	1989E	1990E	Growth 1987–1990E
U.S.	1,864.7	2,016.3	2,120.1	6.6%	2,260.6	2,410.5	2,570.3	6.6%
EBIT	217.2	293.3	323.6	22.1%	345.1	367.9	392.3	6.6%
EBIT margin	11.6%	14.5%	15.3%		15.3%	15.3%	15.3%	
International	2,676.7	3,628.6	4,109.2	23.9%	5,091.4	6,308.3	7,816.2	23.9%
EBIT	672.8	888.0	1,108.9	28.4%	1,374.0	1,702.4	2,109.3	23.9%
EBIT margin	25.1%	24.5%	27.0%		27.0%	27.0%	27.0%	
Total revenue	4,541.4	5,644.9	6,229.3	17.1%	7,352.0	8,718.8	10,386.4	18.6%
Total EBIT	890.0	1,181.3	1,432.5	26.9%	1,719.0	2,070.3	2,501.6	20.4%

Source: Based on information presented in appendices of the Coca-Cola Company's 1987 Annual Report.

revenue and EBIT. Without going into detail about the financials (which I will do later in this chapter) it should have been very clear to an investor at the time that Coca-Cola was a superb business with strong tailwinds.

The management rounds out the discussion of the core soft drinks business by discussing the mostly positive operating developments in countries across the world: some restructuring in Germany, strong organic growth in Japan, the Philippines, and Brazil. They also mention that continued consolidation of bottlers has been driving efficiency gains in distribution. All of this is positive, but would likely have seemed like the icing on the cake: nice, but only reinforcing the conclusion that Coke was a superior business.

Although the financial significance of the soft drinks division to the overall Coca-Cola business is clear, management presents a less-detailed picture when discussing the other two business divisions—foods and equity investments. For foods, a potential investor finds out that the business is involved primarily with the marketing and production of fruit juices under the brand name Minute Maid. Specifically, the business has historically focused on selling frozen concentrate but is now undergoing a restructuring aimed at redirecting the business toward selling chilled (refrigerated) orange juice. Management notes that although Minute Maid is the market leader in the frozen concentrate segment, it places second in the chilled category, which is the faster-growing segment for American consumers. As such, management is investing significant resources in realigning the business and supporting the launch of new products. Financially, while revenues in the business division grew seven percent from $1.32 billion to $1.41 billion, operating income decreased from $120 million to $67 million. Adjusting for provisions related to restructuring of the division of $36 million, the operating earnings figure is less negative but still would have shown a $17 million decrease. All in all, this division seemed to be performing poorly, but the management strategy for turning it around appears quite sensible.

The last division, equity investments, is an aggregation of stakes in businesses where Coca-Cola is the minority owner. Foremost this included Coca-Cola's 49 percent ownership stakes in its primary bottling partners—Coca-Cola Enterprises (CCE) in the United States and T.C.C. Beverages in Canada. It also included lesser stakes in bottling partners— Coca-Cola Bottling Co., Johnston Coca-Cola Bottling Group, and New York Coca-Cola Bottling Company, as well as those of several overseas bottlers. In addition to stakes in bottling companies, Coca-Cola also had a 49 percent stake in Columbia Pictures Entertainment. Columbia Pictures Entertainment resulted from the merger in September 1987 between Columbia Pictures, a company 100 percent owned by Coca-Cola since 1982, and Tri-Star, which was partly owned by Coca-Cola. The company already at that time was one of the major motion picture studios and also owned a chain of 300 theatres. While all these companies were unconsolidated subsidiaries, meaning that their financial figures were not in the revenue and income attributed to Coca-Cola, they were clearly large successful businesses with value.

Before turning to the detailed financials of Coca-Cola, I want to discuss briefly how the management team at Coke might have looked to a potential investor at the time. Roberto Goizueta had been CEO and chairman of Coca-Cola since 1980, and Donald Keough had been COO and president since 1981. Thus, in early 1988, Coke had a management team that was clearly proven and one with a fantastic financial history, even if the news flow during their tenure was not always positive. It is clear from financial reports between 1985 and 1987 that the management team focused intensely on shareholder returns and key operating metrics. The three metrics that they discuss specifically in their overall assessment of their own performance, for instance, make it clear that they care about returns on capital for shareholders and in tangible cash terms (see figure 14.3).

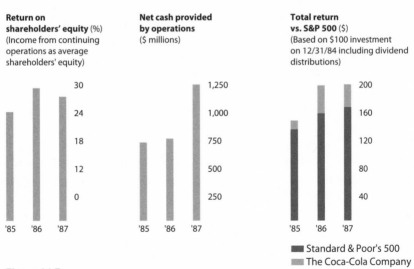

Figure 14.3.
Key financial indicators.

Turning to the 1987 financial statements of the company, the 10-year selected financial data on pages 34 and 35 of the annual report shows that Coca-Cola had grown revenues in each of its last 10 years with only one exception (1982). On the operating income line, there again was growth all but one year (1984). On the earnings per share front, there is a perfect record of increased EPS in each of the last 10 years. These financials are reminiscent of those of the American Express investment, and to any analyst of the day they should have been clear signs of an extremely consistent company. The actual figures show that between 1977 and 1987 Coca-Cola averaged 12 percent per annum growth both in revenues and EPS. This is without considering developments in minority stakes or any disbursements of spin-offs in the interim.

Zooming in on the financial year 1987, the fact that Coca-Cola overall had a 10 percent revenue and 12 percent operating income[5] growth year-over-year is hardly surprising given the performance of each individual division, as discussed previously. What is important, however, is the analysis of the compounding ability of the business in terms of returns on capital employed. At year-end 1987, looking at the balance sheet, Coca-Cola has tangible capital base as follows:

Table 14.3.

Category	Amount in $	As a % of revenues
PPE	$1598m	20.9%
Inventories	$777m	10.1%
Accounts receivables	$672m	8.8%
Accounts payables	−$1430m	−18.7%
Total capital employed (TCE)	$1617m	21.1%

The NOPAT calculation is as follows:

Table 14.4.

Operating income* (EBITA)	$1360m
Adjustment for tax** (34% rate)	−$462m
NOPAT	**$898m**

*Given the limited amount of amortization, I have taken Coca-Cola's reported operating income as EBITA, once again adjusted for exceptional items.

**In October 1986 the Tax Reform Act of 1986 (TRA86) was passed, lowering the top corporate tax rate from 46% to 34%. 1987 was a transition year, and a potential investor would have known to expect a 34% top tax rate going into 1988.

Based on these figures, the ROTCE is 55.5 percent. This is significantly higher than 20 percent, which is my personal internal benchmark for a high ROTCE business. It shows that Coca-Cola is able to run both a capital light business and one that is very profitable in relation to its capital intensity. Coke is clearly benefiting from not having to consolidate the capital requirements of its bottlers. From an internal compounding perspective, Coca-Cola compounds very well with its greater than 10 percent growth and high ROTCE. As a potential investor, I would have known that Coke was a great fundamental business from the prior analysis, but the numbers here would have shown me that Coke is truly one of the amazing businesses.

Finally, one must look at the valuation a potential investor would have seen at the time. Coca-Cola reported the 52-week low, high, and year-end prices of its stock in its annual report. In 1987 the low was $29, the high was $53.13, and the year-end price was $38.13. Assuming that in early 1988 the price was still roughly around the range of the year-end, a potential investor would have seen Coca-Cola stock priced at roughly $40 per share. In fact, although an investor at the time would not have read Buffett's 1988 end of year shareholder's letter, the share price figures just referenced are consistent with the cost basis for the Coca-Cola stock that Buffett paid in 1988. As detailed in his letter, the share price he paid was $41.8.[6]

Given the other information detailed in the annual report, the calculation of enterprise value (EV) would be as follows:

Table 14.5.
Calculation of enterprise value

Share price	$40.00
Number of shares outstanding*	375 million
Market capitalization	$15,000 million
Net financial debt**	$1,237 million
EV	**$16,237 million**

*At year-end 1987 372m shares were reported outstanding; 5.6m further share options were outstanding. As exercise prices were reported only in a range between $10 and $45, I have assumed 3m shares should be counted.
**Net financial debt was calculated based on $1,685m current loans, debts, $213m current portion of LT debt, $803m LT debt, cash balance of $1,017m, marketable securities of $451m, and pension liabilities of $4m.

As previously calculated in the discussion on financial performance, the EBITA adjusted for exceptional items was $1,360 million. Looking at EV/EBITA one sees the following:

Table 14.6.
EV/EBITA multiple

EV/EBITA	1987
EBITA	$1,360 million
EBIT margin	17.8%
EV/EBITA	11.9×

Based on the 1987 EV/EBITA figures, Coca-Cola was trading at an
11.9× EV/EBITA. This is clearly a high number. But in assessing this multiple, no value is attributed to the several unconsolidated businesses. Let me
try to address this issue now.

Ideally, for the value of unconsolidated businesses—especially when
some of them are listed entities—one takes a sum-of-the-parts valuation
based on market values for those unconsolidated entities. Because those
numbers are not readily available, I will consider their balance sheet values as attributed to by Coca-Cola—fully knowing that these values likely
understate the true value of the unconsolidated entities.[7] As evidence of
this, note that in the 1987 annual report under note three of the Notes to
Consolidated Financial Statements, in the discussion of the partial flotation
of T.C.C. there was an accounting gain made when Coca-Cola revalued the
business from the historical cost basis to the market price.

Based on the balance sheet values, the unconsolidated entities have a
value of $2,548 million. If one adjusts the EV taking this value into consid-
eration, the EV drops to $13,689 million. The adjusted EV/EBITA multiple
is then:

Table 14.7.
Adjusted EV/EBITA multiple

EV/EBITA	**1987 adj.**
EBITA	$1,360m
EBIT margin	*17.8%*
EV/EBITA adj.	**10.1×**

The price 10.0× EV/EBITA is not dirt cheap, but it seems to be a very
good price given the quality of the business. Assuming that there is even
more hidden value in those nonconsolidated entities that are carried at cost
basis, the adjusted EV/EBITA multiple would be even lower.

Looking at the PER multiple, I have calculated both the as-reported figures as well as an adjusted figure, subtracting the value of the unconsolidated entities from the market capitalization. The adjusted market capitalization is $12.452 billion; this leads to an adjusted share price of $33.21 based on the 375 million shares outstanding.

The PER multiple is roughly consistent with the EV/EBITA multiple. It should be noted that due to the lower corporate tax rate introduced in the United States in 1988 compared to 1987, the EPS would have been expected to be higher in 1988 even if operating earnings was identical; so a potential investor, without considering any growth, would have been able to calculate a lower PER for 1988 than the 13.7×.

Still, a 13.7× PER multiple, like the 10.1× EV/EBITA multiple, is a great price only for a really great business—like Coca-Cola. A conservative investor at the time, like one today, would probably be willing to pay no more than approximately 7× EV/EBITA or 10× PER for a business that was not growing. Given this, I must conclude that Buffett does pay for growth here. There were multiple tailwinds in the core soft drinks business which seemed almost obvious: (1) international expansion on the back of higher per ounce consumption in nondeveloped markets and (2) continued efficiency gains from consolidation and increased density of distribution networks. Moreover, the growth had both a very long historical consistency as well as a clear vision for decades into the future. Still, in the end Coca-Cola seems to be a clear case where Mr. Buffett does pay what most investors would consider a very fair price for a great business.

The rest of the story about this fabled Buffett investment included Buffett investing over one billion dollars into Coca-Cola between 1988 and 1989. This represented approximately 25 percent of all of Berkshire's market value at the time.

It is easy to look in hindsight and see the miraculously accurate and profitable investment that Buffett made in Coca-Cola. However, looking without hindsight, one other lesson I draw from this case is about sorting

Table 14.8.
PER multiple

PER	1987	1987 adj.
Share price	$40.00	$33.21
EPS (adjusted)	$2.43	$2.43
PER	**16.5×**	**13.7×**

out the real risks from the fake risks. It was clear from all the media stories and also some data on market shares that Coke was clearly facing competition from Pepsi Cola in the 1980s. However, the historical numbers do not tell the story of a crippling competitive war. From the perspective of the Coca-Cola parent company, it seemed that the biggest part of the business was international, and overall that business and Coca-Cola as a whole were doing fabulously throughout the decade. Although one could argue that Buffett only invested in 1988 and after the episode with New Coke, the larger lesson to me seems to be that he was able to focus on the concrete data and the overall picture, which was that Coca-Cola was a great business, was very successful, and would continue to be more successful in the future.

Table 14.9.

Financial summary (1977–1987)
($ in millions except per share data)

Year ended Dec. 31	Unit	1987	1986	1985	1984	1983	1982	1981	1980	1979	1978	1977
Summary of operations												
Net operating revenues		7.658	6.977	5.879	5.442	5.056	4.760	4.836	4.640	3.895	3.423	2.733
Cost of goods		3.633	3.454	2.909	2.738	2.580	2.472	2.675	2.594	2.101	1.854	1.531
Gross profit		4.025	3.523	2.970	2.704	2.476	2.288	2.161	2.046	1.794	1.569	1.222
Selling, administrative, and general expenses		2.665	2.446	2.163	1.855	1.648	1.515	1.441	1.366	1.150	967	694
Provisions for restructured operations and disinvestment		36	180	—	—	—	—	—	—	—	—	—
Operating income		1.324	897	807	849	828	773	720	680	644	602	528
Interest income		207	139	145	131	90	119	85	56	46	41	32
Interest expense		279	197	190	127	77	76	34	30	10	7	6
Equity income		118	156	164	117	84	46	20	14	18	17	19
Other income (deductions), net		—	33	66	12	2	11	−20	−13	−7	−18	−12
Gain on sale of stock by former subsidiaries		40	375	—	—	—	—	—	—	—	—	—
Income from continuing operations before income taxes		1.410	1.403	992	982	927	873	771	707	691	635	561
Income taxes		494	469	314	360	374	379	339	313	306	284	251
Increase from continuing operations		916	934	678	622	553	494	432	394	386	351	310
Net income	Mio $	916	934	722	629	559	512	482	422	420	375	331
Per share data												
Income from continuing operations	$	2.43	2.42	1.72	1.57	1.35	1.27	1.17	1.06	1.04	0.95	0.84
Net income	$	2.43	2.42	1.84	1.59	1.37	1.32	1.30	1.14	1.13	1.01	0.89
Dividends												
Cash	$	1.12	1.04	0.99	0.92	0.89	0.83	0.77	0.72	0.65	0.58	0.51
In-kind	$	0.90	—	—	—	—	—	—	—	—	—	—
Year-end position												
Cash and marketable securities	Mio $	1.468	869	835	734	559	254	344	235	153	325	351
Property, plant, and equipmen,net	Mio $	1.598	1.538	1.482	1.284	1.247	1.233	1.160	1.045	976	833	688
Total assets	Mio $	8.356	7.484	6.246	5.211	4.550	4.212	3.373	3.152	2.710	2.439	2.144
Long-term debt	Mio $	803	908	739	631	428	423	132	121	22	15	15
Total debt	Mio $	2.702	1.610	1.139	1.229	520	493	227	213	130	69	57
Shareholders' equity	Mio $	3.224	3.515	2.979	2.778	2.921	2.779	2.271	2.075	1.919	1.740	1.578
Total capital	Mio $	5.926	5.125	4.118	4.007	3.441	3.272	2.498	2.288	2.049	1.809	1.635
Financial ratios												
Income from continuing operations to average shareholders' equity	%	27.2	23.8	23.5	21.8	19.4	19.6	19.9	19.7	21.1	21.2	20.6
Total debt to total capital	%	45.6	31.4	27.7	30.7	15.1	15.1	9.1	9.3	6.3	3.8	3.5
Cash dividend payout	%	46.0	43.1	53.7	58.0	65.3	62.8	59.5	63.2	57.6	57.4	57.5
Other data												
Average shares outstanding	Mio $	377	387	393	396	408	390	372	372	372	372	369
Capital expenditures	Mio $	300	346	412	300	324	273	279	241	309	234	203
Depreciation		152	151	130	119	111	104	94	87	77	61	55
Market price per share at Dec. 31	$	38.13	37.75	28.17	20.79	17.83	17.33	11.58	11.13	11.50	14.63	12.42

Source: The Coca-Cola Company, *1987 Annual Report*, 34–35.

Table 14.10.
Consolidated balance sheet (1986–1987)
($ in thousands)

| | Year ended Dec. 31 | |
Assets	1987	1986
Current assets		
Cash	1,017,624	606,848
Marketable securities, at cost (approximate market)	450,640	261,785
Trade accounts receivable, less allowances of $13,429 and $11,657	672,160	672,568
Inventories	776,740	695,437
Prepaid expenses and other assets	674,148	932,630
Notes receivable—Columbia Pictures Entertainment, Inc.	544,889	—
Total current assets	4,136,201	3,169,268
Investments and other assets		
Investments in affiliates	—	—
Columbia Pictures Entertainment, Inc.	989,409	1,436,707
Coca-Cola Enterprises Inc.	749,159	709,287
T.C.C. Beverages Ltd.	84,493	87,696
Other	435,484	212,194
Receivables and other assets	289,000	217,046
Total investments and other assets	2,547,545	2,662,930
Property, plant, and equipment		
Land	112,741	98,842
Buildings and improvements	763,317	695,029
Machinery and equipment	1,488,464	1,390,689
Containers	275,120	287,672
Total	2,639,642	2,472,232
Less allowances for depreciation	1,041,983	934,679
Total property, plant, and equipment	1,597,659	1,537,553
Goodwill and other intangible assets	74,155	114,377
TOTAL ASSETS	8,355,560	7,484,128
Liabilities and shareholders' equity		
Current liabilities		
Accounts payable and accrued expenses	1,430,193	1,198,407
Loans and notes payable	1,685,408	697,743
Current maturities of long-term debt	213,609	4,628
Dividends payable in-kind	335,017	—
Accrued taxes, including income taxes	454,313	344,141
Total current liabilities	4,118,540	2,244,919
Long-term debt	803,352	907,676
Deferred income taxes	209,880	239,813
Due to Columbia Pictures Entertainment, Inc.	—	576,741
Total liabilities	5,131,772	3,969,149
Shareholders' equity		
Preferred stock, $1 par value—authorized: 100,000,000 shares; no shares issued and outstanding	—	—
Common stock, $1 par value—authorized: 700,000,000 shares; issued: 415,977,479 shares in 1987 and 414,491,987 shares in 1986	415,977	414,492

(continued)

Table 14.10. (*Continued*)

Assets	Year ended Dec. 31	
	1987	1986
Capital surplus	338,594	299,345
Reinvested earnings	3,783,625	3,624,046
Foreign currency translation adjustment	−5,047	−118,087
Total	4,533,149	4,219,796
Less treasury stock, at cost (43,621,336 shares in 1987; 29,481,220 shares in 1986)	1,309,261	704,817
Total shareholders' equity	3,223,888	3,514,979

Source: The Coca-Cola Company, *1987 Annual Report*, 36–37.

Table 14.11.
Income statement (1985–1987)
($ in thousands except per share data)

Year ended Dec. 31	1987	1986	1985
Net operating revenues	7,658,341	6,976,558	5,879,160
Cost of goods	3,633,159	3,453,891	2,909,496
Gross profit	4,025,182	3,522,667	2,969,664
Selling, administrative, and general expenses	2,665,022	2,445,602	2,162,991
Provisions for restructured operations and disinvestments	36,370	180,000	—
Operating income	1,323,790	897,065	806,673
Interest income	207,164	139,348	144,648
Interest expense	279,012	196,778	189,808
Equity income	118,533	155,804	164,385
Other income, net	34	33,014	66,524
Gain on sale of stock by former subsidiaries	39,654	375,000	—
Income from continuing operations before income taxes	1,410,163	1,403,453	992,422
Income taxes	494,027	469,106	314,856
Income from continuing operations	916,136	934,347	677,566
Income from discontinued operations (net of applicable income taxes of $7,870)	—	—	9,000
Gain on disposal of discontinued operations (net of applicable income taxes of $20,252)	—	—	35,733
NET INCOME	916,136	934,347	722,299
Per share			
Continuing operations	2.43	2.42	1.72
Discontinued operations	—	—	0.12
Net income	2.43	2.42	1.84
Average shares outstanding	377,372	386,831	393,354

Source: The Coca-Cola Company, *1987 Annual Report*, 38.

Part III

The Late Years (1990–2014)

Increasing in size, Berkshire Hathaway entered the 1990s with a total book value of several billion dollars. Warren Buffett had by this time become a well-known investor, first among other investors and later becoming the household name he is today. During this period, Buffett continued investing in more private transactions and also in larger, very well-known businesses. A key aspect during this period was that Buffett now had to invest with the huge size that Berkshire had grown to; investing such large amounts presented a potential difficulty, but it also presented a potential advantage—the fact that more capital also meant more deal flow and the ability to provide capital when others could not. The later part of these years saw Buffett preoccupied with finding good ways of deploying large amounts of capital, or, in his own words, unloading the "elephant gun." He also continues his focus on organically building Berkshire's core businesses, especially insurance.

The economic context between 1990 and 2014 varied widely and was eventful to say the least. In late 1990 the United States entered the first Gulf War, and experienced a full-blown, albeit short, recession. Stock prices collapsed, including Berkshire's, which was down significantly from its price a year before. This was a time for great purchases in the classic sense of buying war scares, and Buffett would partake in this with his purchase of Wells Fargo. Soon, however, the decade turned from pessimism to great jubilation. By the year 2000, it was a bull market in stocks, the likes of which had not been witnessed in many decades. At the core of this most recent bull market was the development of the Internet and the technology revolution behind it. While many of the companies in this sector proved more creative than profitable, it did not prevent a delirious market from proclaiming a new age of innovation and justifiable valuations.

As all manias are eventually followed by panics, the Internet bubble finally burst in the early 2000s. In 2002 the U.S. and world economies were in the midst of another recession. The year before, in September 2001, terrorist attacks on the Twin Towers in New York City had shaken the whole world to its foundation. The years that followed 2002 were years of recovery. Leading this recovery was a new bubble forming in housing prices. By 2007, the Dow had reached over 14,000, significantly higher than the Dow was even in 2000, which had been a bit above 11,000.

In the background, however, deep-seated issues with the indebtedness of sovereign states as well as the consequences of the loose lending policies of commercial banks for mortgages began to emerge. Things turned ugly quickly, and from the heights of 2007 the economy fell into a deep recession by 2008. Accompanying this financial pain was great turmoil in the financial markets. One of the biggest financial institutions, Lehman Brothers, would be one of the victims to fall in the fray. After successive rounds of bailouts of the financial institutions in the developed world, and massive amounts of capital injections to prevent a 1930s type depression, an economic recovery ensued more rapidly than anticipated. The Dow would rise to over 10,000 by the end of 2009. However, some of the deep-seated issues as well as the aftermath of the huge injections of paper money did not disappear by 2010. There was still great financial uncertainty in 2011. One of the developments during this period was the increase in commodity prices, especially in gold and oil. During this time, Buffett sensibly tried to take advantage of investment opportunities where possible, and one of his latest large acquisitions, Burlington Northern, was made during the economic turmoil of 2009.

15

1989: US Air Group

As with the Salomon deal, Warren Buffett's 1988 investment in US Air involved preferred shares: a $358 million purchase of preferred stock with a mandatory redemption in 10 years at a dividend rate of 9.25 percent and a right to convert into common shares at a price of $60 per share. The common shares were valued at around $35 per share at the time, reflecting a total market capitalization for US Air of approximately $1.5 billion. Although the investment was profitable in the end, the US Air deal is often cited as an example of an investment mistake for Buffett. Even in his own annual letters, Buffett discusses the shortcomings of the investment and his failure to correctly identify its investment prospects. For instance, in his annual letter to shareholders year-end 1996, Buffett states:

> I liked and admired Ed Colodny, the company's then-CEO, and I still do. But my analysis of US Air's business was both superficial and wrong. I was so beguiled by the company's long history of profitable operations, and by the protection that ownership of a senior security seemingly offered me, that I overlooked the crucial point: US Air's revenues would increasingly feel the effects of an unregulated, fiercely competitive market whereas its cost structure was a holdover

Figure 15.1.

from the days when regulation protected profits. These costs, if left unchecked, portended disaster, however reassuring the airline's past record might be.

It is easy to criticize investment decisions in hindsight. A more interesting question is, what would a potential investor realistically have seen in US Air at the time? To answer this, we must turn to the US Air annual report for 1988, the latest full-year report before Buffett's purchase.

The report begins with financial highlights, showing that US Air made a net income of $165 million on revenues of $5.71 billion in 1988. The prior year was also profitable for the company, with a net income of $194 million on $3 billion of revenues. The overall picture, from these financial highlights and the ensuing operating review by Chairman and President Ed Colodny, was that US Air was a profitable business undergoing huge changes in scope. The company had just completed the integration of its acquisition of Pacific Southwest Airlines (PSA) and was starting to integrate Piedmont Airlines, which was to merge in 1989. Together, these two acquisitions had more than doubled the size of US Air's operations, adding routes throughout the United States. Organically, at year-end 1988, US Air had confirmed orders for 83 new airplanes (order value of $2 billion) to be delivered between 1989 and 1991, with an optional 108 airplanes (order value of $3 billion). The confirmed orders alone would add 20 percent to US Air's total existing jet fleet.

In addition to rapid growth, there are three other notable takeaways from the annual report. First, while revenues increased exponentially in 1988 (by 90 percent from 1987), net income actually decreased. Some of this divergence can be attributed to exceptional costs related to merger integration and a one-off write-down of BAC 1-11 aircraft (outdated aircraft in its fleet), but even adjusting for these costs, US Air's operating earnings (pre-exceptional costs) increased by only 36 percent—much slower than revenue growth. A closer inspection of the income statement shows that the culprit was operating expenses, which had increased even faster than revenues—by 97 percent. Within the category of operating expenses, personnel costs, rentals and landing fees, and aircraft maintenance costs grew fastest. Although a one-year dramatic increase in operating costs does not indicate permanent cost inflation, it certainly raises a concern about how controllable some of these costs were. Were landing fees charged by airports and pilot wages increasing unchecked, as rapid growth in air-traffic squeezed resources? What exposure was there to fuel cost increases, and were there any controls over these costs?

The second takeaway builds on the first, as it brings up even more risks and uncertainties that should have been apparent to a potential investor: debt and operating leases. To fund the two large acquisitions—PSA and Piedmont—US Air issued $1 billion of new debt in 1987 in the form of a credit agreement. A portion of this was repaid in 1988 by issuing commercial paper, but at the end of that year US Air still had significant financial debt of approximately $1.5 billion,[1] which had covenants, repayment schedules, and all the other risks of significant debt. Making things much riskier, US Air had noncancellable operating leases of $6.4 in addition to financial debt (as detailed on page 23 of the report). These are the obligations that US Air had committed to pay for the future lease of aircraft, ground facilities, and other equipment. Compared to US Air's operating earnings of $434 million, the gross value of this amount was absolutely huge. As with the interest due on financial debt, these costs would be no problem if business went well. But if business were to deteriorate, these payment obligations could become problematic, and the company would risk insolvency.

The third notable fact relates to US Air's business economics, which has two aspects: (1) uncertainty and (2) mediocrity.

(1) Uncertainty: In assessing the quality of the business, a key element is what returns on capital employed it can generate. To calculate this, we must first be able to accurately estimate a steady-state earnings level. For US Airways, this is anything but easy. The first challenge is earnings cyclicality. US Air's selected financial data in table 15.1 show that net income margin can be more than twice as high (around 7.5 percent) in good years than in bad years (around three percent).

To smooth out the cyclicality, a potential investor could use the average last three years' net income margin of 4.9 percent. This may be appropriate for a business that has year-to-year cyclicality but is otherwise in a steady state. However, US Air had neither of these characteristics. Instead, it faced general business cyclicality that had no predictable timeline and was difficult to forecast. It was certainly not in steady state, as its rapid string of acquisitions masked both exceptional integration costs as well as potentially different margins inherent to the original US Air business and the acquired businesses. Although all these factors add greatly to uncertainty, an investor would still ordinarily be able to ballpark a sustainable earnings figure (by assuming average historical margins with some adjustments and calculating for new steady state revenues based on summing the revenue of US Air and its acquisitions) if it were not for an even more significant complication: The entire airline industry was in a state of fundamental change. The operating statistics table from the US Air report shows this best (see table 15.2).

More and more passengers were traveling by air, and the average distance traveled was increasing. At the same time, revenue per passenger

Table 15.1.
Selected financial data
($ in thousands except per share data)

	1988	1987	1986	1985	1984	1983	1982	1981	1980	1979	1978
Income statement											
Operating revenues	5,707	3,001	1,835	1,765	1,630	1,432	1,273	1,110	972	729	567
Operating expenses	5,273	2,682	1,666	1,597	1,483	1,304	1,194	1,052	880	677	533
Operating income	434	319	169	168	192	128	79	58	92	52	34
Net income	165	195	98	117	122	81	59	51	60	33	32
Fully diluted earnings per share	3.81	5.27	3.33	3.98	4.46	3.22	2.88	2.66	3.59	2.24	2.82
Dividends per common share	0.12	0.12	0.12	0.12	0.12	0.12	0.12	0.12	0.09	—	—
Balance sheet											
Total assets	5,349	5,257	2,147	1,951	1,621	1,318	1,062	881	715	533	404
Long-term debt	1,419	1,870	454	474	430	350	334	303	236	184	144
Stockholders' equity	2,070	1,895	1,058	956	737	615	459	353	272	216	167
Shares of common stock outstanding	43.8	43.2	27.3	26.9	23.0	22.8	19.8	17.1	12.0	11.9	9.9
Book value per share	47.28	43.90	38.77	35.44	31.89	26.77	22.89	20.34	18.43	13.85	11.82

Source: US Air Group, *1988 Annual Report*, 30–31.

Table 15.2.
Operating statistics (1982–1988)

		1988*	1987	1986	1985	1984	1983	1982	1981	1980	1979	1978
Revenue passengers	Mio $	32.5	24.8	21.7	19.3	17.0	16.2	14.6	13.4	14.2	14.1	12.8
Average passenger journey	Miles	533.3	527.7	513.5	504.8	480.5	446.5	415.2	404.6	385.3	359.1	318.1
Revenue passenger miles	Mio	17,315	13,072	11,155	9,732	8,191	7,245	6,078	5,424	5,476	5,049	4,083
Available seat miles	Mio	28,234	20,014	18,254	16,433	14,098	12,235	10,666	9,383	8,992	7,853	6,721
Passenger load factor	%	61.3	65.3	61.1	59.2	58.1	59.2	57.0	57.8	60.9	64.3	60.8
Revenue per passenger mile	C	15.33	14.91	14.93	16.71	18.57	18.42	19.51	18.93	16.26	12.88	12.29
Cost per available seat mile	C	9.34	8.90	8.74	9.45	9.98	10.50	11.07	11.07	9.65	8.46	7.67
Average distance between stops	Miles	437.7	425.2	405.8	395.4	374.3	354.5	339.3	325.6	306.1	284.2	242.6
Break even load factor	%	58.7	57.3	56.4	54.2	51.7	54.6	54.1	54.9	55.6	60.2	56.9
Gallons of fuel consumed	Mio	617	463	435	404	367	327	301	276	273	262	239
Cost per gallon of fuel	C	52.58	54.74	53.85	79.74	84.80	89.08	97.30	103.14	86.74	55.83	39.65
Number of employees at year-end	#	24,337	16,509	14,976	13,789	12,524	11,899	11,046	10,765	10,379	9,741	8,745
Aircraft fleet at year-end	#	226	162	149	143	133	127	119	106	95	90	93

Source: US Air Group, *1988 Annual Report*, 30–31.
*PSA was merged into US Air on April 9, 1988.

mile was coming down rapidly, as airlines scrambled to reduce cost per passenger mile and increase load factors. While increased passenger demand was clearly positive for US Air, the pressure for cost reduction was certainly a negative factor. Adding to the uncertainty, fuel costs had been coming down steadily since the early 1980s, but future prices were unknown. This complexity of fundamental and opposing forces would make an accurate determination of future sustainable earnings almost impossible.

(2) *Mediocrity*: If one were to give US Air the full benefit of the doubt and assume the very successful 1987 year was reflective of its inherent ability to generate returns on capital, the calculation of ROTCE would be as follows (note that each balance sheet figure is given in dollars as well as a percentage of revenues to give both absolute and relative pictures of their importance):

(a) PPE: $3520m (117 percent of revenues)
(b) Other intangibles: $202m (7 percent of revenues)
(c) Inventories: $240m (8 percent of revenues)
(d) Accounts receivables: $343m (11 percent of revenues)
(e) Accounts payables: −$283m (−9 percent of revenues)
(f) Tangible capital employed (TCE): $4022m (134 percent of revenues)

Based on the 1987 operating profit (EBIT) of $319 million, the pretax return on tangible capital employed was 7.9 percent. The after-tax figure, based on an ongoing tax rate of 34 percent, was 5.2 percent. (The corporate tax rate going forward in 1988 was 34 percent; hence, this is used to recognize the intrinsic return on capital of the business.) In either case, the key point is that the US Air business was very capital intensive, with PPE (owned aircraft and facilities/equipment) amounting to more than its revenues. The resulting return on capital, even in a good year, was no higher than its cost of capital—less than eight percent (commercial paper issued by US Air in 1988 carried interest rates of 9.5 percent to 9.9 percent). This seems to point to a business with few inherent structural advantages. It diverges from the other quality businesses Buffett invested in around the same time—Coca-Cola and Wells Fargo—both of which had superior returns on tangible capital employed.

While a potential investor should have seen US Air as a cyclical business that likely had few structural advantages and had significant financial risks, there were also many positive aspects. Foremost, in Edwin Colodny, US Air had a CEO who was well respected and had an impeccable track record. By the late 1980s, Colodny had guided US Air from a small regional airline business with $500 million revenues to one of the largest airlines in the United States (see table 15.1). He was able to do so without having a single year of losses, even when earnings were sometimes volatile. Operationally, the US Air business improved several of its metrics under Colodny's leadership, including passenger load factor and average passenger journey (see table 15.2). If US Airways was a pure execution-based business rather than one with structural competitive advantages, it was one that was well executed.

US Air had many things going for it besides just good management. Considering the operating metrics together with what was really happening, US Air was one of the preeminent U.S. airlines in 1988. It had more jet departures than any other U.S. airline and had formed strong hubs in cities like Baltimore, Cleveland, Philadelphia, and Los Angeles. A pioneer in customer royalty, it also boasted one of the largest club networks, with 28 preferred member lounges at 24 different airports. It had both a good reputation and local density advantages resulting from its size and hub and spoke system.

The list of positives goes on. At year-end 1988, US Air had one of the youngest airline jet fleets in the industry with an average age of 8.9 years. Since younger jets require less maintenance and are more fuel-efficient, this means lower costs compared to peers. The integration with both PSA and Piedmont seemed to be going well, and although US Air was incurring exceptional costs that masked its true earnings per share, there was a convincing rationale for eventual synergies along with a natural improvement in margins as exceptional costs came to an end. For an investor who was looking for the positive side of the company, it would be fair to summarize that US Air was a well-executed business in a rapidly growing industry, and it seemed on the way to consolidating a strong position in certain regional markets. It would also have been correct to conclude that margins in 1988 were penalized by exceptional costs.

All of this analysis leads, finally, to valuation, starting with the valuation of the common equity of US Air. In 1989, the shares traded between a low of $28 and a high of $40.25. Taking $35 as a midpoint around which the stock traded for most of the year, the earnings multiple looks as follows:

Table 15.3.

	FY 1988 actual	1987 actual
EPS (diluted)	$3.81	$5.27
PER	**9.2×**	**6.6×**
EBIT	$434 million	$319 million
EV/EBIT*	**6.6×**	**9.0×**

*The calculation of EV is based on a market cap of $1.53 billion plus net debt of $1.34 billion = $2.87 billion.

Putting aside the earlier discussion about the inability to accurately estimate the sustainable future earnings of US Air, the historical valuation metrics look unassuming for a well-executed and growing business, even one with limited structural advantages. Adjusted for the exceptional costs associated with merger integration and the write-down of BAC 1-11 aircraft, the PER multiple for fiscal year 1988 would have been only 7.2×. Because US Air has significant debt, the PER ratio in general looks cheaper than the EV/ EBIT multiple, although a 6.6× EV/EBIT multiple is also not expensive in absolute terms. This was how the valuation looked for the common shares.

Buffett, however, invested in a private placement acquiring convert- ible preferred shares with the qualities of a fixed yield of 9.25 percent, a conversion right for each share into common shares at $60 per share, and a mandatory redemption 10 years from issuance.

Similar to the setup in the Salomon case, the risk profile of this secu- rity is completely different from common equity. The main value of this security comes from its fixed-income quality of paying preferred dividends, which were to be paid before any other ordinary dividends by the company; the conversion feature was a bonus in case US Air became very successful and its common equity would increase in value from its current $35 per share to $60 per share. What differs in this case, compared to the Salomon case, was that the conversion feature was struck at a price much higher than the prevailing common equity price. This implies that the fixed income component was comparatively more important because reaching the equity conversion would be more difficult. Thus, an investor could consider this specific investment to be one where Buffett purchased a fixed-income security, getting a yield of 9.25 percent, which was roughly comparable to the debt issued by US Air. This security had more risks than actual US Air bonds (because those are senior to preferred shares), but also had the optional value in case US Air became even more successful in the ensuing

10 years. Specifically, looking back at the valuation of common equity, the $60 conversion feature would value US Air at an adjusted PER multiple of 12.4× based on 1988 EPS. This value is not especially expensive on a superficial level, and if US Air was able to continue its historical growth and profitability, this would be more than achievable.

All considered, US Air was an investment case where Buffett's investment was markedly different from the choice an ordinary investor would have had. He invested in a preferred convertible share with a conversion feature at $60 per share, whereas the ordinary investor faced a common equity share at around $35 per share. Focusing specifically on the analysis of the common equity shares, a potential investor would have seen many positive aspects as well as negative ones. On the one hand, US Air looked like a leader in its industry, a well-executed business with a proven management team. On the other hand, it should have been very clear to investors that it would be difficult to predict future earnings due to significant changes in the business and its industry, as well as obviously significant risks from financial debt and operating leases. To a prudent investor, the common shares of US Air would likely have fit in the bucket of "too hard to tell." But again, this was not what Buffett invested in.

The aftermath of the US Air investment is well documented in Buffett's own letters to shareholders. Almost immediately after Buffett's investment in US Air, continued route competition and intensifying pricing pressure in airfares led the entire U.S. airline industry into a lull. When the economic recession struck in 1990 and 1991 during the First Gulf War, the U.S. airline industry was decimated. Between 1991 and 1992, some of US Air's largest peers, including Midway Airlines, Pan Am, America West, Continental, and TWA, went into bankruptcy. Compounding the issues, these carriers—no longer bound by their historical financial obligations—continued operating out of bankruptcy with even lower pricing schemes and cut-throat competition. Between 1990 and 1994, US Air lost an aggregate of $2.4 billion, wiping out its entire shareholders' equity. In 1994, its preferred dividend on the shares owned by Buffett was suspended. Buffett wrote off three-quarters of his $358 million investment in US Air preferred shares and tried—unsuccessfully—to sell the shares in 1995 at 50 percent of face value.[2]

Luckily for Buffett, business gradually improved, and when US Air finally had a good full year in 1995, the dividend on the preferred shares resumed. In fact, because Buffett had been cautious enough to structure his initial deal to include a penalty for preferred dividends that were missed, he even received

Table 15.4.
Consolidated balance sheet (1987–1988)
Years ended Dec. 31
($ in thousands)

	1988	1987
Assets		
Current assets		
Cash and cash equivalents	78,000	232,577
Receivables, net	381,127	343,170
Materials and supplies, net	265,310	239,838
Prepaid expenses	97,088	80,530
Total current assets	821,525	$896,115
Property and equipment		
Flight equipment	3,117,121	3,162,995
Ground property and equipment	824,230	642,444
Less accumulated and depreciation	778,100	591,800
Total property and equipment	3,163,251	3,213,639
Purchase deposits	405,448	306,440
Total property and equipment, net	3,568,699	3,520,079
Other assets		
Goodwill, net	623,889	576,857
Other intangibles, net	189,678	202,463
Other assets	145,087	61,239
Total other assets	958,654	840,559
TOTAL ASSETS	5,348,878	5,256,753
Liabilities and stockholders' equity		
Current liabilities		
Current maturities of long-term debt	85,643	71,402
Accounts payable	371,146	283,437
Traffic balances payable and unused tickets	318,883	297,485
Accrued expenses	433,381	341,086
Total current liabilities	1,209,053	993,410
Long-term debt, net of current maturities	1,332,872	1,798,226
Deferred credits and other liabilities		
Income taxes	340,769	344,508
Deferred gains and other liabilities	396,672	225,691
Total deferred credits and other liabilities	737,441	570,199
Total liabilities	3,279,366	3,361,835
Stockholders' equity:		
Preferred stock*	—	—
Common stock**	44,411	43,801
Paid-in capital	1,068,958	1,050,637
Retained earnings	982,904	823,111
Common stock held in treasury***	−26,761	−22,631
Total stockholders' equity	2,069,512	1,894,918
TOTAL LIABILITIES AND STOCKHOLDERS' EQUITY	5,348,878	5,256,753

Source: US Air Group, *1988 Annual Report*, 17.
*Without nominal or par value, authorized 1 Mio shares issuable in series.
**Par value $1 per share; authorized 75 Mio shares, issued 44,411,000 shares and 43,801,000 shares, respectively.
***635,000 and 632,000 shares, respectively, and other.

Table 15.5.
Consolidated income statement (1986–1988)
Years ended Dec. 31
($ in thousands except per share data)

		1988	1987	1986
Operating revenues				
Passenger transportation		5,273,955	2,775,581	1,709,050
Other		433,037	225,503	126,149
Total operating revenues	'000 $	5,706,992	3,001,084	1,835,199
Operating expenses				
Personnel costs		1,944,428	1,039,471	687,389
Aviation fuel		638,453	377,602	237,946
Travel agency commissions		382,718	203,623	124,154
Rentals and landing fees		510,740	200,397	83,778
Aircraft maintenance		337,564	155,782	73,140
Depreciation and amortization		229,729	127,630	93,191
Other		1,229,768	577,361	366,237
Total operating expenses	'000 $	5,273,400	2,681,866	1,665,835
Operating income	'000 $	433,592	319,218	169,364
Other income/expense				
Interest income		12,573	22,474	22,633
Interest expense, net of capitalized interest		−123,206	−88,828	−31,488
Write-down of BAC 1-11 aircraft and spares		−33,000	—	—
Other		−20,445	3,501	9,393
Total other income/expense	'000 $	−164,078	−62,853	538
Income before taxes and equity in net income of Piedmont	'000 $	269,514	256,365	169,902
Provision for income taxes		104,150	101,080	71,550
Income before equity in net income of Piedmont		165,004	155,285	98,352
Equity in net income of Piedmont		—	39,364	—
NET INCOME	'000 $	165,004	194,649	98,352
Earnings per share				
Primary	$	3.81	5.28	3.34
Fully diluted	$	3.81	5.27	3.33
Shares used for computation:				
Primary		43,304	37,728	31,560
Fully diluted		43,315	37,802	31,695

Source: US Air Group, *1988 Annual Report*, 16.

Table 15.6.
Cash-flow statement (1986–1988)
Years ended Dec. 31
($ in thousands)

	1988	1987	1986
Cash flows from operating activities			
Net income	232,577	336,158	349,667
Adjustments to reconcile net income to cash provided by operating activities			
Depreciation and amortization	165,004	194,649	98,352
Deferred income taxes	229,729	127,630	93,191
Write-down of BAC-11 aircraft and spares	−3,739	57,294	65,020
Equity in net income of Piedmont, net of dividends	33,000	—	—
Loss/gain of sale of property	—	−37,508	—
Other	2,119	−6,184	−7,213
Changes in certain assets and liabilities net of effects of purchase of subsidiaries	3,299	9,339	609
Decrease/increase in receivables	−37,957	64,512	10,597
Decrease/increase in materials, supplies and prepaid expenses	−43,483	−7,028	−23,532
Increase/decrease in traffic balances payable and unused tickets	21,398	−37,530	27,485
Increase/decrease in accounts payable and accrued expenses	139,209	−8,915	18,290
Net cash provided by operating activities	508,579	356,259	282,799
Cash flows from investing activities			
Payment for purchase of subsidiaries, net of cash acquired:			
Piedmont	—	−1,476,705	—
PSA	—	−313,291	—
Suburban	—	—	−8,432
Additions to property and equipment	−544,985	−503,251	−266,614
Decrease/increase in purchase deposits	−99,008	27,805	−25,054
Proceeds from disposition of property	564,433	353,607	24,076
Investment in Covia Partnership	−113,133	—	—
Other	−15,285	19,052	5,715
Net cash used in investing activities	−207,978	−1,892,783	−270,309
Cash flows from financing activities			
Issuance of debt	127,241	1,905,450	5,799
Repayment of debt	−591,510	−965,085	−35,507
Issuance of common stock	14,302	517,268	7,048
Treasury stock	—	−20,043	—
Dividends	−5,211	−4,647	−3,339
Net cash provided by/used for financing activities	−455,178	1,432,943	25,999
Net increase/decrease in cash and cash equivalents	−154,577	−103,581	−13,509
Cash and cash equivalents at end of year	78,000	232,577	336,158

Source: US Air Group, *1988 Annual Report*, 18.

extra payments above the unpaid 9.5 percent dividends. By 1997, the business had improved, and the common equity that had traded as low as $4 per share had risen to $73 per share—enough to make the conversion feature of Buffett's preferred shares valuable.[3] Subsequently, in March 1998, the shares were called in for redemption. In total, Buffett's investment in US Air generated dividends of more than $250 million in the eight years he had held them and were profitable through the conversion feature of the securities. Despite going through huge fundamental issues, and becoming the most infamous Buffett mistake, US Air was in fact a profitable investment.

16

1990: Wells Fargo

After Iraq attacked Kuwait in August 1990, the United States entered a full-blown recession. On the one hand, stock prices—including Berkshire's—collapsed, down more than 25 percent from their high a year before. On the other hand, valuations finally came back down to earth after the great bull market run of the 1980s. Also in 1990, California real estate was taking a turn for the worse, and all indications seemed to point to a severe and lengthy period of misery for banks that wrote mortgages. This was especially troubling for Wells Fargo because it was the bank that had written more mortgages in California than any other. However, Wells Fargo was also one of the most profitable banks in the nation, with an especially strongly entrenched franchise in California. It was chaired by Carl Reichardt, who had a reputation as a true efficiency-minded executive.

In its 1989 annual report,[1] the Wells Fargo management team—led by President Paul Hazen and Chairman and CEO Carl Reichardt—gave a clear description of their main business divisions, starting on page one. (Note that the 1989 annual report, dated March 6, 1990, would have been the latest full annual report available to a potential investor in early/mid-1990.) Wells Fargo was organized into four divisions. Although financial figures are not broken down in the annual report along these business divisions, the management discussion gave enough

Figure 16.1.

information to understand what—and more important, how—the businesses were doing.

The first division was the retail and branch banking division. This was described as the largest division, generating the bulk of the bank's $36.4 billion in deposits and also approximately 40 percent of its outstanding loan portfolio of $41.7 billion. The loans made in this division came in the form of consumer, small business, and home mortgage loans. In 1989, the company focused on building a core branch network in California and pursued a strategy of what it called "strengthening customer ties." This meant acquiring branch networks, including Bank of Paradise in Butte County, Valley National Bank of Glendale, the American National Bank of Bakersfield, and the Torrey Pines Group of San Diego County. It also meant divesting many of Wells Fargo's international offices and forming partnerships abroad instead.

The second division—commercial and corporate banking—provided commercial enterprises with loans. This division also provided fee-based services to commercial customers, including cash management and transaction processing. During the year, the focus in this division was also on building additional density in California. This included traditional commercial businesses as well as a significant portion of agricultural businesses.

The third division—real estate lending—provided real estate loans, including both mortgages and construction loans. Together with the loans provided by the commercial and corporate division, these loans accounted for the remaining 60 percent of the bank's outstanding loan portfolio totaling $41.7 billion. This division was also concerned with community development and had some marquee projects funded with Wells Fargo financing, including some of the largest social housing projects at the time in Los Angeles.

The last business was the investment management business. This included an index fund manager called *Wells Fargo Investment Advisors* and a private banking division that managed the wealth of private individuals and trusts. The former had assets under management of $80 billion and the latter assets under management of $34 billion. Some of the new product offerings being introduced in this division included Product Maximizer, which offered investors with accounts over $250,000 full securities brokerage and advisory services.

All in all, what seemed clear from the discussion in the annual report is that the four divisions of Wells Fargo acted as one integrated overall business; this one entity was supported by retail branches with diverse offerings for individuals as well as businesses. As such, the ensuing discussion about Wells Fargo's financial performance also focused on the overall business.

According to those financials, in 1989 net income was $601.1 million and $11.02 on a per share basis. Compared to the previous year, net income increased by 17 percent, and EPS increased by 20 percent. Return on assets (ROA) was 1.26 percent, and return on equity (ROE) was 24.5 percent. These were improvements compared to a ROA of 1.14 percent and 24.0 percent in 1988. In absolute terms, these returns were significantly above the industry average for banks. Just to give perspective: A 24 percent return on equity means that for $100 of a bank's money, the bank is getting a return of $24 in that year. This is a very healthy return by any standard.

Management next details how the $601.1 million net income was generated by breaking down net interest income and noninterest income. The single largest contributor to interest income was the loans made by the bank. On the interest cost side, the largest single cost related to funding source were different forms of savings deposits. Major generators of noninterest income included diverse transaction fees and commissions, services charges on deposit accounts, and income from trust and investment management. Based on these figures, Wells Fargo would have seemed to a potential investor to be very much a deposit bank whose bulk of business was serving depositors and making loans. There were no significant businesses involving derivatives or alternative business models.[2]

The management next discusses the balance sheet figures, going into detail on those assets and loans that are at the core of the bank's income generation. On the asset side, loans were the focus and made up $41 billion of the $48.7 billion in total assets at year-end. The corresponding average balances during the year were $39.4 billion in loans and $47.8 billion in total assets. By category, management discusses positive developments in several of the loan categories with some comments. I have summarized this information in table 16.1.

Table 16.1.
Loan development by category

Category	Avg. balance	YOY change	Comments
Commercial loans	$14.2 billion	+14%	Growth in corporate, midmarket loans
Real estate construction	$4.4 billion	−4%	
Real estate mortgage	$11.7 billion	+19%	Growth in 1–4 family first mortgages
Consumer	$7.6 billion	+6%	
Other	$1.5 billion	−48%	Significant decrease in foreign loans
Total	**$39.4 billion**	**+7%**	

As one can see, the overall asset growth stems primarily from increases in corporate and midmarket loans and growth in one to four family real estate mortgages. Most of these loans were in the state of California because Wells Fargo had a primary interest in California.

Here, we should take a brief look at the investing environment in the banking industry at the time because a potential investor would consider the context quite important. In 1989, the banking industry of the United States was in a period of significant consolidation and "cleansing." In the wake of a general economic slowdown predicated by the high interest rates (tightening of credit markets) of the 1980s, along with a real estate recession (1986–1991), many of the savings and loan associations as well as the weaker banks were having serious issues. Those institutions that had not been prudent in their lending practices were regularly making negative news, and many, in fact, went bankrupt. Although this period was also marked by stronger banks that were able to consolidate the assets of these weaker players—often at favorable valuations—it was difficult to tell the good players from the bad. In total, between 1980 and 1990, the number of S&Ls was said to have been reduced by roughly 50 percent and the number of commercial banks by 20 percent.

As a result of this turmoil, banking assets in general were heavily sold down. There was a fear that Wells Fargo would face a fate to that of some of the lesser banks. Taking a look at the stock price of Wells Fargo in 1990, for the period that a possible investor would have considered the shares, one would have seen wild swings in prices with a steep drop in Q3 and Q4 1990 (this, as it happens, is when Warren Buffett purchased his shares).[3] These fears were not completely unfounded. Wells Fargo, as mentioned previously, was significantly exposed to real estate loans both in construction and mortgages. The bulk of these loans were made in California, which after years of property price increases, was certainly at risk of suffering a real estate price correction.

However, the financial numbers presented by Wells Fargo in the 1989 annual report showed positive financial developments. A potential investor would also have considered the risk metrics reported by Wells Fargo. They came in the form of capital ratios and loss reserve developments of loan losses. In terms of capital ratios, Wells Fargo reported a tier 1 risk-based capital ratio of 4.95 percent at year-end 1989. Tier 1 capital is based on common stockholders' equity and qualifying preferred stock. Compared to the ratio at year-end 1988 of 4.57 percent, this was an improvement. It was also significantly above the level stipulated then by the Federal Reserve Board

Table 16.2.
Loans 90 days or more past due and still accruing
Year ended Dec. 31
(In millions)

	1989	1988	1987	1986	1985
Commercial, financial, and agricultural	**$46.4**	$34.6	$51.5	$71.1	$46.1
Real estate construction	**2.3**	30.7	6.1	11.2	14.3
Real estate mortgage	**28.6**	26.9	41.3	65.4	42.0
Consumer	**47.8**	35.9	35.3	62.9	43.5
Lease financing	**1.7**	2.1	1.3	1.7	0.2
Foreign	—	—	—	3.7	1.5
Total	**$126.8**	**$130.2**	**$135.5**	**$216.0**	**$147.6**

Source: Based on Wells Fargo, *1989 Annual Report*, p. 15, table 12.

(FRB), which was four percent.[4] When looking at overdue and bad loans, one sees in table 16.2 that the total amount of loans 90 days or more past due was $126.8 million, representing 0.32 percent of loans in 1989.

This was less than the comparable $130.2 million figure in 1988, both in dollar terms and as a percentage of total loans. All this would have seemed fairly reassuring. The same would have been the conclusion looking at management's discussion of allowances for loan losses. At year-end 1989, the allowance for loan losses totaled 1.77 percent of total loans, lower than the two percent figure in 1988. This was based on the best judgment of the management. In the end, the fears regarding the collapse of Wells Fargo from its exposure to real estate loans were, from what I could tell, not reflected in the financials reported by Wells Fargo in early 1990. This is not to say that Wells Fargo would never have issues with its exposure in California real estate; but if one believed in the management team and the financials of the company, one would not have seen evidence of a deterioration of the business at this time from the reported numbers. Wells Fargo seemed to be a well-run bank with above-average metrics both in terms of income and its risk profile. Moreover, it seemed to be improving those already impressive metrics year after year for the last several years.

I turn now to valuation. Given the knowledge that Buffett paid an average of $57.88 per share for his purchase in Wells Fargo in 1990,[5] one can draw two conclusions. First, Buffett had purchased the bulk of his stake in Wells Fargo in Q3 and Q4 1990, as prices during the year only dipped below $60 per share during those quarters. Second, the price ranged between $42.75 and $80.13; if one assumes that the price a potential investor had at

Table 16.3.
Calculation of market capitalization

Share price	$58.00
Number of shares outstanding*	54.98m
Market capitalization	**$3,189m**

*Shares outstanding as reported at year-end 1987 included 51.10 million common shares and 4.5 million preferred shares. I have assumed a $50 per share price of the preferred shares as they were redeemable by the company at a price of approximately $50 per share and had a yield at the time slightly below that of the 10-year bond rate. The resulting valuation is equivalent to 3.88 million shares of common stock. I have not considered stock options because the company quotes them to be "not material."

the time was $58.00 per share (roughly the average price for Buffett) the valuation would have looked as described in the following paragraphs.

Based on the consolidated financial statements presented in the 1989 annual report, which is included at the end of this chapter, the market capitalization of Wells Fargo would have been $3.2 billion.

Because Wells Fargo is a bank, I would have focused on the PER and P/B metrics in making the valuation of the company. I would take enterprise value as less relevant given the highly leveraged (in terms of financial assets and debt) balance sheet inherent to a bank.

Based on the historical 1989 net earnings, Wells Fargo would have been trading at approximately five times net earnings. This is very cheap if one believes in the credibility of the balance sheet presented by the management, that is, if there were not very significant write-offs to be taken on the assets from loans gone bad. If an investor had purchased Wells Fargo at its 1990 low of $42.75, the PER ratio would have been at an even more incredible 3.9 times last year's net earnings. Finally, although as a value investor I would not have cared about the dividend yield itself, the fact that the management intended to pay almost $4 per share in dividends in 1990 would have seemed a very confident signal about the prospects of the company. In addition, Wells Fargo was also buying its own shares at this time.

Table 16.4.
PER multiples

PER	1988	1989
Share price	$58.00	$58.00
EPS as reported	$9.20	$11.02
PER	6.3×	5.3×

Moving on to the P/B valuation, one can see that the shareholders' equity totaled $2,861 million at the end of 1989. As the market capitalization was $3,189 million, the P/B ratio at the end of 1989 would have been 1.1×. This meant that the business was valued at slightly more than its book value based on the $58 per share value. Although this is not necessarily bargain-basement cheap for a bank, it is certainly very cheap for a bank that makes a ROE of more than 20 percent. A potential investor might have thought through it like this: Given a bank that earns a ROE equal to its cost of capital, the fair net worth should be roughly equal to the book value; but if a bank or business earned, say, a return of 16 percent when the average cost of capital is eight percent, then it should be roughly worth twice as much as book value. A business like Wells Fargo, assuming that its ROE of 24 percent was sustainable, clearly should be worth even more than that. Hence, a valuation of 1.1 times book value is very cheap for Wells Fargo, given that it has a proven track record of earning a return greater than 20 percent.

To give a calibration on the actual valuation of Wells Fargo, consider that in order for Wells Fargo to have a 10 times PER or two times P/B, which is more fair (but still conservative) at a share price of $58 per share, its earnings would need to be cut roughly in half from $601 million to $300 million. Given that bad loans outstanding were $126 million, this would mean that bad loans would have to more than triple to impair the earnings of 1989 by a sufficient amount to justify the share price. Moreover, this impairment would have to be ongoing indefinitely into the future—a scenario that seems fairly unlikely. Thus, I would have considered there to be a meaningful *margin of safety*.

A last comment on the core business quality before concluding: It should be mentioned that Wells Fargo seemed to have several specific advantages and strengths in addition to what is presented in the numbers. First, its management team was not only very competent, but also had been with the company for many years. They also had been around during the real estate recessions of 1973 to 1975 and 1981 to 1982, giving confidence that their loan practices had been conservative. Management also speaks intelligently and sensibly in their annual report, which I would have found indicative of a competent management team. Second, although Wells Fargo ranked third of all banks at the time in total assets in California, it was the largest middle market lender, commercial real estate lender, and second in terms of retail deposits. In effect, it had a competitive and well-known area of expertise, and management planned on building on those strengths.

In sum, to a potential investor in early/mid-1990 Wells Fargo seemed to be a very well-run bank with clearly better-than-industry-average financial metrics that were improving year-over-year. Its strategy focused on better serving its California customers. While this meant a sensible focus and improving operations, it also meant exposure to California real estate loans that would have concerned some investors. However, based on its capital ratios, loan loss metrics, and commentary of loan loss allowances, there were few facts that should have deeply concerned investors already at that time. The valuation of Wells Fargo's stock at approximately five times PER and 1.1 times P/B seems like a deep discount considering the earnings power and risks of the business seen at that time.

Based on this knowledge, it seems that Buffett's investment in Wells Fargo was a case where he purchased a good business that had historically been superior to peers, run by a good management team he trusted, at an outstanding valuation. This case differs from his investments in Coca-Cola and American Express because the inherent quality of the business and its growth economics were perhaps associated with much more risk and less favorable underpinnings—though in the case of Wells Fargo, he also did not pay for any growth. It also seems that Buffett trusted the positive key financial metrics provided by the management in the annual reports and did not rely on the negative circumstantial evidence of other banks' failures when assessing the future of Wells Fargo. It is likely that Buffett's judgment about Wells Fargo's risks included more primary research on loan losses, but his conclusion was certainly consistent with the positive data and outlook presented by the Wells Fargo management at the time.

Following Buffett's purchase in 1990, and after reporting a good set of numbers for fiscal year 1990, Wells Fargo did go through increasing pressure on loan losses in 1991. Specifically, issues related to loans made in commercial real estate caused Wells Fargo to increase its loss allowance to $1.65 billion or 3.73 percent of total loans (about double the allowance in 1989). However, the 1991 annual report also showed that in terms of Wells Fargo's stock price, it would trade between $48 and $97 in that year, significantly higher on average than the year before. The reality was that there were some risks that the market saw correctly, but that the margin of safety presented by the valuation in 1990 already was more than priced in any future negative news. In the slightly longer term, Wells Fargo recovered to become a very successful bank and continues to be one of Berkshire Hathaway's largest positions with enormous unrealized gains today.

Table 16.5.
Income statement (1987–1989)
Year ended Dec. 31
($ in millions except per share data)

	1989	1988	1987
Interest income			
Loans	4,582.5	4,889.5	3,602.5
Interest-earning deposits	3.7	10.2	99.4
Investment securities	281.0	268.7	250.8
Trading account securities	0.1	3.8	7.6
Federal funds sold	2.9	5.3	7.7
Total interest income	4,870.2	4,177.5	3,967.5
Interest expense			
Deposits	1,810.1	1,560.3	1,463.5
Short-term borrowings	645.3	370.2	364.8
Senior and subordinated debt	256.2	274.9	337.6
Total interest expense	2,711.6	2,205.4	2,165.9
Net interest income	2,158.6	1,972.1	1,801.6
Provision for loan losses	362.0	300.0	892.0
Net interest income after provision for loan losses	1,796.6	1,672.1	909.6
Noninterest income			
Domestic fees and commissions	283.7	278.2	270.8
Services charges on deposit accounts	246.7	219.6	180.6
Trust and investment services income	178.2	153.7	156.5
Investment securities losses	−2.7	−4.3	−12.9
Other	72.8	35.0	5.0
Total noninterest income	778.7	682.2	600.0
Noninterest expense			
Salaries	631.3	619.8	599.3
Employee benefits	149.2	152.4	151.5
Net occupancy	178.5	166.8	178.7
Equipment	137.3	135.8	132.9
Other	478.2	444.3	458.1
Total noninterest expense	1,574.5	1,519.1	1,520.5
Net noninterest income	−795.8	−836.9	−920.5
Income/loss before income tax expense/benefit	1,000.8	835.2	−10.9
Income tax expense/benefit	399.7	322.7	−61.7
Net income	601.1	512.5	50.8
Net income applicable to common stock	573.6	486.7	28.0
Per common share			
Net income	11.02	9.20	0.52
Dividends declared	3.30	2.45	1.67
Average common shares outstanding	52.1	52.9	53.8

Source: Wells Fargo, *1989 Annual Report*, 22.

Table 16.6.
Balance sheet (1988–1989)
Year ended Dec. 31
($ in millions)

	1989	1988
Assets		
Cash and due from banks	2,929.8	2,563.2
Interest-earning deposits	5.1	322.1
Investment securities (market value $1,704.9 and $3,799.8)	1,737.7	3,970.4
Federal funds sold	6.3	27.0
Loans	41,726.9	37,670.0
Allowance for loan losses	738.6	752.1
Net loans	40,988.3	36,917.9
Premises and equipment, net	679.6	688.0
Due from customers and acceptances	211.0	244.9
Goodwill	352.6	373.4
Accrued interest receivable	389.9	365.7
Other assets	1,436.3	1,143.9
TOTAL ASSETS	48,736.6	46,616.5
Liabilities and stockholders' equity		
Deposits		
Noninterest-bearing—domestic	8,003.2	7,105.5
Noninterest-bearing—foreign	—	7.0
Interest-bearing—domestic	28,153.7	26,580.3
Interest-bearing—foreign	273.4	1,376.0
Total deposits	36,430.3	35,068.8
Short-term borrowings:		
Federal funds borrowed and repurchase agreements	2,706.7	2,207.2
Commercial paper outstanding	3,090.4	2,747.7
Other	44.3	47.4
Total short-term borrowings	5,841.4	5,002.3
Acceptances outstanding	211.0	244.9
Accrued interest payable	100.8	110.1
Service debt	695.2	923.0
Other liabilities	751.2	693.9
Total	44,029.9	42,043.0
Subordinated debt	1,845.8	1,994.1
TOTAL LIABILITIES	45,875.7	44,037.1
Stockholders' equity		
Preferred stock	405.0	405.0
Common stock—$5 par value, authorized—150 million shares; issued and outstanding 51,074,971 shares and 52,546,310 shares	255.4	262.7
Additional paid in capital	274.1	389.7
Retained earnings	1,930.7	1,528.2
Cumulative foreign currency translation adjustments	−4.3	−6.2
Total stockholders' equity	2,860.9	2,579.4
TOTAL LIABILITIES AND STOCKHOLDERS' EQUITY	48,736.6	46,616.5

Source: Wells Fargo, *1989 Annual Report,* 23.

17

1998: General Re

On December 21, 1998, Berkshire Hathaway acquired 100 percent of General Re Corporation for $22 billion, using both cash and stock. From a strategic viewpoint, the rationale for the acquisition was that Berkshire, a company with extremely strong cash generation from its operating businesses, was an ideal candidate to absorb the volatility involved in a large-scale reinsurance business.[1] The line of thinking went that Berkshire did not need to worry about short-term financial volatility in one business segment, and General Re would be able to write more business profitably after being acquired than as a standalone. Berkshire also would have access to General Re's capital to potentially better invest those assets. Lastly, Berkshire would gain additional expertise in insurance and a broader international distribution network.

Before jumping into the details of the acquisition, one must note the financial environment in which this acquisition took place. The stock market had been on a tear in the years immediately before 1998, with the S&P index generating more than 20 percent year over year in 1995, 1996, and 1997. It was on the way to doing so again in 1998. Mirroring the bull years in the general market, the insurance industry had also enjoyed a string of good years. As noted in Warren Buffett's 1997 annual letter to clients, dated February 1998,[2] Berkshire's insurance business had generated five consecutive years of profitable underwriting.

To delve into the investment case of General Re, one must start with its fundamentals. In the description of the business in its 1997 year-end report filing, General Re presents itself as a global business with four main divisions:

Table 17.1.
Overview of operations

Segment	Revenues	% total revenue	% total operating earnings
North American property/casualty	$3967m	48%	63%
International property/casualty	$2706m	33%	23%
Life/health insurance	$1277m	15%	6%
Financial services	$301m	4%	8%
Total	**$8251m**	**100%**	**100%**

As table 17.1 shows, General Re's insurance business centered on reinsuring property and casualty risks, with the company's most profitable segment in North America.

The report gives further detail on the North American property/casualty segment, stating that it was principally focused on direct underwriting of treaty and facultative reinsurance. Treaty reinsurance refers to reinsurance that is set by a framework contract and that automatically covers all of a certain class of risks passed on by the primary insurer to the reinsurer. Facultative reinsurance involves the underwriting of individual risks through specific contracts. (There are two other kinds of reinsurance—pro rata reinsurance, which reinsures for a defined proportion of an overall risk by the reinsurer, and excess reinsurance, which describes the nonproportional risk assumed when a reinsurer insures a risk above a specified limit to be paid by the primary insurer.) In focusing on these two types of reinsurance, General Re assumed risks either written as framework contracts or as underwriting per individual risk. The percentage in this division between casualty and property was approximately 60 percent to 30 percent, with the remaining 10 percent falling under specialty lines.

The second division—international property/casualty reinsurance—was quite similar in nature to the first business, with 61 percent of this division's gross written premium coming in property reinsurance and 39 percent coming in casualty reinsurance. The main difference is the international nature of this segment, which underwrote reinsurance in 150 countries.

This international segment was the result of a 1994 acquisition of a controlling stake in Cologne Re based in Germany.

The third business division—global life/health reinsurance—was also partly a result of the Cologne Re acquisition and was also an international business, with 38 percent of premiums written in Europe, 47 percent of premiums written in North America, and the remainder in the rest of the world. Unlike the first two businesses, the main reinsuring in this division was based on individual and group life and health policies. Most of the life business was written on a proportional basis, while most of the health business was written on an excess (nonproportional) basis.

The last business—financial services—was a small business that provided numerous professional services like real estate brokerage and real estate management, as well as dealing in derivative and structured products. The derivative and structured products segment offered major corporations, insurance companies, and financial institutions customized offerings to manage risks.

Overall, as a potential investor, I would not have seen anything especially remarkable in the business setup. General Re was likely more exposed to certain kinds of risks as a result of its involvement in global casualty and property and some life and health insurance, but it would be difficult to judge its business quality without looking more closely at its financial metrics. In my experience with insurance businesses, the key judgment about the performance of a company comes down to whether the company is run conservatively and for profit, or for growth. In order to determine this, it is crucial to look at the numbers the company presents and the assumptions underpinning these numbers. Here, a bit more explanation is needed in order to take a closer look at how this information plays out in the case of General Re.

General Re's annual report of 1997 provides a wonderfully detailed 11-year history of key financials, covering the years from 1987 to 1997. It shows that revenues increased from $3.1 billion in 1987 to $8.3 billion in 1997, representing a 10-year CAGR of 10.2 percent. Likewise, net income increased from $511 million to $968 million, albeit at a lesser CAGR of 6.6 percent. Note that for General Re, as with most insurance businesses, the bulk of revenues came in the form of earned premiums. Earned premium is revenue from customers as their time under a policy expires and is hence recognized over time (e.g., John Smith pays for a one-year auto insurance policy and seven months have expired—seven months' revenue is recognized).

On the cost side, the first major cost comes from claims that are incurred and must be paid (e.g., John Smith subsequently requires auto repair for an accident). The total cost of claims is called the loss expense, and this figure as a percentage of total earned premiums is called the *loss ratio*. In addition to the cost of claims themselves, the insurance company also has costs associated with running the insurance business, such as selling and underwriting. This cost in sum, divided by the total earned premiums, is called the *expense ratio*. If one adds up the cost of claims and the cost of operations, one arrives at the total cost of underwriting. This total cost of underwriting divided by the total earned premiums is called the *combined ratio*. As a figure, the lower the combined ratio the better; it means either better underwriting decisions leading to fewer claims per earned amount or an efficiently run insurance operation with low operating expenses, or both.

In the lingo of insurance, a combined-ratio below 100 percent means that the earned premiums were sufficient to cover the total costs of underwriting. When the combined ratio is over 100, it means that it costs the insurance company more to pay for claims and other costs than it earned through premiums. The difference must then be made up by the investment income or other forms of earnings, or the company will suffer an overall loss.[3] In the insurance industry a combined ratio of 100 or below is considered good.

It may seem strange to say that achieving a total cost equivalent to total premium revenue is a "good performance." However, insurance businesses almost always receive their premiums before they have to pay for claims. In some reinsurance businesses, where the risks underwritten are long term, there may be years between when a customer pays his or her premium and when a claim is made. Thus, an insurance company is able to hold cash that is essentially the customer's. This amount, which appears on the balance sheet and is called *float*, is available for the insurance company to invest in order to generate investment income. As such, the total underwriting performance (revenue minus cost) is simply the cost of generating the float capital for the insurance company. If the company can generate an investment return superior to this total underwriting cost, it will be profitable as a firm. Hence, the bar of what is considered acceptable in terms of underwriting performance is lower than a combined ratio of 100 percent. A combined ratio of 100 percent means that the company is generating float for free. An insurance company does not have to perform that well to generate a positive return given that it is able to generate any investment return. As such, the industry as a whole usually operates at a combined ratio above 100 percent, with investment returns making up for a shortfall in underwriting performance.

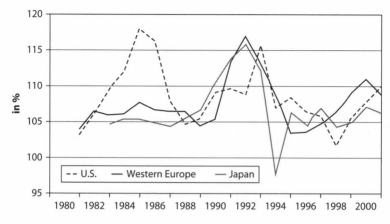

Figure 17.1.

Figure 17.1 shows a graph from a study conducted by Swiss Re on the overall underwriting performance for insurance companies between 1980 and 2000.[4] This graph presents the combined ratio of the overall nonlife insurance industry in the United States, Western Europe, and Japan.

As one can see, while the ratio varied with insurance cycles with peaks around 1984 and 1993 and troughs around 1988 and 1993, the long-term average combined ratio was significantly above 100 percent for the industry in each region.

So where does General Re's performance fall? In its 1997 report, the company reported loss, expense, and combined ratios for its largest two divisions in the North American and international property/casualty divisions; I have summarized these in table 17.2.

As one can see, on the whole, the underwriting performance of General Re in the North American property/casualty business was quite consistent, with an 11-year average combined ratio of 100.6 percent. This meant that the total underwriting costs were roughly equivalent to the net premiums—and further, that the underwriting performance of General Re was better than average.

Analyzing the breakdown of claims costs and operational costs in a bit more detail, one sees that over the 11-year period, General Re was able to bring down its loss ratio from 75 percent to 68 percent, but much of this improvement was negated by increased operational costs, which as a percentage of premiums written increased from 25 percent to 31 percent in that timeframe. Thus, while underwriting decisions had been good and

Table 17.2.
Summary of operations

North American property/casualty	1997	1996	1995	1994	1993	1992	1991	1990	1989	1988	1987	11-year avg.
Loss ratio	68.4%	69.0%	67.3%	71.4%	70.0%	78.8%	72.0%	67.5%	69.7%	70.7%	74.5%	70.8%
Expense ratio	30.8%	30.1%	32.3%	30.5%	31.1%	29.3%	29.3%	31.5%	28.3%	28.8%	24.7%	29.8%
Combined ratio	**99.2%**	**99.1%**	**99.6%**	**101.9%**	**101.1%**	**101.3%**	**101.3%**	**99.0%**	**98.0%**	**99.5%**	**99.2%**	**100.6%**

International property/casualty	1997	1996	1995	1994	1993	1992	1991	1990	1989	1988	1987	11-year avg.
Loss ratio	72.1%	73.2%	77.0%	69.2%	75.1%	80.2%	75.8%	71.5%	62.4%	64.4%	64.2%	71.4%
Expense ratio	30.3%	28.9%	25.8%	29.4%	30.9%	32.8%	35.2%	37.5%	33.4%	31.3%	31.9%	31.6%
Combined ratio	**102.4%**	**102.1%**	**102.8%**	**98.6%**	**106.0%**	**113.0%**	**111.0%**	**109.0%**	**95.8%**	**95.7%**	**96.1%**	**103.0%**

improving in the North American business, operationally the business had grown a bit fatter. Buffett may have seen this as an area of possible improvement.

Regarding the international casualty/property division, General Re (which in this segment was mostly Cologne Re prior to 1994) had a more volatile performance with an average combined ratio over the period of 103 percent. There was a particularly weak period between 1990 and 1993, when the combined ratio averaged above 109 percent. Looking at the loss ratio and expense ratio separately, an investor at the time may have concluded that this was caused by a combination of less conservative underwriting and poor operational efficiency starting in 1990. Although operational efficiency as represented by the expense ratio was back down by 1997, the loss ratio of 72 percent in 1997 was still much higher than the loss ratios in the late 1980s. This loss could be the remnants of poor underwriting decisions or simply a result of a very favorable insurance environment in the late 1980s.

All in all, General Re, as captured by its two core casualty/property reinsurance divisions, seemed to be a decent but not an amazing reinsurance business. As a potential investor, I would have seen a slightly different story in the North American and international businesses, with the former improving in underwriting but not operational efficiency and the latter recovering from some poor years.

However, as I mentioned previously, it is not just the numbers that are important, but also the assumptions behind them. As many reinsurance policies have infrequent but large claim risks, the actual claims associated with a policy often will not come for many years after a policy is first written and premiums are earned. Thus, the management or underwriting team has to make estimates of the future claims associated with a certain tranche of written policies. This means that many of the figures previously presented, particularly the loss ratios and the combined ratios, depend significantly on the assumptions of the management. If management wanted, it could estimate very few losses in any particular year, increasing the likelihood that they would need to adjust estimates upward in the ensuing years. This is why in the analysis of an insurance company a potential investor is heavily dependent on the conservatism of the management in estimating those losses and on writing business in accordance with those conservative estimates.

Without going into all the esoteric details around reserve setting and insurance accounting, one of the few ways an investor can ascertain if management really has been conservative in their underwriting is to look at the development of individual years of underwriting as they progress over time. This is captured in what is called a loss reserve development table. For General Re's North American business, this table from its 10K form is summarized in table 17.3. The two top rows of numbers represent the best estimate of liabilities for each underwriting year in the year they were made, i.e., 1987 is based on the estimate made in 1987, and 1997 is based on the estimate in 1997. The development of those estimates is then traced for each underwriting year in each column as the years pass. For the 1987 underwriting year, there are 10 years of figures. For the 1997 years, on the other hand, there is simply one estimate.

Looking at table 17.3, one can see that for the underwriting years between 1987 and 1991, all the liability estimates had significant negative developments since their initial estimate. For example, the estimate of the liabilities associated with policies underwritten in 1987 was first calculated at approximately $4.7 billion. Over the next 10 years, this increased almost 30 percent, to $6.1 billion. Clearly, management had not been conservative enough when they first made their estimates of liabilities. Over time, they had to add to reserves to fill this gap. For the liabilities associated with the 1987 underwriting year, about $250 million was added in year six (1993) and year seven (1994), and about $300 million was added in year eight (1995). It is likely that this information would have been something of a red flag to a potential investor in 1997. What it means is that for years like 1987, the management clearly had not been conservative enough when they first made their estimates of liabilities.

Were I considering investing in General Re in 1997, I would want to be convinced that (a) the management team was significantly more conservative than they seemed to have been in 1987 and (b) that the reserve additions for years that were underreserved are now completed, i.e., no additional reserve-adding would be needed. The dangers of underreserving have been revealed through many examples in history. The one I am most familiar with is the more recent case of UK auto insurers between 2002 and 2010. During that time the UK motor (automobile) insurance industry faced a tumultuous period with an industry combined ratio that started below 100 in 2002 and ended at around 115 by 2010. During this eight-year stretch, many companies were required to add to their reserves repeatedly and some of them had to exit lines of business altogether. The lesson from this case is that when reserves are added by an insurance company, this is often only the first step in rectifying a problem that takes

Table 17.3.
Analysis of North American net claims and claim expense development

		1987	1988	1989	1990	1991	1992	1993	1994	1995	1996	1997
Net liability for unpaid claims and claim expenses	Mio $	4.738	5.217	5.549	5.842	6.230	6.635	6.803	7.029	7.385	8.741	8.881
Net liability reestimated as of:	Mio $											
1 year later		4.903	5.185	5.537	5.856	6.286	6.775	6.767	7.042	7.337	8.563	
2 years later		4.927	5.247	5.481	5.778	6.352	6.850	6.845	6.868	7.055		
3 years later		4.991	5.166	5.502	5.906	6.475	6.994	6.739	6.731			
4 years later		4.983	5.236	5.683	6.091	6.638	6.935	6.703				
5 years later		5.044	5.420	5.900	6.319	6.635	6.979					
6 years later		5.284	5.642	6.173	6.326	6.720						
7 years later		5.528	5.958	6.190	6.442							
8 years later		5.855	5.979	6.319								
9 years later		5.882	6.139									
10 years later		6.066										
Cumulative (deficiency) redundancy		−1.328	−922	−770	−600	−490	−344	100	298	330	178	—
Cumulative amount of net liability paid through:	Mio $											
1 year later		747	812	927	905	1.044	1.291	1.207	1.176	1.253	1.584	—
2 years later		1.354	1.436	1.584	1.613	1.955	2.195	2.063	1.959	2.142		
3 years later		1.846	1.903	2.115	2.332	2.570	1.850	2.617	2.677			
4 years later		2.209	2.320	2.689	2.769	3.071	3.300	3.179				
5 years later		2.546	2.814	3.025	3.184	3.437	3.754					
6 years later		2.965	3.085	3.362	3.481	3.808						
7 years later		3.203	3.375	3.618	3.806							
8 years later		3.472	3.611	3.890								
9 years later		3.695	3.858									
10 years later		3.923										

several adjustments to rectify, and, further, some companies can hide their underreserving for several years through trying to "outgrow" their problem by generating additional revenues and float. At times companies did this by writing cheap policies that were not conservative, thereby creating

Table 17.4.
Analysis of international net claims and claim expense development
($ in millions)

	1994	1995	1996	1997
Net liability for unpaid claims and claim expenses	3.289	4.352	4.664	4.560
Net liability reestimated as of:				
1 year later	3.545	4.134	4.141	
2 years later	3.316	3.776		
3 years later	3.100			
Cumulative increase/decrease in net liability, including foreign exchange	−189	−576	−523	
Less: increase/decrease due to foreign exchange	285	591	533	
Cumulative (deficiency) adjusted for foreign exchange	−96	−15	−10	
Cumulative amount of net liability paid through:				
1 year later	408	800	1.060	
2 years later	704	1.569		
3 years later	1.571			

a long-term problem while trying to solve a short-term one. Of course, an investor looking at General Re in 1987 would not have had access to this exact case study, but he or she would have been able to anticipate these types of problems as the logical outcomes of reckless underwriting.

> Because loss costs must be estimated, insurers have enormous latitude in figuring their underwriting results, and that makes it very difficult for investors to calculate a company's true cost of float. An experienced observer can usually detect large-scale errors in reserving, but the general public can typically do no more than accept what's presented.
>
> —Buffett to Berkshire Hathaway investors, February 27, 1998.

There are a few aspects of General Re that would, however, have appeased the nervous investor. The development of underwriting in the years between 1993 and 1996 seemed much more positive, with reserve releases rather than additions. And even for those earlier years that were underreserved, the rate of reserve increases stabilized somewhat. This indicates that in the last few years the business was much more conservatively operated.

Having covered the bases on the underwriting side, one must now turn to the income side of the General Re business. In 1997, General Re had an investment income pretax of $1.29 billion and after tax of $969 million. This return was generated from insurance investments totaling $24.6 billion, suggesting a pretax return of 5.2 percent and after-tax return of 3.9 percent. The shareholders' equity in the business was $8.16 billion at the end of the year, suggesting a pretax ROE of 15.8 percent and an after-tax return of 11.9 percent. These are also fairly decent numbers, but not outstanding. Wells Fargo, for instance, had an ROE of 24 percent in the year before Buffett's investment.

As shown in the consolidated balance sheet (see table 17.9), the bulk of the investments—about $16 billion—were in fixed income products, as could be expected for an insurance business trying to minimize risk and match the duration of assets and liabilities. Although not formally detailed, note that there is also $352 million of revenue associated with noninsurance and investment revenues, presumably from financial services. Accounting for approximately $100 million pretax operating profits, this seemed to be a highly profitable side business for General Re.

Before I move on to valuation, a few words must be said about the management team of General Re. Because I was concerned about the previous underwriting practices of General Re, I would have been interested in learning whether the company had a rationale for a dramatic improvement toward conservative underwriting sometime around 1993 in the form of a new management team. From the description of the management team in the 1997 annual report, it seems that there was no real change in the management; the CEO, Ronald Ferguson, had held his position since 1987, and the CFO, Joseph Brandon, had been with the company since 1989 (although only since 1997 in the CFO role). Thus, the investor is left in the dark as to the reason for the dramatic change in management's underwriting conservatism. Moving to valuation, an investor has a clear source for what this looked like when Buffett purchased the whole business. In Berkshire Hathaway's announcement document on June 19, 1989 regarding the acquisition of General Re by Berkshire, Berkshire quotes a total acquisition price of $22 billion, which represents $276.50 per share. Calibrating this with the information contained in the 1997 10K document of General Re, one sees that the share price of General Re ranged between $151 and $219 per share with a closing price of $212 per share at year-end. Hence, Buffett paid a premium of approximately 30 percent to the year-end share price of General Re in 1997.

Since General Re is a financial institution, a look at PER and P/B based on the 1997 year-end metrics is warranted:

Table 17.5.
PER multiples

PER	1997	1996
Share price	$276.50	$276.50
EPS as reported (diluted)	$11.76	$10.78
PER	**23.5×**	**25.6×**

Based on the historical earnings of 1997, General Re was trading at a multiple of 23 times. This would seem like a remarkably high multiple to pay even for an outstanding business. The price that Buffett paid for Wells Fargo, another financial company, was a mere six times net earnings per share of the previous full year.

Looking at P/B, one sees the following:

Table 17.6
P/B multiples

P/B	1997	1996
Market capitalization	$22.0 billion	$22.0 billion
Shareholders' equity	$8.16 billion	$7.33 billion
P/B	**2.7×**	**3.0×**

Again, at 2.7 times book value based on 1997 year-end shareholders' equity, General Re seems quite expensive. Wells Fargo traded at a P/B ratio of 1.1 times and had a ROE of 24 percent in the full year prior to the investment. General Re traded at a P/B ratio of 2.7 times and had a ROE of 12 percent after taxes. This seems significantly more expensive.

Had I been considering General Re for investment at the time, I would have seen it as an above-average reinsurance operation, but would have had significant concerns about management's conservatism in underwriting. At 23.5 times 1997 PER and 2.7 times book value, I would have found

General Re very expensive given the business's ability to generate a ROE of 12 percent in 1997. Considering General Re at the price of year-end 1997, $212 per share, the valuation would have been a PER of 18 and P/B of two. I would have found this a more reasonable valuation, but no home run for a business that had grown net income by seven percent per annum over the previous 10 years. As a standalone business, I would not have seen an amazing company. In the actual investment case, it seems that Buffett's investment rationale must have focused on some of the expertise that General Re would bring along with the large float it had, which Buffett likely would have been able to reinvest at healthy returns. As an investment case, potential investors would have been able to find and invest in General Re if they were looking for well-run insurance businesses.

***

Buffett's own explanation for his acquisition of the company, which he provided in a letter to Berkshire shareholders for year-end 1998, shows that he took a somewhat different stance than I deduced based on the aforementioned numbers. Buffett comments that "for many decades, General Re's name has stood for quality, integrity and professionalism in reinsurance—and under Ron Ferguson's leadership, this reputation has been burnished still more . . . there is a lot they can teach us." Along with the positive opinion of the management team and overall business at the time, Buffett goes on to explain that a General Re/Berkshire combination will give the combined business a unique structural advantage of being able to confidently absorb any earnings volatility, which is inherent in a good reinsurance business that writes policies based on expected returns rather than earnings smoothness. Specifically, unlike other publically listed standalone reinsurance companies, General Re would no longer have to worry about being penalized by investors who do not like earnings volatility and can focus solely on writing profitable policies even if they include ones that will likely be volatile. Buffett goes on to describe the ability that General Re would have in expanding Berkshire's worldwide distribution for selling insurance products and the technical abilities in underwriting it would bring to the Berkshire businesses. Surprisingly, in this case Buffett's investment is only partially based on financials—it is also based on business rationales for the acquisition.

Table 17.7.

Eleven-year financial summary (1987–1997)

($ in millions except per share data)

Summary of operations	1997	1996	1995	1994	1993	5yr. CAGR	1992	1991	1990	1989	1988	1987	10 yr. CAGR
CONSOLIDATED													
Total revenues	8.251	8.286	7.210	3.837	3.560	19.5%	3.387	3.207	2.954	2.742	2.719	3.115	10.2%
Net premiums written	6.545	6.661	6.102	3.001	2.524	22.7%	2.349	2.249	2.150	1.898	1.903	2.365	10.7%
Net income	968	894	825	665	711	8.1%	657	657	614	599	480	511	6.6%
Per basic share	12.04	11.00	9.92	7.97	8.28	9.8%	7.55	7.46	6.89	6.52	5.04	5.04	9.1%
Per diluted share	11.76	19.78	9.74	7.86	8.16	9.6%	7.45	7.32	6.76	6.40	5.03	5.03	8.9%
After-tax income excl. realized gains/losses	965	877	788	621	604	15.7%	465	563	566	559	518	458	7.7%
Per basic share	12.00	10.79	9.47	7.43	7.01	17.8%	5.30	6.37	6.35	6.08	5.44	4.52	10.3%
Per diluted share	11.72	10.57	9.30	7.33	6.91	17.4%	5.25	6.25	6.23	5.97	5.44	4.52	10.0%
Investment income before tax	1.288	1.205	1.017	749	755	11.3%	755	752	706	673	570	506	9.8%
Investment income after tax	969	909	787	622	619	9.3%	620	618	581	558	494	435	8.3%
Insurance investments	24.576	23.168	21.061	17.237	12.012	17.5%	10.986	10.471	9.291	8.758	7.831	6.945	13.5%
Total assets	41.459	40.161	34.263	28.116	19.419	23.0%	14.700	12.416	11.033	10.390	9.394	8.902	16.6%
Long-term debt	285	286	150	150	184	8.4%	190	290	290	250	100	100	11.0%
Common shareholders' equity	8.161	7.326	6.587	4.859	4.761	14.1%	4.227	3.911	3.270	3.084	2.695	2.563	12.3%
Operating return on equity (%)	16.9	16.2	16.5	14.5	15.4	—	13.1	17.7	20.0	21.9	21.9	20.4	—
Total return on equity (%)	23.4	14.5	32.9	9.5	18.3	—	15.8	23.6	17.4	24.7	19.5	21.2	—
NORTH AMERICAN PROPERTY/CASUALTY OPERATIONS													
Net premiums written	3.058	3.081	2.964	2.581	2.275	7.0%	2.177	2.122	2.040	1.789	1.780	2.251	3.1%
Investment income before tax	814	727	711	986	705	3.0%	703	703	662	638	539	479	5.45
Pretax income excl. realized losses/gains	849	741	716	599	644	11.7%	489	647	649	612	511	449	6.6%
Statutory surplus	6.309	5.326	4.607	3.770	3.836	12.8%	3.452	3.363	2.902	2.684	2.319	2.009	12.1%
Investments	15.995	14.879	13.481	11.177	11.601	8.8%	10.477	10.003	8.848	8.417	7.532	6.666	9.1%
Net claims and claim expense liabilities	8.881	8.741	7.385	7.029	6.803	6.0%	6.635	6.230	5.816	5.535	5.218	4.739	6.5%
Loss ratio (%)	68.4	69.0	67.3	71.4	70.0	—	78.8	72.0	67.5	69.7	70.7	74.5	—
Expense ratio (%)	30.8	30	32.3	30.5	31.3	—	29.9	29.3	31.5	28.3	28.8	24.7	—
Underwriting combined ratio (%)	99.2	99.1	99.6	101.9	101.1	—	108.7	101.3	99.0	98.0	99.5	99.2	—

(continued)

Table 17.7. (Continued)

Summary of operations	1997	1996	1995	1994	1993	5yr. CAGR	1992	1991	1990	1989	1988	1987	10 yr. CAGR
INTERNATIONAL PROPERTY/CASUALTY OPERATIONS													
Net premiums written	2.268	2.505	2.429	420	249	67.5%	172	127	110	109	123	114	34.9%
Investment income before tax	369	394	247	52	43	51.0%	47	44	39	31	27	24	31.4%
Pretax income excl. realized losses/gains	315	320	200	46	25	67.3%	24	30	25	35	33	26	28.3%
Investments	8.581	8.290	7.535	6.060	589	75.9%	509	469	442	342	299	279	40.9%
Net claims and claim expense liabilities	4.560	4.664	4.352	3.289	253	86.5%	202	164	156	121	109	105	45.8%
Loss ratio (%)	72.1	73.2	77.0	69.2	75.1	—	80.2	75.8	71.5	62.4	64.4	64.2	—
Expense ratio (%)	30.3	28.9	25.8	29.4	30.9	—	32.8	35.2	37.5	33.4	31.3	31.9	—
Underwriting combined ratio (%)	102.4	102.1	102.8	98.6	106.0	—	113.0	111.0	109.0	95.8	95.7	96.1	—
GLOBAL LIFE/HEALTH OPERATIONS													
Net premiums written	1.219	1.075	709	—	—	—	—	—	—	—	—	—	—
Investment income before tax	73	59	40	—	—	—	—	—	—	—	—	—	—
Pretax income excl. realized losses/gains	83	53	50	—	—	—	—	—	—	—	—	—	—
Net policy benefits for life/health contracts	637	523	379	330	—	—	—	—	—	—	—	—	—
FINANCIAL SERVICE OPERATIONS													
Revenues excl. net realized losses/gains	300	269	250	229	211	21.1%	115	100	88	90	101	106	11.0%
Pretax income excl. realized losses/gains	105	100	100	85	58	60.0%	10	1	6	14	27	30	13.3%
COMMON SHAREHOLDERS' INFORMATION													
Average common shares outstanding													
Basic	79.5	80.3	82.1	82.1	84.5		85.7	87.1	88.0	91.3	95.3	101.4	
Diluted	81.9	82.5	84.2	84.0	86.6		87.6	89.0	89.9	93.2	95.3	101.5	
Dividend per common share	2.20	2.04	1.96	1.92	1.88	4.1%	1.80	1.68	1.52	1.36	1.20	1.00	8.2%
Total common dividends	174	163	161	157	159	2.6%	153	146	133	124	114	101	2.6%
Cost of common share repurchases	864	735	35	207	134	—	179	59	236	206	268	274	—
Common shareholders' equity per share	105.40	89.92	80.22	59.35	56.92	16.1%	49.89	45.14	37.50	34.28	29.04	26.20	14.9%
Common share price													
High	219.38	169.38	157.88	128.50	132.75	12.1%	123.13	101.88	93.00	95.75	59.25	68.38	12.1%
Low	151.25	139.13	122.88	102.50	105.38	14.0%	78.63	84.88	69.00	55.00	45.88	48.75	12.0%
Year-end	212.00	157.75	155.00	123.50	107.00	12.9%	115.75	101.88	93.00	87.13	55.25	55.88	14.3%

Source: General Re Corporation, *1997 10K Report*, 7–9.

Table 17.8.

Income statement (1995–1997)

($ in millions except per share data)

	1997	1996	1995
Premiums and other revenues			
Net premiums written			
Property/casualty	5.326	5.586	5.393
Life/health	1.219	1.075	709
Total net premiums written	6.545	6.661	6.102
Net premiums earned			
Property/casualty	5.414	5.618	5.141
Life/health	1.193	1.060	696
Total net premiums earned	6.607	6.678	5.837
Investment income	1.288	1.205	1.017
Other revenues	352	309	292
Net realized gains on investments	4	104	64
Total revenues	8.252	8.296	7.210
Expenses			
Claims and claim expenses	3.788	3.984	3.680
Life/health benefits	883	789	505
Acquisition costs	1.414	1.478	1.345
Other operating costs and expenses	810	727	550
Goodwill amortization	29	21	13
Total expenses	6.924	6.999	6.093
Income before income taxes and minority interest	1.327	1.297	1.117
Income tax expense (benefit):			
Current	254	327	288
Deferred	48	−4	−41
Income tax expense	302	323	247
Income before minority interest	1.025	974	870
Minority interest	57	80	45
NET INCOME	968	894	825
Share data			
Net income per common share:			
Basic	12.04	11.00	9.92
Diluted	11.76	10.78	9.74
Average common shares outstanding:			
Basic	79,502,845	80,251,342	82,085,315
Diluted	81,947,547	82,466,750	84,227,806
Dividends per share to common shareowners	2.20	2.04	1.96

Source: General Re Corporation, *1997 10K Report,* 34.

Table 17.9.

Consolidated balance sheet (1996–1997)
($ in millions)

Assets	1997	1996
Investments		
Fixed maturities, available-for-sale (cost: $15,859 in 1997; $16,298 in 1996)	16.847	16.992
Preferred equities, at fair value (cost: $980 in 1997; $771 in 1996)	1.041	789
Common equities, at fair value (cost: $2,098 in 1998; $1,940 in 1996)	4.748	3.672
Short-term investments, at amortized cost which approximates fair value	1.172	1.019
Other invested assets	768	696
Total insurance investments	24.576	23.168
Cash	193	154
Accrued investment income	358	350
Accounts receivable	1.858	2.663
Funds held by reinsured companies	488	474
Reinsurance recoverable	2.706	2.935
Deferred acquisition costs	476	457
Goodwill	968	1.038
Other assets	962	804
Financial service assets		
Investment securities, at fair value (cost: $790 in 1997; $176 in 1996)	792	179
Trading securities, at fair value (cost: $1,908 in 1997; $2,994 in 1996)	1.859	2.967
Short-term investments, at fair value	129	248
Cash	159	211
Trading account assets	4.313	3.962
Securities purchased under agreement to resell	903	—
Other assets	719	551
Total financial service assets	8.874	8.118
TOTAL ASSETS	41.549	40.161
Liabilities and shareholders' equity		
Liabilities		
Claims and claim expenses	15.797	15.977
Policy benefits for life/health contracts	907	751
Unearned premiums	1.874	1.957
Other reinsurance balances	2.948	3.388
Notes payable	285	286
Income taxes	1.104	732
Other liabilities	997	963
Minority interest	1.032	1.166
Financial service liabilities:		
Securities sold under agreements to repurchase, at contract value	1.030	1.985
Securities sold but not yet purchased, at market value	1.190	869
Trading account liabilities	3.664	3.785
Commercial paper	689	140
Notes payable	746	4
Other liabilities	1.032	830
Total financial service liabilities	8.351	7.613
Total liabilities	33.295	32.833
Cumulative convertible preferred stock (shares issued: 1,700,231 in 1997 and 1,711,907 in 1996; no par value)	145	146
Loan to employee savings and stock ownership plan	−142	−144
Common shareholders' equity		
Common stock (102,827,344 shares issued in 1997 and 1996; par value $0.50)	51	51
Paid-in capital	1.109	1.041
Unrealized appreciation of investments, net of deferred income taxes	2.460	1.625
Currency translation adjustments, net of deferred income taxes	−42	−53
Retained earnings	7.492	6.708
Less common stock in treasury, at cost (shares held: 25,393,840 in 1997 and 21,262,113 in 1996)	−2.909	−2.046
Total common shareholders' equity	8.161	7.326
TOTAL LIABILITIES AND SHAREHOLDERS' EQUITY	41.459	40.161

Source: General Re Corporation, *1997 10K Report*, 35.

18

1999: MidAmerican Energy Holdings Company

In October of 1999, Warren Buffett announced a deal to purchase approximately 76 percent of MidAmerican Energy for a per share price of $35.05 in cash, which was a 29 percent premium over the preannouncement closing price. Berkshire Hathaway acquired common shares as well as preferred convertible shares and fixed income securities in this deal, which was structured to give Berkshire Hathaway an economic interest of 76 percent in the company but a voting interest of only just under 10 percent of the company. This structure was adopted in part to avoid breaching any of the complex regulations related to the Public Utility Holding Company Act of 1935 (PUHCA). This act significantly restricted the business activities of holding companies of public utilities, and presumably if Berkshire had a larger voting interest than 10 percent, it would have been subject to these restrictions. In total, Berkshire Hathaway paid approximately $2 billion in this transaction, and there were also two notable coinvestors: Walter Scott, who had been on the board of Berkshire Hathaway since 1988 and had introduced the deal to Buffett, and David Sokol, the entrepreneurial CEO of MidAmerican at the time.[1]

Diving right into the investment case, if I were a potential investor at the time, I would have asked two main questions about the company: Is this a quality business? And is the company for sale at a good price? The

1998 year-end report of MidAmerican is a good place to start because that is the latest annual report that would have been available at the time when the deal was announced in late 1999.

As the annual report shows, MidAmerican was a diversified energy company that was involved foremost with electricity production but also with electricity distribution and "up-stream" gas field exploration. According to the segmental reporting in the notes to financial statements, MidAmerican broke its business into three core business segments and its corporate overheads (see Table 18.1).

The annual report also includes a list of the company's generation plants of the company at year-end 1998.

As we can see, the business segment responsible for the largest portion of income was domestic generation, with most of the U.S. generation plants in Iowa and Illinois. These plants encompass coal, gas, geothermal, hydro, and nuclear power plants. The foreign power plants, which include three power plants in the Philippines and two in England, constitute the assets of the foreign generation segment.

The domestic and foreign generation businesses were similar in their operations. In both, the core activity was building and operating power plants—purchasing fuel, such as coal, and selling electricity. There are nuances to what differentiates more-profitable from less-profitable power plants—their substitute fuels and costs, their technologies, and their efficiency—but the largest difference overall between the two businesses was in government regulation. Power generation is one of the most heavily regulated industries across the world, and as a result, a generation company's profitability is tied substantially to the regulatory environment of the country in which it operates.

In the United States at the time, there were several regulatory agencies and policies that were relevant for MidAmerican. At the national level,

Table 18.1.
Overview of business segments

Segment	Revenue	Operating income	Comments
Domestic generation	$583 million	$314 million	
Foreign generation	$224 million	$143 million	Primarily in Philippines
Foreign utility	$1843 million	$173 million	Primarily in United Kingdom
Corporate	$33 million	−$10 million	
Total	$2683 million	$619 million	

Table 18.2.

Summary of generation plants (1998)

Project[a,b]	Facility net MW	Net MW owned[c]	Fuel	Location	Commercial operation	U.S. $ payments	Power purchaser[d]	Political risk insurance
Projects in operation								
Council Bluffs Energy Center, units 1 & 2	131	131	Coal	Iowa	1954, 1958	Yes	MEC	No
Council Bluffs Energy Center, unit 3	675	534	Coal	Iowa	1978	Yes	MEC	No
Louisa Generation Station, units 1 & 2	700	616	Coal	Iowa	1983	Yes	MEC	No
Neal Generation Station, units 1 & 2	435	435	Coal	Iowa	1964, 1972	Yes	MEC	No
Neal Generation Station, unit 3	515	371	Coal	Iowa	1975	Yes	MEC	No
Neal Generation Station, unit 4	624	253	Coal	Iowa	1979	Yes	MEC	No
Ottumwa Generation Station	716	372	Coal	Iowa	1981	Yes	MEC	No
Quad-Cities Power Station	1,529	383	Nuclear	Illinois	1972	Yes	MEC	No
Riverside Generation Station	135	135	Coal	Iowa	1925–1961	Yes	MEC	No
Combustion turbines	758	758	Gas	Iowa	1969–1995	Yes	MEC	No
Moline Water Power	3	3	Hydro	Illinois	1970	Yes	MEC	No
Imperial Valley	268	134	Geo	Calif.	1986–1996	Yes	Edison	No
Saranac	240	90	Gas	N.Y.	1994	Yes	NYSEG	No
Power Resources	200	100	Gas	Texas	1988	Yes	TUEC	No
NorCon	80	32	Gas	Penn.	1992	Yes	NIMO	No
Yuma	50	25	Gas	Arizona	1994	Yes	SDG&E	No
Roosevelt Hot Springs	23	17	Geo	Utah	1984	Yes	UP&L	No
Desert Peak	10	10	Geo	Nevada	1985	Yes	N/A	No
Mahanagdong	165	149	Geo	Philippines	1997	Yes	PNOC-EDC	Yes
Malitbog	216	216	Geo	Philippines	1996–1997	Yes	PNOC-EDC	Yes
Upper Mahiao	119	119	Geo	Philippines	1996	Yes	PNOC-EDC	Yes
Teesside Power Ltd.	1,875	289	Gas	England	1993	No	Various	No
Viking	50	25	Gas	England	1998	No	Northern	No
Total projects in operation	**9,517**	**5,197**						

[a]The company operates all such projects other than Teesside Power Limited, Quad Cities Power Station, Ottumwa Generation Station, and Desert Peak.

[b]Table 18.2 excludes three projects in Indonesia, two of which are currently in arbitration. One unit became operational in March 1998.

[c]Actual MW may vary depending on operating and reservoir conditions and plant design. Facility net capacity (in MW) represents facility gross capacity (in MW) less parasitic load. Parasitic load is electrical output used by the facility and not made available for sale to utilities or other outside purchases. Net MW owned indicates current legal ownership, but, in some cases, does not reflect the current allocation of partnership distributions.

[d]PNOC-Energy Development Corporation (PNOC-EDC); Government of the Philippines (GOP) and Philippine National Irrigation Administration (NIA) (NIA also purchases water from this facility); Northern Electric plc (Northern). The Government of the Philippines undertaking supports PNOC-EDC's and NIA's respective obligations. Southern California Edison Company (Edison); San Diego Gas & Electric Company (SDG&E); Utah Power & Light Company (UP&L); Bonneville Power Administration (BPA); New York State Electric & Gas Corporation (NYSEG); Texas Utilities Electric Company (TUEC); Niagara Mohawk Power Corporation (NIMO); and MidAmerican Energy Company (MEC).

since the passage of the Public Utilities Regulatory Policies Act ("PURPA") just prior to 1980, independent energy producers were encouraged, and utilities had to buy their electricity. The regulation also extended to price levels. At the state level, there were also numerous regulations, often related to national policies. For example, in Iowa, direct profit regulation stipulated that if MidAmerican's annual jurisdictional return on common equity exceeded 12 percent, some of those profits had to be shared with customers. Likewise, unless MidAmerican's annual return on common equity fell below nine percent, it would not be able to increase its prices.

In England, the regulation of the power generation industry included a full market for electricity trading called the "Pool." Since the phase-in of the Electricity Act of 1989, virtually all electricity generated in England and Wales had to be purchased and sold through this Pool, which set prices. This meant that even if a company produced electricity and sold it as a utility, it had to sell its electricity to the Pool at a specified price and repurchase it from the Pool in order to resell to its utility customers. This and several other measures made price regulation prevalent in England.

Overall, the effect of governmental regulation—both domestic and abroad—was to confine profitability to a band of healthy but not stellar numbers. Within the timeframe of a stipulated contract, an energy company could increase profits if they could increase efficiency, but only for so long. Once regulatory agencies noticed these high profits, new regulation would set in.

The company's final two business segments were foreign utility and corporate. Foreign utility was dominated by the Northern Electric Distribution Limited, which was a distributor of electricity in England. In 1998, this business had approximately 17,000 km of overhead and 26,000 km of underground electricity cables and had rights to supply electricity to approximately 1.5 million customers. In addition to being a distributor of electricity, Northern also supplied and distributed natural gas. Besides Northern, MidAmerican had other businesses, including CE Gas UK Limited, that were involved in gas exploration and production. Hence, abroad, especially in England, MidAmerican had a traditional utility business, including the full value chain of energy supply from exploration to generation to distributing and selling to customers. The final segment of the business, corporate, included corporate functions like legal and finance, but also several niche businesses like Homeservices, which was a realty business belonging to the overall MidAmerican entity.

Turning to the financial statements, in 1998 MidAmerican reported net income of $127 million on a revenue basis of $2.55 billion for the holding company. On a diluted per share basis, this represented $2.01 per share for the 74.1 million shares on a diluted basis outstanding at year-end 1998. Calculating for an operating profit, the EBIT is $491 million. This excludes $220 million in net interest expense, a $93 million provision for income taxes, a $41 million minority interest charge, and $11 million in extraordinary charges. Given the extent of net interest expenses (close to double the net income), the EBIT is probably more reflective of the inherent earnings ability of the business than the net income. In margin terms, EBIT margin was 19.2 percent, and net income margin was five percent.

As a potential investor in the company, I would also consider the capital intensity and return economics of the business and would have calculated for the ROTCE in order to do this. Here, taking an EBIT of $491 and subtracting the 35 percent corporate tax prevalent in 1998, the resulting NOPAT would have been $319 million. The tangible equity base would have looked as follows:

Table 18.3.

Category	Amount in $	As a % of revenues
PPE	$4236m	166%
Inventories	—	0%
Accounts receivable	$528m	21%
Accounts payable	−$306m	−12%
Total capital employed (TCE)	**$4458m**	**174%**

As one can see, the capital employed in the power generation and utility business from MidAmerican is quite significant. In total it is 174 percent of revenues, which is considerably higher than in most production businesses. The resulting ROTCE, based on this TCE and the NOPAT of $319 million, is 7.2 percent. This is fair, but not exceptional. Considering that some of this PPE at year-end was on the balance sheet but did not contribute to the earnings in that year, a less-conservative TCE of year-end 1997, $3731 million, would also be reasonable. Based on this figure, the resulting ROTCE would have been 8.5 percent—better, but still not very good. As an investor, I would have concluded that the ROTCE economics of the MidAmerican business were good but certainly not great.

Of course, there are additional factors to consider. Given that MidAmerican is a utility business with a high level of consistency, it likely had access to very cheap capital and thus was able to generate better returns than suggested by its ROTCE economics. Calculating the ROE is a good way to test this hypothesis. Taking the net income of $127 million on a common equity base of $827 million, the ROE of MidAmerican is 15 percent. This indeed seems to support the hypothesis that MidAmerican was able to achieve fairly good returns from the business at least in part due to its use of financial leverage of reasonably priced capital. Overall, I would conclude that while MidAmerican was a company that was better operated than its peers and also had higher growth, its core business was not inherently a superb compounder.

Finally, valuation: Given the $35.05 per share price that Berkshire Hathaway purchased MidAmerican at, the valuation would have been as follows:

Table 18.4.
EV/EBIT multiples

EV/EBIT	1998	1997
EV*	$7867m	$7867m
EBIT	$491m	$343m
EV/EBIT	**16.0×**	**22.9×**

*Calculation of EV is based on share price of $35.05 × 72.64m diluted shares outstanding at June 30, 1999 plus net debt at June 30, 1999 of $5321m. Net debt is calculated based on figures of $247m cash + $130m marketable securities + $385m restricted cash + $190m equity investments − $2017m parent co. debt − $ 4256m project debt. Note that this sum based on the latest available 10Q report is somewhat lower than the approximate $9 billion EV quoted in the press release document for the acquisition. Two factors explain the divergence: (1) changes in net debt between June 30 and press release date (2) calculation of the value of preferred shares.

Table 18.5.
PER multiples

PER	1998	1997
Share price	$35.50	$35.50
EPS as reported (diluted)	$2.01	Negative
PER	17.4×	Not applicable

These multiples seem extremely high, especially given the previous analysis that MidAmerican was not a great compounder. To be sure, there were one or two businesses within MidAmerican (such as the realty business) that had a clear value but were not considered in the valuation, but unless the earnings were at cyclically depressed levels, MidAmerican would not have seemed undervalued to me as a potential investor at the time. Given the seven percent ROTCE and 15 percent ROE achieved in 1998, I would have considered cyclically depressed earnings unlikely; as power generation clearly seemed to be capital intensive, I would have guessed cyclical high ROTCE to be no more than about 12 or 13 percent. Assuming that in a very good year earnings were 50 percent higher on the same asset basis, the comparable EV/EBIT multiple would have been approximately 11 times, and the PER would have been approximately 12 times—hardly dirt cheap.

The only aspect that would have seemed impressive to be me would have been the growth. Between 1994 and 1998, as the selected financial data show, revenues grew from $154 million to $2.5 billion. Similarly, net income grew from $37 million to $127 million during this period. The commentary in the annual report makes it clear that growth was both organic and acquisitions based. All in all, I would have seen MidAmerican as a stable business with good growth, but only average returns. I would not have seen it as an especially attractive investment, at least with respect to the common equity.

So what might Buffett have seen differently in this case? The October 25, 1999 press release from Berkshire Hathaway about this acquisition offers clues. First, the transaction was not structured as a simple acquisition through the purchase of all common stock. To keep the percentage of voting rights low for regulatory purposes, Berkshire Hathaway was to invest approximately $1.25 billion in common stock and nondividend-paying convertible stock and a further $800 million in a nontransferable-trust preferred stock. As is revealed in the Berkshire annual letter to shareholders, the $800 million trust preferred stock was equivalent to a fixed income security with an 11 percent yield and was considered as such by Buffett. Given this, one can view Buffett's investment in MidAmerican as one in which he only commits $1.25 billion as equity, with the benefit of having an 11 percent fixed-income product with relatively little risk. While the setup is somewhat complicated, this transaction seems akin to a private equity transaction. Buffett and his associates do not purchase the 72 or so million diluted shares outstanding[2] at $35.05 per share, which would have cost approximately $2.5 billion. Buffett only pays $1.25 billion, gets to invest in a fixed-income product yielding 11 percent, and gets a 76 percent ownership of the earnings of the company. The remaining cash is made up with debt in the form of bonds and a smaller $300 million investment by coinvestors Walter Scott and David Sokol. In this setup, it seems that Buffett benefits twice. First, he enjoys a rather attractive fixed-income investment; second, he is able to benefit from leveraging a fairly stable growth business, resulting in higher returns on his equity in

comparison to the moderate ROTCE inherent in the business. While difficult to quantify, it seems that this deal is significantly better than it would be
for an ordinary investor investing in the common equity of MidAmerican.
It also seems clear that avoiding regulatory requirements was not the only
reason the deal was structured in this complex manner.

Another point that seems essential for Buffett in this investment case is
the focus on the management team and the board. In describing the acquisition of MidAmerican, Buffett states, "If I only had two draft picks out
of American business, Walter Scott and David Sokol are the ones I would
choose for this industry."[3] This seems to be a case where Buffett was also
investing in two partners he believed to be superb managers. MidAmerican's annual report does not give a strong sense of the management team,
but from the company's history of growth it is clear that management had
been competent. Buffett clearly benefited from his personal knowledge of
the capacity of the management team.

Reading the commentaries of Buffett about the business in later years,[4]
I was struck by Buffett's keen eye for the numbers. Specifically, he comments that MidAmerican carries a significant amount of amortization of
goodwill (also called purchase price allocation), which was going away.
The 1998 annual report indeed includes a figure of goodwill amortization,
but the figure is hidden in the income statement under the line "depreciation and amortization." Although only $42 million in 1998, the goodwill
amortization should not be counted as a real cost since it is an accounting cost only rather than a cost that a business requires in continuing its
operations. Considering this factor, the true EBIT minus PPA would have
been $533 million rather than $491 million—about 10 percent higher. The
resulting EV/EBIT multiple would change from 16.0 times to an EV/EBIT
minus PPA multiple of 14.6 times—still high but lower than before.

Taking these factors together, Buffett seems to have invested foremost
in a team of managers whom he trusted and believed would continue to
grow the business. He also invested in a specific setup that was likely significantly better than a private investor would have gotten if that investor
had purchased on the common equity at the same price. However, in terms
of price, which is a bit lower than what I would have focused on, Buffett
seems to be paying a full price in comparison to the previous earnings of
the MidAmerican business. Perhaps it is true that, during 1999, which was
the tail-end of a large run of stock prices, Buffett had to pay more than previously and was prepared to pay for a business that would be able to employ
a large amount of capital at a decent, albeit not great, return.

Table 18.6.
Five-year financial summary (1994–1998)
($ in thousands)

	1998[a]	1997	1996[b]	1995[c]	1994
Income statement data					
Operating revenue	2,555,206	2,166,338	518,934	335,630	154,562
Total revenue	2,682,711	2,270,911	576,195	398,723	185,854
Expenses	2,410,658	2,074,051	435,791	301,672	130,018
Income before provision for income taxes	272,053	196,860*	140,404	97,051	55,836
Minority interest	41,276	45,993	6,122	3,005	—
Income before change in accounting principle and extraordinary item	137,512	51,823	492,461	63,415	38,834
Extraordinary item, net of tax	−7,146	−135,850	—	—	−2,007
Cumulative effect of change in accounting principle, net of tax	−3,361	—	—	—	—
Net income/loss	127,003	−84,027	2,492,261	63,415	36,827
Preferred dividends	—	—	—	1,080	5,010
Net income/loss available to common stockholders	127,003	−84,027	492,461	62,335	31,817
Income per share					
Before change in accounting principle and extraordinary item	2.29	0.77*	1.69	1.32	1.02
Extraordinary item	−0.12	−2.02	—	—	−0.06
Cumulative effect of change in accounting principle	−0.06	—	—	—	—
Net income/loss	2.11	−1.25*	1.69	1.32	0.96
Basic common shares outstanding	60,139	67,268	54,739	47,249	33,189

(continued)

Table 18.6. (*Continued*)

	1998[a]	1997	1996[b]	1995[c]	1994
Income per share					
Before extraordinary item and cumulative effect of change in account—diluted	2.15	0.75	1.54	1.22	0.95
Extraordinary item—diluted	-0.10	-1.97	—	—	-0.05
Cumulative effect of change in accounting principle—diluted	-0.04	—	—	—	—
Net income/loss— diluted	2.01	-1.22*	1.54	1.22	0.95
Diluted shares outstanding	74,100	68,686	65,072	56,195	39,203
Balance sheet data					
Total assets	9,103,524	7,487,626	5,630,156	2,654,038	1,131,145
Total liabilities	7,598,040	5,282,162	4,181,052	2,084,474	867,703
Company-obligated mandatorily redeemable convertible preferred securities of subsidiary trusts	553,930	553,930	103,930	—	—
Preferred securities of subsidiary	66,033	56,181	136,065	—	—
Minority interest	—	134,454	299,252	—	—
Redeemable preferred stock	—	—	—	—	63,600
Stockholders' equity	827,053	765,326	880,790	543,532	179,991

Source: MidAmerican Energy Holdings Co., *10K Report 1998,* 61.
[a]Reflects the acquisition of KDG.
[b]Reflects the acquisitions of Northern, Falcon Seaboard, and the Partnership Interest owned for a portion of the year.
[c]Reflects the acquisition of Magma Power Company owned for a portion of the year.
*Includes the $87,000, $1.29 per basic share, $1.27 per diluted share, nonrecurring Indonesian asset impairment charge.

Table 18.7.
Balance sheet (1997–1998)
Years ended Dec. 31
($ in thousands)

Assets	1998	1997
Cash and cash equivalents	1,604,470	1,445,338
Joint venture cash and investments	1,678	6,072
Restricted cash	515,231	223,636
Restricted investments	122,340	—
Accounts receivable	528,116	376,745
Properties, plants, contracts, and equipment, net	4,236,039	3,528,910
Excess of cost over fair value of net assets acquired, net	1,538,176	1,312,788
Equity investments	125,036	238,025
Deferred charges and other assets	432,438	356,112
TOTAL ASSETS	9,103,524	7,487,626
Liabilities and stockholders' equity		
Liabilities		
Accounts payable	305,757	173,610
Other accrued liabilities	1,009,091	1,106,641
Parent company debt	2,645,991	1,303,845
Subsidiary and project debt	3,093,810	2,189,007
Deferred income taxes	543,391	509,059
Total liabilities	7,598,040	5,282,162
Deferred income	58,468	40,837
Company—obligated mandatorily redeemable convertible preferred securities of subsidiary trusts	553,930	553,930
Preferred securities of subsidiary	66,033	56,181
Minority interest	—	134,454
Common stock and options subject to redemption	—	654,736
Stockholders' equity		
Common stock, par value $0.0675 per share*	5,602	5,602
Additional paid-in capital	1,233,088	1,261,081
Retained earnings	340,496	213,493
Accumulated other comprehensive income	45	−3,589
Common stock and options subject to redemption	—	−654,736
Treasury stock—23,375 and 1,658 common shares at cost	−752,178	−56,525
Total stockholders' equity	827,053	765,326
TOTAL LIABILITIES AND STOCKHOLDERS' EQUITY	9,103,514	7,487,626

Source: MidAmerican Energy Holdings Co., *10K Report 1998*, 73.
*Authorized 180,000 shares, issued 82,980 shares, outstanding 59,605 and 81,322 shares, respectively.

Table 18.8.
Income statement (1996–1998)
Year ended Dec. 31
($ in thousands except per share data)

	1998	1997	1996
Revenue:			
Operating revenue	2,555,206	2,166,338	518,934
Interest and other income	127,505	104,573	57,261
Total revenues	2,682,711	2,270,911	576,195
Costs and expenses:			
Cost of sales	1,258,539	1,055,195	31,840
Operating expense	425,004	345,833	132,655
General and administration	46,401	52,705	21,451
Depreciation and amortization	333,422	276,041	118,586
Loss on equity investments in Casecnan	—	5,972	5,221
Interest expense	406,084	296,364	165,900
Less interest capitalized	−58,792	−45,059	−39,862
Nonrecurring charge—asset valuation impairment	—	87,000	—
Total costs and expenses	2,410,658	2,074,051	435,791
Income before provision for income taxes	272,053	196,860	140,404
Provision for income taxes	93,265	99,044	41,821
Income before minority interest	178,788	97,816	98,583
Minority interest	41,276	45,993	6,122
Income before extraordinary item and cumulative effect of change in accounting principle	137,512	51,823	92,461
Extraordinary item, net of tax	−7,146	−135,850	—
Cumulative effect of change in accounting principle, net of tax	−3,363	—	—
Net income/loss available to common stockholders	127,003	−84,027	92,461
Per share			
Income before extraordinary item and cumulative effect of change in accounting principle	2.29	0.77	1.69
Extraordinary item	−0.12	−2.02	—
Cumulative effect of change in accounting principle	−0.06	—	—
Net income/loss	2.11	−1.25	1.69
Per share—diluted			
Income before extraordinary item and cumulative effect of change in accounting principle	2.15	0.75	1.54
Extraordinary item	−0.10	−1.97	—
Cumulative effect of change in accounting principle	−0.04	—	—
Net income/loss	2.01	−1.22	1.54

Source: MidAmerican Energy Holdings Co., *10K Report 1998,* 74.

Table 18.9.
Cash-flow statement (1996–1998)
Years ended Dec. 31
($ in thousands)

	1998	1997	1996
Cash flows from operating activities:			
Net income/loss	127,003	−84,027	92,461
Adjustments to reconcile net cash flow from operating activities:			
Nonrecurring charge-asset valuation impairment	—	87,000	—
Extraordinary item, net of tax	7,146	—	—
Cumulative effect of change in accounting principle	3,363	—	—
Depreciation and amortization	290,794	239,234	109,447
Amortization of excess of cost over fair value of net assets acquired	42,628	36,807	9,139
Amortization of original issue discount	42	2,160	50,194
Amortization of deferred financing and other costs	21,681	31,632	11,212
Provision for deferred income taxes	34,332	55,584	12,252
Income on equity investments	−10,837	−16,068	−910
Income/loss applicable to minority interest	5,313	−35,387	1,431
Changes in other items:			
Accounts receivable	−135,124	−34,146	−13,936
Accounts payable, accrued liabilities, and deferred income	−41,803	29,799	2,093
Net cash flows from operating activities	344,538	312,588	273,383
Cash flows from investing activities:			
Purchase of KDG, Northern, Falcon Seaboard, Partnership Interest, and Magma, net of cash acquired	−500,916	−632,014	−474,443
Distributions from equity investments	17,008	23,960	8,222
Capital expenditures relating to operating projects	−227,071	−194,224	−24,821
Philippine construction	−112,263	−27,334	−167,160
Indonesian construction	−83,869	−146,297	−76,546
Acquisition of UK gas assets	−35,677	—	—
Domestic construction and other development costs	−36,047	−12,794	−73,179
Decrease in short-term investments	1,282	2,880	33,998
Decrease/increase in restricted cash and investments	20,568	−116,668	63,175
Other	−33,787	60,390	−2,910
Net cash flows from investing activities	−990,772	−1,042,101	−713,664
Cash flows from financing activities:			
Proceeds from sales of common and treasury stock and exercise of stock options	3,412	703,624	54,935
Proceeds from convertible preferred securities of subsidiary trusts	—	450,000	103,930
Proceeds from issuance of parent company debt	1,502,243	350,000	324,136

(*continued*)

Table 18.9. (*Continued*)

	1998	1997	1996
Repayment of parent company debt	−167,285	−100,000	—
Net proceeds from revolver	—	−95,000	95,000
Proceeds from subsidiary and project debt	464,974	795,658	428,134
Repayments of subsidiary and project debt	−255,711	−271,618	210,892
Deferred charges relating to debt financing	−47,205	−48,395	−36,010
Purchase of treasury stock	−724,791	−55,505	−12,008
Other	21,701	13,142	10,756
Net cash flows from financing activities	797,338	1,741,906	757,981
Effect of exchange rate changes	3,634	−33,247	4,860
Net increase in cash and cash equivalents	154,738	979,146	322,560
Cash and cash equivalents at beginning of year	1,451,410	472,264	149,704
Cash and cash equivalents at end of year	1,606,148	1,451,410	472,264
Supplemental disclosures			
Interest paid (net of amounts capitalized)	341,645	316,060	92,829
Income taxes paid	53,609	44,483	23,211

Source: MidAmerican Energy Holdings Co., *10K Report 1998*, 76.

19

2007–2009: Burlington Northern

In his 2007 year-end letter to shareholders, Warren Buffett showed an ownership of 60,828,818 shares of Burlington Northern Santa Fe (BNSF) for a cost basis of $4.73 billion. This represented a 17.5 percent stake in the company at an average price of $77.76 per share. This marked Buffett's initial investment in BNSF, which was and remains one of the two largest railroad companies, along with Union Pacific, in North America. In late 2009, Buffett and Berkshire Hathaway purchased all the remaining shares outstanding in BNSF in a deal that gave the company a total market capitalization of $34 billion, or roughly $100 per share for its 341.2 million outstanding shares at the time. The remainder purchased at this time represented a 77.4 percent stake in the company. Berkshire Hathaway had grown its shares from a 17.5 percent stake to a 22.6 percent stake between 2007 and 2010. This chapter looks at the BNSF investment from both the perspective of the initial investment in 2007 as well as the buy-out in 2010. Operating a railroad network is often associated with high capital requirements. BNSF generates the vast majority of its revenue from transporting freight between major North American economic centers, and thus incurs the costs of maintaining a fleet of locomotives and freight cars, an infrastructure of tracks, and a whole network of support facilities including yards, terminals, dispatching centers, and specialized service and maintenance shops. According to

Figure 19.1.

BNSF's 2008 annual report, the railroad had approximately 40,000 employees, 6,510 locomotives, and 82,555 freight cars. Matthew Rose, the CEO and chairman of the company, stated that between 1997 and 2008, BNSF spent $30 billion on improving its rail infrastructure and rolling stock. By any metric, this is a huge amount of money invested. Besides dealing with the day-to-day operations, running a profitable railroad also involves allocating capital wisely on expansion, navigating the competitive landscape, and successfully managing regulatory issues such as trackage rights.

According to the BNSK 2008 annual report the business is segmented into four core divisions and an "other" category. The split by revenue is as follows:

Table 19.1.
Overview of business segments

Segment	Revenue	% of total
Consumer products	$6,064m	34%
Industrial products	$4,028m	22%
Coal	$3,970m	22%
Agricultural products	$3,441m	19%
Other	$515m	3%
Total	**$18,018m**	**100%**

Excluding the Other category, the four core freight businesses generated revenue of $17.5 billion in 2008. As table 19.1 shows, although Consumer Products was the largest segment, Industrial Products, Coal, and Agricultural Products were also significant.

Researching further into the details of each freight category, Consumer Products refers to approximately 90 percent containers (both international shipping containers as well as domestic goods) and 10 percent automotive products. Industrial Products refers to construction products, building products, petroleum products, chemicals/plastics, and food and beverage products. Coal is coal, but refers specifically to BNSF's transportation of U.S. low-sulfur coal originating from the Powder River Basin in Wyoming and Montana. Agricultural Products is the transportation of corn, wheat, soybeans, and other bulk foods, as well as ethanol, fertilizers, and related products. Overall, whichever the product category, BNSF's main business activity is the transportation of bulk products. As seen in figure 19.2, which is taken from its 10-K statement of that year, BNSF does this mostly across the heartland of the central and western United States.

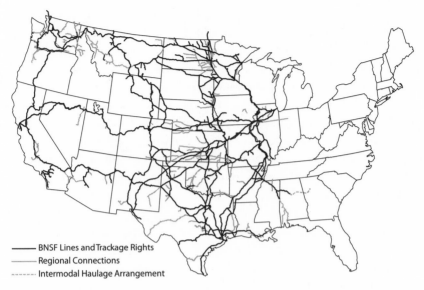

—— BNSF Lines and Trackage Rights
—— Regional Connections
------- Intermodal Haulage Arrangement

Figure 19.2.
Map of BNSF footprint. (*Source*: Union Pacific Corporation, *2007 Annual Report*.)

As is also noted in the 10K statement, the customer interface of BNSF is such that approximately two-thirds of the revenues of BNSF are covered by individual customer contracts of various durations, while one-third of revenues come from customers who pay the common carrier published prices.

As one can see, while average length of hauls have remained roughly in line, the total amount of ton-miles (volume) has increased between one percent and two percent in each of the last two years. The real difference, however, comes from the average revenue per ton-miles—in other words, the price—which increased significantly between four percent and 13 percent in the last two years. Some of this was due to higher fuel prices; but according to BNSF's detailed financials, fuel costs increased by only

Table 19.2.
Operational metrics BNSF

Year ended Dec. 31	2008	2007	2006
Revenue ton-miles (millions)	664,384	657,572	647,857
Freight revenue per tsd revenue ton-miles	$26.34	$23.34	$22.45
Average length of haul (miles)	1,090	1,079	1,071

Source: Based on Burlington Northern Santa Fe, *2008 10K Report*, 10.

$1.7 billion while freight revenues increased by $3 billion. This information indicates that BNSF has pricing power.

Another key aspect in understanding BNSF is recognizing its competitive position. First, BNSF competes with other railroads. Union Pacific, with its 48,000 employees and approximately 8,700 locomotives in 2008, was the largest competing railroad. To understand to what degree BNSF competes with Union Pacific, see the map of operations for Union Pacific in figure 19.3.

As you can see, Union Pacific and BNSF competed on a significant number of routes between the Central Plains and the West Coast.[1] Given this fact, price, timeliness, and quality of service must also be operational aspects on which the two railroads compete. Table 19.3 contains the operational metrics from Union Pacific's 2008 annual report.

By comparing these metrics with those of BNSF, one can draw two conclusions. First, it seemed that BNSF had added trackage or managed

Figure 19.3.
Operational Metrics, BNSF. (*Source*: Burlington Northern Santa Fe Corporation, *2008 Annual Report*.)

Table 19.3.
Operational metrics Union Pacific

Year ended Dec. 31	2008	2007	2006
Revenue ton-miles (millions)	562,600	561,800	565,200
Freight revenue per tsd revenue ton-miles	$30.43	$27.56	$26.17
Operating ratio	77.3%	79.3%	81.5%
Customer satisfaction index	83	79	72

Source: Based on Union Pacific, "Operating/Performance Statistics," *2008 Annual Report,* 35.

volumes slightly better than Union Pacific. Unlike Union Pacific, which saw a very slight decrease in revenue ton-miles during the period from 2006 to 2008, BNSF saw an increase of three percent. Second, like BNSF, Union Pacific was increasing prices. The fact that both railroads were able to increase prices indicates a favorable pricing environment within the industry and an absence of cutthroat price competition between the railroads.

As far as direct competition, Union Pacific was a real competitor to BNSF, but based on the previous analysis, this was likely a respected duopoly with pricing discipline. BNSF seemed to be the better operator of these two players because it had been able to grow revenue ton-miles profitably between 2006 and 2008, although Union Pacific also performed reasonably well.

In addition to the direct competition of alternative railroads, one must also consider the competition from the substitutes available for long distance freight transport, the most obvious of which are transport via truck, water, and aircraft. Given that water transport is limited to areas near waterways, and given the very high price point of aircraft transportation, the most relevant substitute for cargo rail is clearly truck transport.

BNSF Chairman Matthew Rose goes to great lengths in his annual report to detail the advantages of cargo rail over truck transport, noting that "trains transport on average a ton of freight nearly three times as far as a truck on the same amount of fuel." And so while train transport accounts for a bit more than 40 percent of the nation's freight, it only accounts for 2.6 percent of the nation's greenhouse gas emissions.[2] Overall, rail is probably the most efficient, cheap, and environmentally friendly option for regular transport. In fact, Rose states that BNSF's focus should not be on direct competitors like Union Pacific as much as on the opportunity the whole rail industry has in capturing a larger slice of the overall freight transportation pie.

As to the financials of Burlington Northern Santa Fe, from 2000 to 2007, BNSF's revenues increased from $9.2 billion in 2000 to $15.8 billion in 2007. Similarly, EBIT increased from $2.2 billion in 2000 to $3.5 billion in 2007. Net earnings increased from $980 million in 2000 to $1.8 billion in 2007. As a CAGR for the period, the annual growth rates for revenue, EBIT, and net earnings were approximately eight percent, seven percent, and nine percent, respectively. According to the balance sheet of the BNSF business at year-end 2007, its capital requirements and return economics were as described in table 19.4.

As table 19.4 shows, the primary capital employed in the railroad business is tied to PPE: property, plant, and equipment. This category includes the tracks, the maintenance facilities, and the rolling stock, including locomotives and rail cars. Besides the PPE, the business requires very little capital. Based on the $15.8 billion revenues and $3.5 billion EBIT, one can calculate a before-tax return of 10.9 percent. Assuming a tax rate of 30 percent leading to a NOPAT of $2.4 billion, the theoretical after-tax ROTCE would be 7.6 percent.

Although this in itself is not very impressive (a good ROTCE is usually considered to be something above 15 percent), BNSF seemed to have a significantly better marginal return on tangible capital than on its entire capital base. This case is not obvious, but it is fairly straightforward. Out of its approximately $40 billion in gross net PPE, approximately 80 percent was tied to track structure and other roadway.[3] All the locomotives, freight cars, and other equipment together only accounted for approximately $6 billion in gross PPE. Here, while locomotives and freight cars may need replacement every several years, or more may need to be purchased, the core railroad tracks and roadways are mostly costs that have to be incurred once and do not require significant additional capital. Of course, there are some new tracks laid with regional expansion, but the scope of this "marginal capital" is much less than the cost of laying the core tracks. To be specific,

Table 19.4.

Category	Amount in $	As a % of revenues
PPE	$33,583m	213%
Inventories	$579m	4%
Accounts receivable	$790m	5%
Accounts payable	−$2824m	−18%
Total capital employed (TCE)	**$32,128m**	**203%**

BNSF reported its new and maintenance track miles laid in 2006, 2007, and 2008 as 854 miles, 994 miles, and 972 miles, respectively. Out of the approximately 60,000 total operated miles of track for the company, this represents an annual figure of a bit over one percent. New expansion tracks are a fraction of this amount. This is a very small investment in relation to the freight revenue growth, which increased five percent and 14 percent in 2007 and 2008, respectively. Hence, the marginal ROTCE is likely at least two times as high as what is suggested by the 7.6 percent ROTCE, which is based on the total capital of the business.

In total, with a long-term growth rate of about six to eight percent per annum based on railroads being more efficient than other modes of transport, and a high marginal ROTCE of 15 percent or greater, BNSF would have looked attractive to a prospective investor who understood the business economics—a good-quality business with some structural advantages. The major arguments one could make against BNSF are regarding qualitative issues, such as that it is a business with competition and one where good operational execution is critical to success.

This leads naturally to an analysis of the BNSF management team, who are responsible for good execution. At the end of 2007, the team in charge of BNSF included CEO and President Matthew Rose and CFO Thomas Hund. Matthew Rose had been the chairman and CEO of BNSF since 2000. He had joined the company in 1993 and moved up the ranks on the operations side, having held the position of COO before becoming CEO. Before he joined BNSF, he worked in the rail industry as vice president of transportation at a subsidiary of Norfolk Southern Railroad. Rose was clearly a manager with significant experience in operating railroads, and, as discussed previously, as CEO he had a track record of great financial performance, helping his company generate consistent revenue and profit growth. Under Rose's leadership BNSF often outperformed Union Pacific.[4] Thomas Hund was also an executive with extensive background in railroads. He had been the CFO of BNSF since 1999 and had previously held multiple financial positions with BNSF and Santa Fe Railway. Between December 31, 1999 and December 31, 2007, BNSF's shares outstanding (diluted) were reduced by about 23 percent, from approximately 467 million to 359 million, a reduction of about 23 percent, and dividends increased from $0.48 to $1.14. This indicates good capital management on Hund's part. While the BNSF management team members did not seem to own many shares themselves, they seemed to be very experienced and had a very respectable history.

Finally, valuation. Buffett made his purchase of Burlington Northern Santa Fe in several tranches. For his initial purchase of a 17.5 percent stake in the company in 2007, Buffett paid $4.7 billion, valuing the total company at $27.0 billion. On a per share basis, this reflects an average price of $77.78 per share. The conventional valuation multiples for this purchase would have been as follows:[5]

Table 19.5.
Valuation multiples

	2007 expected	2006 actual
EPS (diluted)	$5.10	$5.11
PER	15.3×	15.2×
EBIT	$3.49 billion	$3.52 billion
EV/EBIT	10.1×	10.0×
P/B	2.43×	2.42×

This is not incredibly cheap, but for a well-managed and inherently good-quality business with an understandable reason for having seven percent annual increases in profits and revenues at a high marginal ROTCE, this is a more than fair price for an investor who believes in the value of growth. The key then becomes the certainty of that growth. Given that BNSF had the structural advantage of being a more fuel-efficient form of cargo transport, had a long history of growth, and had a competent management team, as a potential investor, I would have been fairly comfortable with its growth prospects.

When purchasing the remainder of the company in 2010, Berkshire's cost was roughly $100 per share for the 341.2 million shares outstanding that it did not already own. This was roughly 20 percent higher than the cost basis of his initial share purchases in 2007. Looking at year-end 2009 earnings (of which fourth quarter results were likely still not available at the time the purchase was made), the new valuation would have looked as follows:[6]

Table 19.6.
Valuation multiples II

	2009 expected	2008 actual
EPS (diluted)	$5.01	$6.06
PER	19.9×	16.5×
EBIT	$3.26 billion	$3.91 billion
EV/EBIT	13.2×	11.0×
P/B	2.66×	3.06×

Even more than his 2007 purchase, it is clear that the valuation that Buffett pays is not cheap. Even accounting for the premium he would have had to pay to take 100 percent ownership of the company, an investor at the time could have easily thought that the multiple of 11.0× EV/EBIT based on 2008 was based on peak-year earnings in the industry, and that the 13.2× 2009 multiple was a more accurate reflection of the price paid on sustainable earnings. It seems that Buffett either thought he knew better or was confident enough in the growth prospects of BNSF to pay a 13.2× EV/EBIT price.

Most impressive to me was the economic context in which this investment was made. When Buffett made this purchase in late 2009, the United States had just gone through one of the deepest economic recessions of recent times. On November 3, 2009, when the Burlington Northern deal was announced, the Dow was hovering just around 10,000, when in March of that year it had fallen to below 7,000. Looking specifically at Burlington Northern Santa Fe, the year-end operating performance (which would not have been available at the time Buffett purchased his shares) was roughly in line with the performance BNSF achieved in 2006, a full three years prior. But despite the fear abounding in the market and the short-term poor performance of BNSF, Buffett had the fortitude to invest the largest stake in his career at a time of relative uncertainty. He saw an opportunity to purchase a high-quality business with decent growth and high marginal ROTCE and was confident enough to pay a price others would have considered expensive—especially in 2009. Here I can only guess that Buffett chose to stick to a good investment that he had come to known well, over other surely interesting investment candidates in late 2009.

To sum up, it seems that Buffett first invested in BNSF as a good business with good management at a fair price. In 2009, he then took an opportunity to pay "only" an approximate 25 percent premium to his initial purchase price to take private a business he knew well but at a time where both the market uncertainty and the company specific momentum were still uncertain. For any seasoned investor, doing this takes a lot of courage regardless if one has to answer to shorter-term investors in one's fund or not.

INTERVIEW WITH MATT ROSE

On December 21, 2009, Burlington Northern Santa Fe Corporation (BNSF) posted on its intranet a video of CEO Matt Rose interviewing Warren Buffett, CEO of Berkshire Hathaway Inc. (Berkshire Hathaway), on matters related to Berkshire Hathaway's acquisition of BNSF. A transcription of the interview follows:

BNSF Video News
Interview with Warren Buffett
Interviewer: Matt Rose
December 3, 2009

MKR: Hi, I'm Matt Rose. Welcome to this special edition of BNSF Video News. As you all know, we've been in the news a lot with the major announcement that we have the future ownership position of BNSF being acquired by Berkshire Hathaway. So I've been asked a lot of questions around, what does this mean for BNSF, what does it mean for the individuals that work for BNSF, what does it mean for customers, and what does it mean for the communities in which we operate? And so I thought, who better to ask these questions to than Warren Buffett, chairman, chief executive officer of Berkshire Hathaway. We have a great treat. We've got Warren with us today at this taping, so we're going to get right into it. I've asked about 20 people to send in a number of questions, of "ask-Warren" questions, and they did. They sent in about 150 questions. We're only going to ask about 15 to 20. We'll see how we do on time. So let's get right into it. Again, Warren, welcome, thank you for joining us. The first one is, why BNSF, and why now?

WB: Well, uh, you know, I love railroads. I mean, you go back 70 years when I used to be going down to Union Station every Sunday, and so I've watched it for years. And, and we couldn't have done this 20 years ago, in terms of the size of Berkshire. But Berkshire piles up. We don't pay out any dividends, so we pile up 8 or 9 or 10 billion dollars a year, and you know, this is a dream for me, you know, getting a chance to buy a wonderful railroad like this, and uh, I couldn't be happier about it.

MKR: So, the next one. In announcing the acquisition, you said it's an all-in wager on the economic future of the United States. Buffett, who has been building up his rail holdings for several years, said in the statement, I love these events. So would you please just share your perspective and thoughts on the future of the rail industry?

WB: Well, it has to do well if the country does well, and the country is going to do well. So, you know, I don't know about next week or next month or even next year, but if you look at the next 50 years, this country is going to grow, it's going to have more people, it's going to have more goods moving, and rail is the logical way for many of those goods to travel, and probably a greater percentage all the time, just in terms of, of cost efficiency, in terms of fuel efficiency, in terms of environmentally-friendly. So there's no way rail is going to lose share, and I think the pie is going to grow, and I think the rail share of the pie is going to grow.

MKR: So the next question. You said in the past, you'd rather buy a great business at a fair price than a fair business at a great price. What does BNSF meet the definition of a great business?

WB: Well, it's a great business in that you know it's going to be here forever, to start with. I mean, the hula-hoop business came and, you know, went, and then, you know, the pet rocks and all that kind of thing. And even television set manufacturers have, you know, moved over to Japan. All of that sort of thing. The rail business is not going to go anyplace. It's going to be right here in the United States. There's going to be four big railroads that are moving more and more goods. So it's, it's, it's a good business. It, it can't be, it can't be something like Coca-Cola or Google, because it's, you know, it's a public service type business, too, and it has, it has a fair amount of regulation that is part of the picture. But it'll be a good business over time. It will make sense for this country to want railroads to continue to invest more and more money, in terms of ex-panding and becoming more efficient. So you're on the side of society, and society will largely be on your side. Not every day, but most of the time.

MKR: Well, I think our 40,000 employees definitely agree with that. Alright, so the next one. Historically, are companies more profitable after join-ing Berkshire Hathaway, and if so, why?

WB: Well, you can run the business exactly as you see fit. You don't have to please banks. You don't have to please Wall Street. You don't have to, you know, you don't have to please media or anybody else. Basically, it frees up the managers of our businesses to do exactly what they love to do, which is to run their businesses. And, and, and there's no home really like Berkshire that can offer that.

MKR: Alright. The next question is, and I didn't ask this, will Berkshire di-rectly be involved in the management of BNSF, and will the manage-ment structure change?

WB: No, it won't. It's very simple. We've got 20 people in Omaha, and there isn't one of them that knows how to run a railroad.

MKR: Alright, next question. Will this transaction impact employment lev-els positively or negatively?

wb: Well, I don't think it changes anything, really, in that respect. I mean, you'll be running the railroad, and you'll run it in an efficient way, and when times are good, you're going to have more people employed than when times are bad. But nothing in our ownership really has any effect on employment.

mkr: Okay. So, this came from one of our locomotive engineers. He said, will rail labor have access to you regarding issues? How do you balance negotiating fair wages, health care, and a good work environment with Berkshire Hathaway earnings?

wb: Well, you'll do it just like you've managed it in terms of BNSF earnings. And there will be no involvement by me or anybody else in Omaha in terms of labor or in terms of purchasing or in terms of what locomotives you buy, anything of the sort. It's—we bought it because it was well-managed. If, if, if we had to bring management to BNSF, both of us would have been in trouble.

mkr: Okay. The next question came from our finance group. Will there be a significant, will there be significant BNSF asset sales to pay down the eight-billion-dollar acquisition debt?

wb: Not a dime. Not a dime.

mkr: Next question. Will Berkshire continue to invest the capital needed to maintain the BNSF infrastructure?

wb: Well, it'd be crazy if we didn't. You know, we're not going to, we're not going to buy a business and starve it. You got where you are because you were willing to make the investments ahead of time to pay it off 3, 5, 10 years down the road, and that's, that's part of the railroad business, and it'll stay part of the railroad business.

mkr: You've heard me talk about regulatory risk. We've been talking to our employees about that for a number of years. And the question is, uh, what's your perspective on the regulatory risk in our industry, from what you know about it?

wb: Well, Matt, it'll never go away, in the sense that, people, you know, you will always have people that are bothered by what you're charging, and you know, whether it's in some farmer in a pasture or wherever. And the very fact that it has a utility aspect to it. Now it has an entrepreneurial aspect to it, too, but it has a utility aspect to it. So it's always going to be regulated. There always will be some tension between shippers and railroads, and they will all, there will always be some people who will try and use political influence to affect rates. But in the end, the country needs railroads to spend lots and lots and lots of money merely to stay in the same place, but then beyond that, to grow, and, and it would be crazy of society to deny you a reasonable rate of return.

MKR: Another question from the finance group. Will BNSF capital requests now have to compete internally with other Berkshire interests?

WB: Not in the least. No.

MKR: I thought it was a good question. Okay, next question. In 10 years, how will you evaluate the acquisition of BNSF, whether or not it's been successful?

WB: Well, I—I'll measure it against my own standard, which is that I have made a bet on the country doing well. And if I'm wrong on that, that's my fault and not anybody at BNSF's fault. But I will look at it how it does compared to other railroads. I'll look at how railroads are doing versus trucking and all of that. But in the end, I don't really worry about that very much. I, I've seen what's been done here. I think I know how the country is going to develop. I think the West is going to do well. I'd rather be in the West than the East. So I really don't have much of a worry about that.

MKR: The next question is, how should be BNSF support the long-term goals of Berkshire Hathaway, and what expectations have you established for the BNSF management team?

WB: You should, you should really be doing it as if you had the same 250,000 owners you have now. I mean, their interests are the same, you know, as Berkshire's will be, and, and I don't really see any difference. We want this railroad run as well as it can be. We'd love it every, every, every car you can steal away from the Union Pacific [unintelligible], but we want Union Pacific to do well, too. I mean, we're both going to do well, too. I mean, we're both going to do well, you know, in the years ahead. And, and, you know, if we thought it needed changing, we wouldn't be here.

MKR: Okay, this was a question from one of the employees. I heard Berkshire's eliminated company-sponsored pension plans at some companies. What are the plans for the BNSF pension plans, and what factors do you take into consideration when evaluating whether to maintain a pension plan at a company you acquire?

WB: Yeah. That will be up to the management. I mean, there may be changes in benefits that the government legislates. I mean, who would have guessed 401Ks would have come along 40 years ago or something of the sort. But you'll make those determinations just like you make all other determinations.

MKR: BNSF has developed a pay structure that encourages employees to take ownership of the company by basing a portion of the compensation on corporate performance. How will this change after the merger?

WB: Well, the people who have been involved in any kind of a pay-for-performance-type arrangement, whether it's stock or anything else, will undoubtedly have a pay-for-performance type of compensation, which, you know, you'll work out, basically.

MKR: Okay, so there were just a lot of questions on your view of the national economy and philosophy around this. A couple of questions. One, it's been said recently that the rising national debt may be the next economic crisis. Do you agree, and what should be done about it?

WB: Well, I actually wrote an article about that a few months ago. I mean, it is a problem, but if, if you sat down at the start of every year going back to 1776, you could have written down a bunch of problems in the United States. We aren't perfect at avoiding them, but we're pretty darn good at solving them. I mean, you know, we've even had a civil war in this country, you know, let alone a Great Depression, world wars, and flu epidemics and all that sort of thing. So the country always has problems. The country always solves them. And I don't know whether business comes back in 3 months or 6 months, but I know this: in the next 100 years, we're probably going to have 50 bad years, I mean 15 bad years in the United States, and we're probably going to have, you know, another 15 so-so, and we'll probably have 70 good ones, something like that. I don't know the order in which they're going to come, but overall, this country works. We started out with 4 million people in 1790, and look at what we've got now. And it's because of the system.

MKR: Next question. Do you promote management collaboration among the subsidiary companies?

WB: Yeah, we, we tell them if they can find ways to do things among themselves that benefit both parties, go to it. But we don't, we don't force anything through Omaha. We've got, for example, a carpet company that worked out something with our insulation company, Johns Manville, in terms of back hauls, for example. And we've got other companies cooperated on getting special discounts by buying computers cause of mass purchasing power. But we've never ordered anything from Omaha. We don't convene people to do that or anything. The managers do get to know each other, and sometimes they figure out things to their mutual advantage.

MKR: Okay, the next question is, it's thought that Berkshire Hathaway has not previously invested in heavily unionized companies. Given that,

what are Mr. Buffett's views of the role of unions in private-sector businesses generally, and at BNSF in particular?

WB: Yeah, we probably have, I'm sure we have more than a dozen businesses that are, are anywhere from moderately unionized to very heavily
unionized. The *Buffalo News* we've probably got, I don't know, 12 or 13
unions. In See's Candies, we've got unions. We've got, we've got unions at
CTB, our farm equipment company. We've got lots and lots of unions.
And there, you know, we—it's a question of the industry, to a great extent, and, and uh, and what the management has done in the past, and
so on.

MKR: You've acquired some terrific private and family-run companies where
the owners have great passion for their business. What traits have made
those companies so successful, and how can the BNSF family of 40,000
employees apply those principles in our work and lives?

WB: Yeah, well, we, we do—we look for companies where the managers
are passionate about the business. It makes a real difference. I mean,
anybody that's enthused about something just brings something extra
to the decision-making and the work every day. So I wouldn't, I really wouldn't be here today unless I thought you were passionate about
the business. I mean, it's crazy to have some bureaucratic type going
through the motions every day running a business. It won't work in
America. And, and it's, it's an important ingredient. You do find quite
often in family businesses, and you probably find it a little less often
in, in, in the professionally managed operation, but I'm sure it exists at
BNSF.

MKR: Closing comments?

WB: Closing comments is, I'm happy to be here. This—I had to wait until I
was 79, but it's still a boyhood dream come true.

MKR: Well, Warren, I get the question a lot, of how life will change. It's been
a little frustrating, I think, for some of our employees, because at the
end of the day, truly, this is mainly about corporate structure. Instead of
shareholders, we now have Berkshire Hathaway and yourself. What our
employees continue to be focused on, of course, every day, is improving safety, getting more freight to the railroad, taking cost out, and, and
going deeper into our customer supply chain. And we look forward to
a great relationship with Berkshire Hathaway, and we're delighted that
you took this time to come and spend it on our video news, and I'm
sure it means a lot to all of our employees. Thanks very much.

WB: Thanks for inviting me.

Table 19.7.
Income statement (2006–2008)
Year ended Dec. 31
($ in millions except per share data)

	2008	2007	2006
Revenues	18,018	15,902	14,985
Operating expenses			
Fuel	4,640	3,327	2,856
Compensation and benefits	3,884	3,773	3,816
Purchased services	2,136	2,023	1,906
Depreciation and amortization	1,397	1,293	1,176
Equipment rents	901	942	930
Materials and other	1,148	959	780
Total operating expenses	14,106	12,316	11,464
Operating income	3,912	3,486	3,521
Interest expense	533	511	485
Other expense, net	11	18	40
Income before income taxes	3,368	2,957	2,996
Income tax expense	1,253	1,128	1,107
NET INCOME	2,115	1,829	1,889
Earnings per share:			
Basic earnings per share	6.15	5.19	5.23
Diluted earnings per share	6.08	5.10	5.11
Average shares:			
Basic	343.8	352.5	361.0
Dilutive effect of stock awards	4.0	6.4	8.8
Diluted	347.8	358.9	369.8

Source: Burlington Northern Santa Fe Corporation, *2008 10K Report,* 39.

Table 19.8.
Balance sheet (2007–2008)
Year ended Dec. 31
($ in millions)

Assets	2008	2007
Current assets		
Cash and cash equivalents	633	330
Accounts receivable, net	847	790
Materials and supplies	525	579
Current portion of deferred income taxes	442	290
Other current assets	218	192
Total current assets	2.665	2.181
Property, plant, and equipment, net	30.847	29.567
Other assets	2.891	1.836
TOTAL ASSETS	36.403	33.583
Liabilities and stockholders' equity		
Current liabilities		
Accounts payable and other current liabilities	3.190	2.824
Long-term debt due within one year	456	411
Total current liabilities	3.646	3.235
Long-term debt and commercial paper	9.099	7.735
Deferred income taxes	8.590	8.484
Pension and retiree health and welfare liability	1.047	444
Casualty and environmental liabilities	959	843
Employee separation costs	57	77
Other liabilities	1.874	1.621
Total liabilities	25.272	22.439
Stockholders' equity		
Common stock, $0.01 par value, 600,000 shares authorized; 541,346 and 537,330 shares issued, respectively	5	5
Additional paid-in capital	7.631	7.348
Retained earnings	12.764	11.152
Treasury stock, at cost, 202,165 shares and 189,626 shares, respectively	−8.395	−7.222
Accumulated other comprehensive loss	−874	−139
Total stockholders' equity	11.131	11.144
TOTAL LIABILITIES AND STOCKHOLDERS' EQUITY	36.403	33.583

Source: Burlington Northern Santa Fe Corporation, *2008 10K Report,* 40.

Table 19.9.
Cash-flow statement (2006–2008)
Year ended Dec. 31
($ in millions)

	2008	2007	2006
Operating activities			
Net income	2.115	1.829	1.889
Adjustments to reconcile net income to net cash provided by operating activities:			
Depreciation and amortization	1.397	1.293	1.176
Deferred income taxes	417	280	316
Employee separation costs paid	−15	−21	−27
Long-term casualty and environmental liabilities, net	150	26	−55
Other, net	81	183	−43
Changes in current assets and liabilities:			
Accounts receivable, net	191	20	−127
Change in accounts receivable sales program	−250	—	—
Material and supplies	54	−91	−92
Other current assets	−31	12	99
Accounts payable and other current liabilities	−132	−39	53
Net cash provided by operating activities	3.977	3.492	3.189
Investing activities			
Capital expenditures	−2.175	−2.248	−2.014
Construction costs for facility financing obligation	−64	−37	−14
Acquisition of equipment pending financing	−941	−745	−1.223
Proceeds from sale of assets financed	348	778	1.244
Other, net	−241	−163	−160
Net cash used for investing activities	−3.073	−2.415	−2.167
Financing activities			
Net increase/decrease in commercial paper and bank borrowings	−161	−584	283
Proceeds from issuance of long-term debt	1.150	1.300	300
Payments on long-term debt	−217	−482	−467
Dividends paid	−471	−380	−310
Proceeds from stock options exercised	91	142	116
Purchase of BNSF common stock	−1.147	−1.265	−730
Excess tax benefits from equality compensation plans	96	121	95
Proceeds from facility financing obligation	68	41	—
Other, net	−10	−15	−9
Net cash used for financing activities	−601	−1.122	−722
Increase/decrease in cash and cash equivalents	303	−45	300
Cash and cash equivalents:			
Beginning of year	330	375	75
End of year	633	330	375
Supplemental cash-flow information			
Interest paid, net of amounts capitalized	538	494	462
Income taxes paid, net of refunds	820	680	779
Noncash asset financing	258	461	109

Source: Burlington Northern Santa Fe Corporation, *2008 10K Report*, 41.

20

2011: IBM

In November 2011, Warren Buffett announced on CNBC's television show *Squawk Box* that Berkshire Hathaway had taken a $10.7 billion position in IBM—5.5 percent of the company's shares outstanding. Explaining the purchase, Buffett said that although he had been reading the annual reports of the company for the past fifty years, he had only recently realized how important its business was for IT organizations around the world. However, after reading the 2010 annual report, Buffett began buying shares.

IBM was founded by Charles Ranlett Flint in 1911 as the Computing-Tabulating-Recording Company (CTR). CTR dealt in late-nineteenth-century technologies such as commercial scales and industrial time recorders. By 1924, under the leadership of Thomas J. Watson Sr., the company was ready to expand internationally and focus on new products. To reflect these new goals, Watson renamed the company International Business Machines Corporation (IBM). Watson would become an iconic leader, best known for instituting an almost reverent fervor in IBM employees. Professionalism and customer focus were key signatures, and the new direction of the company was built around its motto: "Think."

Since these founding decades, IBM had been a research and development powerhouse. The company played a major role in developing record-keeping and calculating machinery between 1930 and 1980, serving

Figure 20.1.

both commercial enterprises (developing, for instance, the American Air-lines booking system, SABRE) as well as the government (building the record-keeping system used for Social Security, as one example). In 2013, Bloomberg noted that IBM had secured more US patents than any other company for the twentieth straight year.[1] Its inventions included the auto-mated teller machine (ATM); the floppy disk; the hard drive disk; the magnetic stripe card; the Universal Product Code (UPC); the scanning tunneling microscope; and the AI system "Watson" that famously com-peted in—and won—on the game show *Jeopardy!* in 2011. Over the course of its history, the core business of IBM had been serving the systems, cal-culations, and processing needs of their diverse international customers in customized ways.

Since the year 2000, IBM had augmented some of its more robust divisions, while shifting away from others. In 2002, it acquired PwC Con-sulting, a move that was meant to strengthen its Global Business Services (GBS) division that focused on IT systems, integration, and implemen-tation consultancy. In 2005, IBM sold its personal computer business to Lenovo. It also made numerous acquisitions in software, enterprise, and cloud services, including Micromuse, SPSS, Ascential, FileNet, ISS, Cog-nos, Kenexa, and SoftLayer Technologies. IBM's strategic focus in the last decade has been to build its software division.

To understand what an investor considering IBM would have seen in early 2011, we must turn to the company's 2010 annual report. The report starts with a personal note from Samuel Palmisano, IBM's chair-man, president, and CEO, describing the company's transformation into an international, high-margin products and services business, and how this transformation will put IBM in a strong position in the decade to come. On page five of his letter, Palmisano presents a clear roadmap to the future (the 2010 Road Map). The vision is clear: IBM will achieve clear success as tracked by IBM's earnings-per-share performance over the next five years. The three drivers for achieving this will be (1) operating leverage, (2) share repurchases, and (3) growth. For Palmisano, operating leverage means shifting to increasingly higher-margin business and improving productiv-ity in the company. As for share repurchases, Palmisano states a specific target of distributing $50 million in share buy-backs and $20 million in dividends over the next five years. Growth is much more complicated, but a few areas for targeted growth are discussed. For instance, China, India, and Brazil were identified as "growth markets," where IBM was in the pro-cess of nearly doubling its number of branch locations. Palmisano presents a goal of increasing the share of growth market revenues from 20 percent to 30 percent by 2015. Palmisano also discusses the area of business analytics and optimization, pointing to a megatrend toward ever-increasing data for businesses and to the value that IBM can deliver in helping companies utilize these data to improve decision making. A third area of growth is cloud computing, where IBM can help clients develop their own private clouds as well as utilize IBM's cloud-based infrastructure. Finally, Palmisano addresses what he calls "Smarter Planet," referring to a broad bucket of new IT-driven solutions in high-growth industries like healthcare, retail, banking, and communications.

Overall, it seems from the annual report that IBM has a CEO and chairman with a very clear vision of how to increase IBM's intrinsic value for shareholders within the next five years. As a potential investor, I would have appreciated Palmisano's directness and his specific targets in achieving value for shareholders. I would still have been skeptical, however, about how the growth would be achieved.

As far as the actual business of IBM, the company breaks itself down into five separate business segments. I have presented them in the same order as IBM presented them in its annual report.

As table 20.1 shows, by far the most significant divisions are the Global Technology Services, Global Business Services, and the Software divisions. Together they make up 79 percent of revenues and 83 percent of pretax profits. In fact, because the Software division has such a high margin, it makes up a larger proportion of overall pretax profits than any other business segment, at 44 percent. As a potential investor, I would have focused on understanding the two Global Services divisions and the Software division.

Table 20.1.
Overview of business segments

Business unit	FY 2010 revenues	% of total	Gross margin	PBT margin
Global Tech. Services	$38.2 billion	38%	34.7%	14.1%
Global Business Services	$18.2 billion	18%	28.3%	13.5%
Software	$22.5 billion	23%	86.9%	35.8%
Systems and Tech.	$18.0 billion	18%	38.5%	8.4%
Global Financing	$2.2 billion	2%	51.3%	48.0%
Other	$0.7 billion	1%	N/A	N/A
Total	**$99.8 billion**	**100%**	**21.5%**	**19.5%**

Global Technology Services (GTS): An investor with a limited knowledge of the industry would probably have understood just the basics of this business—that it provides four major infrastructure and business process services to clients: (1) Strategic Outsourcing Services, which includes outsourcing of whole IT activity and/or the execution of business processes such as HR to a cheaper location like India; (2) Integrated Technology Services, which increases enterprise efficiency or productivity; and (3) Technology Support and (4) Maintenance Services, which offer product support services and maintenance of software platforms and systems. The annual report does not provide much greater detail than this, and an investor with no other information would likely have found it very difficult to understand the core business of IBM in GTS. Only those well versed in IBM's structure and in the industry would understand that GTS is primarily a technology consulting business, focused on helping clients implement the capabilities mentioned previously. As such, its customer interface consists of sales personnel, who sell solutions and the implementation of solutions directly to chief technology officers, chief marketing officers, and other managers of major corporate customers. Competitors that offered similar services would have included Accenture, Deloitte, Infosys, and Cognizant.

Global Business Services (GBS): According to IBM's annual report, Global Business Services primarily offers customers help in two areas. The first, *Consulting and Systems Integration,* is a broad set of services that help customers develop and implement IT solutions. This includes installing third-party software, like SAP or Oracle, and also includes some of the business analytics and optimization solutions that IBM highlights as a growth area. The second, *Application Management Services,* is primarily a customized software and software support business where IBM helps customers develop and maintain software solutions for specific business purposes. Again, a potential investor with limited technology knowledge would likely have understood only the basics of this business, which could be summed up as a mix of consulting and customized software solutions implementation.

Software: For IBM, Software describes numerous software platforms that the company ownes and supports. This is primarily middleware, the class of enterprise software used by companies to integrate information from different systems software from different functions. There are five distinct platforms that IBM mentions: Websphere software, Information Management software, Tivoli software, Lotus Software, and Rational software. In addition to middleware, IBM also supports customized operating systems—tailored versions of the main software that provides the interface for running a system.

Table 20.2, which IBM provides in the annual report, shows the year-on-year growth rates for subgroups of middleware. As this shows, middleware is a growth category, with WebSphere and Tivoli being the fastest growers.

In terms of how software is sold by IBM, approximately two-thirds of revenue is annuity based, coming from recurring license fees and postcontract support. The other one-third of revenues comes from one-time or spot revenues. This includes postcontract support, product upgrades, and technical support.

As far as competition in the software area, IBM solutions competed directly and indirectly with numerous other software providers such as Oracle, Microsoft, and niche players like Software AG. Assessing the business quality of the core IBM businesses is not straightforward. In software it would have seemed clear to a potential investor that customer stickiness was high and capital intensity very low. The GTS and GBS businesses, meanwhile, are more complex. Some of the services they provided—like specialized IT implementation of data analytics—would have seemed like areas where IBM likely had a competitive advantage built over time. Other services, like business consulting or outsourced services, would have appeared to be more commoditized with numerous credible competitors.

Table 20.2.
Overview of IBM's software revenue by subcategories
($ in millions)

For the year ended Dec. 31	2010	2009*	Yr.-to-yr. change	Yr.-to-yr. change adjusted for currency
Software external revenue:	$22,485	$21,396	5.1%	4.8%
Middleware	$18,444	$17,125	7.7%	7.5%
Key branded middleware	13,876	12,524	10.8	10.7
WebSphere			20.8	20.6
Information management			8.6	8.3
Lotus			(2.3)	(2.1)
Tivoli			15.0	15.1
Rational			4.8	4.8
Other middleware	4,568	4,602	(0.7)	(1.2)
Operating systems	2,282	2,163	5.5	4.9
Other	1,759	2,108	(16.6)	(17.0)

*Reclassified to conform to 2010 presentation.
Source: IBM, 2010 Annual Report, 28.

A potential investor at the time may have concluded that IBM was a complex mix of software solutions and people services, where approximately 40 percent (matched with the software profits) were highly recurring, high-quality revenues and 40 percent (associated with consultancy and business services) were based on a range of both low- and higher-quality revenues facing different sets of competitive offerings. For this second component of revenues, which are people services, asset light, but execution heavy, the investor would likely realize the high dependence on good execution.

Before moving on to the financial analysis of IBM, let me just touch upon the last two business divisions of IBM that make up approximately 20 percent of revenues. According to IBM's annual report, the business *Systems and Technology* provides customers with business solutions based on advanced computing power and storage capabilities. In layperson terms, this means mostly hardware solutions like customized servers and add-on products—in particular, IBM's designated System z, Power Systems, and System x. The last business division, *Global Financing*, is responsible for helping to finance some of the customer purchases made for IBM's products.

Turning to the financial statements, one notes that on pages 10 and 11 of the annual report IBM provides a 10-year snapshot of its business for the metrics of pretax profits, EPS, free cash flow, and margins. Pretax profits increased from roughly $11 billion to $21 billion in ten years. Referencing the business divisional pretax profits, one can see that most of this growth came from the GTS/GBS and the Software businesses (see figure 20.2).

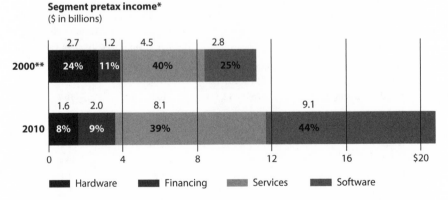

Segment pretax income*
($ in billions)

*Sum of external segment pretax income not equal to IBM pretax income.
**Excludes Enterprise Investments and not restated for stock-based compensation.

Figure 20.2.
IBM pretax development (2000–2010). (*Source*: IBM, *2010 Annual Report*, 10.)

Table 20.3.
Overview of total capital employed

Category	Amount in $	As a % of revenues
PPE	$14.1 billion	14%
Intangibles	$3.4 billion	3%
Inventories	$2.5 billion	3%
Accounts receivable	$10.8 billion	11%
Financing receivables	$26.8 billion	27%
Accounts payable	−$7.8 billion	−8%
Deferred income	−$11.6 billion	−12%
Total capital employed (TCE)	**$38.2 billion**	**38%**

The increase in pretax profits is matched by the other metrics, with EPS and free cash flow both more than doubling during that period. For all profitability measures, the annual rate over the previous ten years was greater than six percent per annum. Moreover, there is an increase in the gross margin from 37 percent to 46 percent and an increase in PBT margin from 12 percent to 20 percent. All these financials look Buffettesque; except for one down year in 2003, IBM had increased all key metrics year after year. The evidence points to an obviously successful transformation of the IBM business.

One area that seems underemphasized in the annual report is revenues. In fact, in the entire 10-year discussion, there does not seem to be any mention of revenues in the year 2000. The investor would be forced to turn to previous annual reports to find out that revenues in 2000 were $85 billion compared to revenues in 2010 of $100 billion. This comes out to an annual compounded rate of growth of approximately 1.6 percent—definitely less impressive than the development of other metrics.

Analyzing the business economics of IBM further, IBM's capital requirements and return economics are shown in table 20.3.

As this table shows, IBM's core business is not capital intensive. There is some PPE involved, but for the most part capital requirements relate to working capital, including financing receivables.

All in all, the TCE of IBM equals 38 percent of revenues, and with an EBIT of $19.8 billion, the calculated pretax ROTCE is 52 percent. Assuming a normalized 30 percent tax rate, the comparable after-tax ROTCE is 36 percent. This is a very good return on capital and this is clearly the basis for IBM's ability to return capital back to shareholders in the form of dividends and share repurchases. In terms of the financials, a potential investor would have found IBM to be a highly profitable, cash-generating business, whose only fault was a very modest growth in revenues. From the initial analysis, there would have been reason to believe that this was partly justified by the structural transformation of the business. Of course, one also would have preferred the top line to be growing strongly, as in the case of American Express or even BNSF.

Besides the fundamental business activity and the financials, a potential investor also would have considered the management team in place at IBM. Sam Palmisano served as the chairman, president, and CEO, so he was clearly the man in charge. Palmisano's professional background was within IBM; he joined Big Blue in 1973 as a salesman and worked his way up to the position of COO, which he held immediately before he was appointed CEO in March of 2002. Palmisano succeeded the well-known and much-admired Lou Gerstner. Gerstner had been credited with saving IBM from bankruptcy in the 1990s, as competitors eroded its PC business. Palmisano took over the business after the collapse of the tech bubble and was known as the executive who led new initiatives to transform IBM in the post-Gerstner period. Palmisano's key contributions up to this time included taking IBM into more diversified consulting capabilities (including the purchase of PwC's consulting practice in 2002) as well as championing growth areas such as data analytics and cloud computing. He also made the controversial decision to sell IBM's PC group to Lenovo in 2005. As the financials show, he was focused on profitability of the business. Based on these facts, the financial performance of IBM during his tenure, and his communication of a very specific vision and goal for IBM, a potential investor would likely have found him to be both a proven and capable executive. He delivered the goods.

Before turning to the valuation of IBM and what a potential investor faced with the prospect of investing in IBM would have concluded, I want to address two other aspects of IBM that I find relevant from the analysis. First, it was clear that IBM was an acquisition machine. During the period between 2000 and 2010, as noted in the annual report, IBM purchased 116 companies. The net cost of acquisitions during this period was $27 billion, or roughly one fifth of the cash flow generated by IBM. In pursuing these acquisitions, Palmisano focused on acquiring services capabilities or software platforms that would be plugged-into IBM's distribution network. This was one major source of growth for IBM and seems to have generated significant value for the business. As a potential investor in IBM, I would have viewed its M&A track record positively, recognizing IBM as a platform that can quickly integrate and ramp up distribution for bolt-on acquisitions.

Second, IBM had a large pension liability. On the balance sheet, the net deficit reported in 2010 was $13 billion. The notes section of the annual report shows the full extent of these obligations. IBM had both U.S. and international defined benefits plans, and the gross amount of total estimated liabilities was $99 billion. Against this amount, IBM also had fair value of plan assets of $86 billion. This is a significant amount and also a risk potential. With most other companies that have pension deficits, there is a cash amount required of the company to correct the shortcoming over time. As one can see in the cash-flow statement, in the previous three years 2010 included, IBM paid approximately $2 billion a year in cash for the purpose of correcting this deficit. This is real money that would not be available for share buybacks or dividends or investing into the company. It also represents approximately 15 percent of the cash flow generated after tax for IBM in a year. Besides the immediate negative impact, the large gross value of the estimated liability means there is a significant risk arising from actuarial changes. Specifically, the $99 billion gross liability is only an estimated amount depending on assumptions made about the longevity of participants, the discount rate, the inflation of salaries, and so on. Hence, minor changes in assumptions could have major absolute dollar implications for how much IBM would owe in the future. For example, it seems that between 2009 and 2010, IBM changed its discount rate assumption from 5.6 percent to 5.0 percent in evaluating the gross liability of U.S. defined pension plans. This alone had the actuarial effect of increasing IBM's liability by $1.5 billion. IBM's assumptions, at cursory glance, seem to be on the less-conservative side; as a potential investor, this would be one long-term risk I would keep in mind. Aside from this risk, IBM seemed like a well-performing, good-quality business with strong economics.

I now turn to the valuation of the investment. As mentioned earlier, Buffett bought his stake in IBM in the first half of 2011. According to the Berkshire letter to shareholders of that year, the average price Buffett paid was $169.87 per share.[2] In total this amounted to 5.5 percent of outstanding IBM shares, and it should be noted that given the very large size of IBM, Buffett more or less purchased the stock like anyone else would, as common shares and as a public investor. According to his interview on CNBC's *Squawk Box*, Buffett had not even known Samuel Palmisano very well on a personal level. So this is perhaps his one investment where Buffett was most like an ordinary investor looking at a company.

The conventional valuation multiples for this purchase would have been as follows:

Table 20.4.
Calculation of enterprise value

Share price	$169.87
Number of shares outstanding*	1228 million
Market capitalization	**$208.6 billion**
Net financial debt and pensions deficit**	$29.8 billion
Enterprise value	**$238.4 billion**

*Based on shares outstanding on December 31, 2010 as reported on page 16 of the *2010 Annual Report* for IBM.
**Included were cash and marketable securities of $11.7 billion, ST and LT debt of $28.6 billion, and net pension deficit of $ 12.9 billion.

Table 20.5.

	2010 actual	2009 actual
EPS (diluted)	$11.52	$10.01
PER	14.7×	17.0×
EBIT	$20.1 billion	$18.5 billion
EV/EBIT	11.9×	12.9×
FCF yield on mkt. cap*	7.8%	7.2%

*I have used IBM's reported FCF of $16.3 billion, which is roughly in line with my own calculation of FCF (based on cash earnings after tax minus estimated maintenance CAPEX). Reported FCF in 2009 was $15.1 billion.

Given that IBM looked like a good-quality business with a strong track record of financial performance and proven management, the valuation looks still reasonable, although not cheap. At earnings multiples of 11.9× EV/EBIT and 14.7× PER, the share price would not have fully valued the growth in earnings if IBM were to continue on the trajectory of the previous 10 years. Note also the free cash yield of IBM. A combination of factors—including having less required maintenance CAPEX than depreciation and amortization (partly due to having less hardware than before) as well as lower than usual tax rates (partly due to overseas business and previous tax losses)—meant that IBM had an unusually high cash conversion from earnings. In fact, from my analysis, IBM had a cash earnings conversion ratio from EBIT over 80 percent for every year since 2003. The cash earnings yield of almost eight percent is quite healthy. This is especially attractive considering that management had already promised to put a significant amount of this cash flow into share buybacks and dividends. Overall, as a potential investor in IBM, I would have found this case to be quite attractive. I would have especially liked the solid financial performance, the proven management team, and the fair valuation, although I would have been concerned about not fully grasping the complexities of the business, and also about the defined benefit pension schemes.

Buffett's View

Buffett has spoken about his investment in IBM in several interviews, including the famous interview on CNBC's *Squawk Box* in November 2011 where he first announced Berkshire's purchase. IBM was also mentioned in his annual report of that year. In the Berkshire annual report, Buffett refers to IBM as a wonderful business and one of his largest four investments along with Coca-Cola, American Express, and Wells Fargo. Specifically, Buffett comments that CEOs Lou Gerstner and Sam Palmisano have done a superb job in transforming IBM, and says that their operational and financial management accomplishments had been truly extraordinary and brilliant, respectively. Buffett goes further to detail what astute capital allocation IBM had performed over the years with respect to share buybacks. He remarks that he would not mind if the share price languished, because IBM would then be able to accumulate more shares for the same price and increase the ownership of every existing shareholder by more.

On *Squawk Box*, Buffett went on to say that before he started purchasing shares, he had paid particular attention to the precise targets Samuel Palmisano had given shareholders about where IBM would be financially in the future. Impressively, Palmisano achieved what he set out to do. Buffett mentioned speaking to quite a few IT organizations within Berkshire's subsidiaries about IBM, and the takeaway from all these discussions was the strength of the role that IBM played and the "stickiness" of those relationships.

[IBM is] a company that helps IT departments do their job better . . . it is a big deal for a big company to change auditors, change law firms. The IT departments . . . very much get working hand in glove with suppliers . . . there is a lot of continuity to it.

—Warren Buffett, interview on *Squawk Box*,
CNBC, November 14, 2011.

Buffett was clearly enthusiastic about IBM and said that the company had a reverence for shareholders that he found unique among large corporations. At the end of the interview, when asked why he was buying IBM even though it was a technology company and its share price was at an all-time high, Buffett replied that he considers everything, including technology companies, but he just had not found a company he thought he could understand before. When asked about how he felt about purchasing IBM at an all-time high share price, Buffett said that he absolutely did not care about the share price. He had bought control of GEICO at an all-time high share price, and BNSF as well.

Considering all this, IBM seems to be a unique case where a potential investor would have seen a picture similar to the one Buffett saw. The superb financials, management,[3] cash flows, as well as the astute capital allocation in the form of dividends and share-buy backs, would all have been recognizable to a potential investor. Buffett did benefit a bit extra from the discussions he had with Berkshire subsidiaries' IT departments, which further convinced him of his positive assessment of the IBM business, but overall, his decision was based on the criteria discussed earlier, and he was willing to pay a fair valuation to invest in IBM.

Table 20.6.
Income statement (2010)
Year ended Dec. 31
($ in millions except per share data)

	2010	2009	2008
Revenues:			
Services	56.868	55.128	58.892
Sales	40.736	38.300	42.156
Financing	2.267	2.331	2.582
Total revenue	99.870	95.758	103.630
Cost:			
Services	38.383	37.146	40.937
Sales	14.374	13.606	15.776
Financing	1.100	1.220	1.256
Total cost	53.857	51.973	57.969
Gross profit			
Expense and other income:			
Selling, general, and administrative	21.837	20.952	23.386
Research, development, and engineering	6.026	5.820	6.337
Intellectual property and custom development income	−1.154	−1.177	−1.153
Other expense/income	−787	−251	−298
Interest expense	368	402	673
Total expense and other income	26.291	25.647	28.945
Income before income taxes	19.723	18.138	16.715
Provision for income taxes	4.890	4.713	4.381
NET INCOME	14.833	13.425	12.334
Earnings per share of common stock:			
Assuming dilution	11.52	10.01	8.89
Basic	11.69	10.12	9.02
Weighted-average number of common shares outstanding			
Assuming dilution	1,287,355,388	1,341,352,754	1,387,797,198
Basic	1,268,789,202	1,327,157,410	1,369,367,069

Source: IBM, *2010 Annual Report*, 62.

Table 20.7.
Balance sheet (2010)
Years ended Dec. 31
($ in millions)

Assets	2010	2009
Current assets		
Cash and cash equivalents	10.661	12.183
Marketable securities	990	1.791
Notes and accounts receivable—trade (net of allowances of $324 and $217)	10.834	10.736
Short-term financing receivables (net of allowances of $342 and $438)	16.257	14.914
Other accounts receivable (net of allowances of $10 and $15)	1.134	1.143
Inventories	2.450	2.494
Deferred taxes	1.564	1.730
Prepaid expenses and other current assets	4.226	3.946
Total current assets	48.116	48.935
Plant, rental machines, and other property	40.289	39.596
Less: accumulated depreciation	26.193	25.431
Plant, rental machines, and other property, net	14.096	14.165
Long-term financing receivables (net of allowances of $58 and $97)	10.548	10.644
Prepaid pension assets	3.068	3.001
Deferred taxes	3.220	4.195
Goodwill	25.136	20.190
Intangible assets, net	3.488	2.513
Investments and sundry assets	5.778	5.379
TOTAL ASSETS	113.452	109.022
Liabilities and equity		
Current liabilities		
Taxes	4.216	3.826
Short-term debt	6.778	4.168
Accounts payable	7.804	7.436
Compensation and benefits	5.028	4.505
Deferred income	11.580	10.845
Other accrued expenses and liabilities	5.156	5.223
Total current liabilities	40.562	36.002
Long-term debt	21.846	21.932
Retirement and nonpension postretirement benefit obligations	15.978	15.953
Deferred income	3.666	3.562
Other liabilities	8.226	8.819
Total liabilities	90.279	86.267
Stockholders' equity:		
Common stock, par value $20 per share and additional paid-in capital*	45.418	41.810
Retained earnings	92.532	80.900
Treasury stock, at cost (shares: 2010—933,806,510; 2009—821,679,245)	−96.161	−81.243
Accumulated other comprehensive income/loss	−18.743	−18.830
Total stockholders' equity	23.046	22.637
Noncontrolling interests	126	118
Total equity	23.172	22.755
TOTAL LIABILITIES AND STOCKHOLDERS' EQUITY	113.452	109.022

Source: IBM, *2010 Annual Report*, 63.
*Shares authorized: 4,687,500,000; shares issued: 2010—2,161,800,054; 2009—2,127,016,668.

Table 20.8.
Cash-flow statement (2008–2010)
Year ended Dec. 31
($ in millions)

	2010	2009	2008
Cash flow from operating activities			
Net income	14.833	13.425	12.334
Adjustments to reconcile net income to net cash provided by operating activities:			
Depreciation	3.657	3.773	4.140
Amortization of intangibles	1.174	1.221	1.310
Stock-based compensation	629	558	659
Deferred taxes	1.294	1.773	1.900
Net gain/loss on asset sales and other	−801	−395	−338
Change in operating assets and liabilities, net of acquisitions/divestitures:			
Receivables (including financing receivables)	−489	2.131	274
Retirement related	−1.963	−2.465	−1.773
Inventories	92	263	−102
Other assets/other liabilities	949	319	1.268
Accounts payable	174	170	−860
Net cash provided by operating activities	19.549	20.773	18.812
Cash flow from investing activities			
Payments for plant, rental machines, and other property	−4.185	−3.447	−4.171
Proceeds from disposition of plant, rental machines, and other property	770	330	350
Investment in software	−569	−630	−716
Purchases of marketable securities and other investments	−6.129	−5.604	−4.590
Proceeds from disposition of marketable securities and other investments	7.877	3.599	6.100
Nonoperating finance receivables, net	−405	−184	−16
Divestiture of businesses, net of cash transferred	55	400	71
Divestiture of businesses, net of cash acquired	−5.922	−1.194	−6.313
Net cash used in investing activities	−8.507	−6.729	−9.285
Cash flow from financing activities			
Proceeds from new debt	8.055	6.683	13.829
Payments to settle debt	−6.522	−13.495	−10.248
Short-term repayments/borrowings less than 90 days, net	817	−651	−6.025
Common stock repurchases	−15.375	−7.429	−10.578
Common stock transactions, other	3.774	3.052	3.774
Cash dividends paid	−3.177	−2.860	−2.585
Net cash used in financing activities	−12.429	−14.700	−11.834
Effect of exchange rate changes on cash and cash equivalents	−135	98	58
Net change in cash and cash equivalents	−1.522	−558	−2.250
Cash and cash equivalents January 1	12.183	12.741	14.991
Cash and cash equivalents December 31	10.661	12.183	12.741
Supplemental data			
Income taxes paid—net of refunds	3.238	1.567	2.111
Interest paid on debt	951	1.240	1.460
Capital lease obligations	30	15	41

Source: IBM, *2010 Annual Report*, 64.

Part IV
Lessons Learned

21

Evolution of Buffett's Investment Strategy

Warren Buffett's long investment career, as exemplified by the notable investments I have reviewed, is not defined by only one type of investment or investing strategy; his approach has clearly evolved between 1957 when he started his first investment partnership and today. Retracing the journey through the characteristics of his various investments can help one understand this evolution.

Most striking about the companies Buffett invested in early on—such as the Sanborn Maps Company, Dempster Mill, or Berkshire Hathaway—is that they traded at incredibly cheap prices compared to the value of the assets they held. This did not always mean paying a low earnings multiple (say, about 5× PER). Indeed, both Sanborn Maps and Dempster Mill had little earnings at the time of Buffett's investment and thus would have had high earnings multiples. Rather than just evaluating PER, Buffett seemed to be looking for companies that traded below the clearly realizable value of the assets they had. Sanborn Maps, for instance, had an investment portfolio worth more than the price he paid for the whole company; in Dempster Mill there was inventory that he knew was sellable; and in the case of Berkshire Hathaway, there was a combination of cash and realizable working capital.

Aside from just cheap investments, from very early in his career Buffett was focused on the fundamental businesses he invested in. He was not just interested in net-nets, but in companies that had positive earnings and (when possible) positive developments in underlying business prospects. Sanborn Maps, for example, was a business that had been in a structural decline for years due to technological change—but it was still a business making a positive profit margin and had in fact stabilized in the years preceding the investment. This means that Buffett did not have to worry about the business burning all its cash on unprofitable operations. Buffett also identified situations where there were operational improvements in the works—or where he could be a catalyst for such positive developments.

Another important aspect to Buffett's investment strategy is that even during this early period of the partnership years, he paid keen attention to a business's management team. Although his criteria for evaluating such teams evolved with time, in his earliest investments (such as Dempster Mill and Berkshire Hathaway) he already showed great interest in selecting great operating managers. And it should be said that Buffett, even in his early work, was not just a one-trick pony focused only on finding cheap companies. As the Texas National Petroleum investment shows, Buffett also invested in merger arbitrage situations (including in fixed income products), and his detailed analysis and understanding of the risks demonstrated his familiarity with this type of investment. He also dabbled in control investments where he took an active part in bringing change; at both Dempster Mill and Berkshire Hathaway, for example, he played a key role in influencing the operations of the business after he took over.

To summarize Buffett's early investment strategy: He focused foremost on finding companies that were cheap in comparison to the value of realizable assets they had, but he was still familiar with other kinds of investments and pursued those when they seemed especially attractive. The real foundation for his later thinking about investments seemed to be his scrutiny of each investment case—many of them smaller businesses with tangible assets—from the lens of a business owner. He assessed both the key people and assets involved in a business, and evaluated their likely effect on the future development of the business. From the beginning, his strategy was clearly more involved than the simple Graham style calculation of net-nets.

By the middle years of his career (from 1968 to about 1990), Buffett seemed to place increasing importance on the quality of the business. He shifted from focusing on the value of a business's assets toward evaluating its sustainable earnings power. Looking at the investments that Buffett made in this period—whether it was a private investment like See's Candies, a turnaround situation like GEICO, or a branded franchise like

Coca-Cola—the key rationale was always attractive long-term earnings. Buffett still purchased great companies at great valuations when possible, but seemed to become much more comfortable paying higher earnings multiples—15× PER in several instances—which is more than most value investors would consider.

Buffett's definition of quality included both quantitative and qualitative aspects. Quantitatively, he gravitated increasingly to those businesses with consistent growth and a high return on tangible capital employed (ROTCE). Notably, Buffett was not fixated on extremely high growth or particularly attractive valuation; rather, mid-single digit growth that was extremely consistent and driven by an understood structural cause seemed to be the key criteria. This was certainly the case with the several branded goods investments. When Buffett invested in Coca-Cola in 1987, increased global consumption had helped the company grow revenues and operating income in nine out of the previous ten years. Similarly, when he published See's Candies financials after his purchase of the business in 1976, he showed that increasing like-for-like revenues at stores had led to five straight years of revenue growth and four out of five years of income growth. Even when Buffett bought companies for cheaper prices compared to their earnings, this consistent growth was often still present. For example, the *Washington Post* had grown revenues ten out of ten years and operating income eight out of ten years in the period before Buffett's purchase. In almost all instances over this middle period of his career, Buffett invested in companies that could consistently deliver an ROTCE of above 20 percent after tax. Investing in companies that had consistent growth and high ROTCE meant that Buffett was indeed investing in compounders—ones with a long track record of consistent growth to depend on.

Just as his quantitative evaluation of businesses evolved, Buffett came to place even greater trust in his ability to understand the qualitative aspects of business operations. With his investment in American Express and later in GEICO, he risked a large portion of his portfolio based on key qualitative insights that others, and the market at large, were not able to see. In the case of American Express, he understood that the Salad Oil Scandal would not have a long-term effect on the company's ability to generate profits, and he realized that other parts of the business (such the new credit card division) would position it to grow significantly in the future. When it came to GEICO, he recognized that the business had inherent competitive advantages in insurance and that a turnaround was likely.

The *Buffalo Evening News* was another investment driven by Buffett's qualitative insights. Buffett purchased that business based not primarily on its historical earnings (which would have made the valuation seem very excessive), but on his deep knowledge of what the business could fundamentally become—one with a much higher margin and higher return, with very sticky revenues and pricing power. He understood this in part because of his experience in media, mentoring Katherine Graham at the *Washington Post* and Tom Murphy at Capital Cities. This investment would in a few short years validate Buffett's trust in his own qualitative insights, as profits increased more than tenfold a few years after his purchase.

Finally, in these middle years, Buffett did not just shift his focus to higher-quality businesses, but also built increasing expertise in several business areas that he would come to revisit time after time—notably, insurance, media, and retail brands. While he did invest in companies in other industries, Buffett built an extremely strong understanding of business frameworks in these particular areas. He developed, for example, a keen sense of how to evaluate the underwriting of insurers by looking at loss, expense, and combined ratios, and assessing the kinds of risks management teams were taking. On the investment side, Buffett had clear perspectives about how to determine an insurer's competency managing float.

Buffett's expertise within these industries was not limited to the conceptual; he also built a network of resourceful people, including many CEOs. Within media, for instance, his close relationships with associates like Katharine Graham and Stan Lipsey were clearly instrumental in helping Buffett find and evaluate investment opportunities. His trust in management continued to play a central role in his investment decisions, but during these middle years he started to focus not only on their trustworthiness and operational ability, but also on their competence in allocating capital wisely. In certain instances like with Katharine Graham at the *Washington Post*, Buffett himself provided guidance on how to be conservative with making acquisitions and capital expenditures.

In the late years of Buffett's career, since 1990, his challenge has been to invest ever-growing amounts of capital for Berkshire Hathaway. An obvious resulting change in his investment strategy has been the much greater emphasis on large companies. But in terms of his investment style, Buffett still seemed to maintain the qualitative focus that he honed during the middle years. Whether it was correctly assessing the mortgage crisis faced by Wells Fargo or his own admitted failure to understand the competitive dynamics faced by US Air, Buffett's primary concern is his ability to understand fundamental insights better than other investors. In the service of this aim, he has gone back to the same industries—and at times, even the same companies—that he became expert in decades earlier.

Take, for example, General Re. By the time of Buffett's investment, Berkshire already had a significant insurance operation of its own and was owner of insurance companies like GEICO, and Buffett knew the General Re owners. This experience gave him an understanding of the business that surpassed most other analysts. This knowledge was not lost on General Re's management. As the story goes, when Buffett first met with them to discuss his purchase of the company, he said: "I'm strictly hands-off. You guys run your own business. I won't interfere." But when he subsequently started speaking about GEICO and quoting numbers, the team was amazed, and the chief underwriter Tad Montross exclaimed, in so many words: "Holy cow! This is hands off?"[1] Buffett stuck to his circle of competence, but his competence in those areas was always impressive and often beyond what he admitted to.

Even though Buffett followed the same overall investment philosophy and continued to add to his vast expertise in certain industries, working with huge amounts of capital forced him to evolve aspects of his strategy. Foremost, Buffett started to seek investments in companies that were not only very large and often more mature, but also where large amounts of capital could be intelligently deployed. Some of Buffett's most recent investments, like MidAmerican Energy and Burlington Northern Santa Fe, exemplify this new approach.

MidAmerican Energy, as discussed earlier in the book, was primarily involved in building and efficiently operating several dozen power plants in the United States and around the world. The infrastructure required billions of dollars to build and maintain. When Buffett invested in the business in 1998, MidAmerican Energy had property, plant, and equipment of $4.2 billion on its books, which represented 166 percent of its revenues of that year. Because of the heavy capital requirements of the business, its after-tax returns, while relatively stable, were modest—usually in the high-single or low-double digits. The clear value for Buffett was that he could deploy large amounts of capital organically and at reasonable rates of return. This value was further enhanced through the unique structure Buffett used in investing in the company, which involved several different share classes and made some of the return more or less guaranteed.

Similarly, in the case of the railroad business Burlington Northern Santa Fe, the requirements for capital were immense. Along with laying and maintaining tracks, the company was faced with continual upkeep on locomotives, freight cars, and support facilities like yards, terminals, and dispatching centers. While the marginal return on capital of railroads was higher than the return based on the total capital employed, this was still a business that required billions of dollars of investments over a few years. As with MidAmerican Energy, for BNSF Buffett paid a price to earnings multiple above 15 times—hardly the dirt cheap price of some of his early investments. Instead, the key investment case for these two businesses—both of which Berkshire would soon own 100 percent—was that they required a large amount of invested capital and produced reasonable returns.

Further evidence of Buffett's focus on deploying large amounts of capital is the structuring of investments as preferred or convertible shares with a fixed-income characteristic. This was the case with the US Air investment (covered in this book) as well as with Goldman Sachs, General Electric, Bank of America, and Burger King (not covered in this book). Buffett, during these late years, seems willing to accept slightly lower returns for being able to deploy large amounts of capital.

All in all, what I find most astounding is that Buffett's investments were not limited to only cheap stocks or businesses with a high return on capital, nor were they limited specific aspects (like growth) or deep value. Buffett's career evolved steadily, driven partly by the opportunities that were present in the market, partly by Buffett's own development, and partly by the resources and limitations of the assets he managed. Some investment criteria, such as a trustworthy and capable management team, remained constant throughout his career. Other aspects, such as consistent growth and the ability of a company to compound or the necessity of a company for large amounts of capital, developed over time. This evolution allowed Buffett to maneuver from successfully managing a private investment partnership to successfully managing one of the largest investment vehicles in the world.

22

What We Can Learn from Buffett

Over the years, Warren Buffett has discussed almost every topic related to investing, either through one of his letters to shareholders or in an interview or article. Drawing from these discussions, one could assemble a laundry list of investment advice that includes anything from how to look at risk versus reward to how to think about portfolio concentration. But since this book focuses on what an investment analyst working at the time would have seen when considering the companies Buffett invested in, I will keep my learning points to those that I think are most critical to becoming a better investor. These lessons learned represent my own best interpretation of the major takeaways from analyzing Buffett's twenty key investments (as covered in this book) and include a combination of ideas I found especially insightful as well as those that are fundamental enough to deserve restating—even if they are not new to a well-studied value investor. As such, this list is by nature at least partially subjective. I encourage the reader to draw additional lessons based on his or her own view of the evidence presented.

A. Quality of Information

Most value investors who have followed Buffett know that he believed in conducting fundamental research and investing in a concentrated fashion once this research was done. Investing, according to Buffett, should be like having a punch card with only twenty holes, each representing one investment that an investor could make over his whole lifetime. Generally less understood, however, is what good research meant to Buffett and why it made sense for him to be concentrated rather than diversified in his investments.

One fact that stood out to me when analyzing Buffett's investments was the quality of information he had on the companies in which he invested. Take Burlington Northern Santa Fe, for example. When Buffett looked to invest in the company, the level of information that he had (and, I would argue, that any dedicated analyst would have been able to obtain) was extremely high. In its publically available annual reports, BNSF included not only detailed financial information, but also the most relevant operating metrics of its rail business. This included, among other things, revenue ton-miles traveled, freight revenue per thousand tons, and customer satisfaction scores. These metrics were reported consistently over several years, so potential investors have the relevant objective data they need to really understand how the business is performing year to year. Even more important, the annual report—written by long-time CEO and Chairman Matthew Rose—clearly explains each major area of the business and the key drivers in each. He details that the consumer products area, for instance, consists of 90 percent domestic and international goods transport (whose volumes depended on international trade traffic) and 10 percent automotive products distribution (whose volumes depended on the success of the regional car industry). He goes on to detail the capital requirements of the business over time and discusses why, for those product categories, rail is a more efficient method of transportation than the alternatives (most notably, trucking). Enough verifiable and objective data are thus available to support a qualitative insight necessary for a sound investment. In this case, Buffett's insight was that future capital intensity would decrease with higher network density in such a rail business, meaning that returns on marginal capital employed would continue to improve, and that with this ever-increasing efficiency, the rails share of the overall product transport mix would likely continue to increase for many more decades.

Over and over, across very different cases, one constant in Buffett's investing was an abundance of relevant objective data for the companies in question. For American Express, Buffett had information to support his qualitative insights into the long-term potential of credit cards and travelers cheques as well as the localized and short-term damage of the Salad Oil Scandal. Similarly, for Coca-Cola, objective data were available to confirm that international expansion and increasing consumption (in 8-oz. servings per year) across different countries would drive growth. So while it is certainly true that Buffett was diligent in learning about all aspects of a business, Buffett focused especially on investment cases that could be bolstered by concrete objective data points.

This information did not always come from annual reports, but industry data as well. The Association of American Railroads published detailed operational data (such as operating ratios and downtimes) on a monthly basis for every major railroad in the United States. This gave investors a measure of not only how one railroad performed month to month and year to year, but also how it compared to others. Similarly, in the case of *Buffalo Evening News*, circulation figures for Buffalo area newspapers and advertising data at the industry level were available. Buffett gravitated toward industries where the level of objective data available was high—further supporting the lesson that access to high-quality information is crucial for successful investing. Without high-quality information to support one's qualitative insights, the best path is probably just not to invest.

A likely result of this is Buffett's strategy of revisiting certain industries again and again. I would argue that Buffett increasingly focused his investments in a select few industries because this helped him hone and understand what high-quality information meant and how to deploy this knowledge repeatedly. For example, knowing the detailed subscription numbers, churn rates, and operating margins of the *Washington Post* undoubtedly helped in evaluating the investment case for the *Buffalo News*. On the whole, it also seems that the industries Buffett revisits—media, insurance, and branded products—were ones with ample objective industry information. By having great objective information, Buffett could confidently make the big bets that defined his concentrated approach to investing.

B. Consistency of Earnings Growth

Most investors who have followed Buffett associate him with investments in "high-quality" businesses, where high-quality denotes a company with an enduring brand name (like Coca-Cola or American Express) or one that's a "compounder" with high returns of capital. While both of these criteria were part of Buffett's consideration, what I want to highlight, and what I believe is even more important, is the consistency of performance, specifically of revenue and earnings.

Let me explain. Most value investors look for businesses with "moats"—durable competitive advantages. For many, this means time spent actively searching for network effects, switching costs, scale benefits, and other such qualitative signs of advantages. On the quantitative side is detailed analysis of current earnings and returns. The preferred metric, which is also roughly what Buffett looked at, is cash earnings after considering maintenance (CAPEX for maintenance). Another frequent quantitative focus for value investors is return on tangible capital employed as defined by either the aforementioned earnings divided by total capital employed or some form of marginal capital employed. While all of these factors are relevant and worthy of scrutiny, the lesson gleaned from analyzing Buffett's investments is that all of them are secondary to being able to make a dependable prediction of the future prospects of a company.

The majority of the investments covered in this book were in companies that had extremely consistent revenue and earnings growth in the years preceding Buffett's investment. Many of these companies had grown revenues or earnings nine out of the previous ten years—remarkable given that few companies perform at this level. Buffett clearly valued consistent historical financials and good data, and used this to understand the qualitative reasons for a business's consistent growth (in revenue or earnings) and the rationale that such performance would continue. His insight about American Express, for example, was that more international travel would mean a greater need for American Express's travelers cheques. For Burlington Northern Santa Fe, his insight was that cargo transport by rail would continue to take market share from trucking, and that this would continue because of the inherently more fuel-efficient nature of rail transport. But why is looking for consistently good performance even more important than looking for competitive advantages or compounders or current earnings? I will address competitive advantages first.

In my experience, explicitly looking for competitive advantages is quite imprecise. Sometimes one can articulate and understand an actual competitive advantage, but one must have consistent historical financials or data of some sort to confirm this. Otherwise, explicitly looking for competitive advantages can lead to finding moats that simply do not exist in a meaningful way. Take, for example, the once-common argument that BlackBerry had a moat with its subscription model and its private servers. While some of that may have been true, financially this simply did not matter as the business's revenue shrunk by over 80 percent between 2011 and 2014, and earnings became negative.[1] Looking for evidence in the form of numbers and objective data seems to be a more dependable way of determining an actual structural advantage—rather than just theorizing one.

When it comes to compounders and current earnings (which many investors will devote disproportionate time to calculate precisely to the nth degree), the argument is even more straightforward. Determining current earnings is important; it gives an investor a sense of what the valuation of the business is. And understanding the return on capital of a business is important as well; without a return on capital that is significantly higher than the cost of capital, a business cannot compound. However, the true value of a business is the aggregate of its future earnings. It does not matter so much if an investor gets current earnings exactly right at $80 or $82 or $79—it matters much more if the future earnings in five years are around $700 or $15 or $3000. Similarly, while having a high return on capital is one requirement for compounding, if the future prospects of a company are unclear, then having a high return on capital is clearly insufficient. A business that has a wonderful 50 percent return on capital employed but that grows its revenues or earnings zero percent has exactly zero benefit from its high return on capital compared to a company with lesser returns, since it will not be able to reinvest its earnings into growing the business.

Given this, I now believe that rather than spending 80 percent of one's research time determining with extreme accuracy what current earnings in the last year were or a establishing a precise return on capital for a business, one should spend significantly more time looking for businesses with great consistency in earnings growth and finding quality data that support a clear rationale why this growth is occurring. One should not fall victim to the phenomenon of being precise but wrong.

C. Letting Opportunities Drive Your Investment Style

In today's world of investing, many investors define their investment strategy by one approach, such as "value," or "growth," or "event driven." Buffett transcended such types; he did not invest only in cheap net-nets or only quality businesses or only preferred shares. Instead, he matched his investment strategy to market conditions and his personal investment setup.

One can take a closer look at how Buffett did this. In his 1961 year-end partnership letter, Buffett details three types of investments that are at the core of his partnership's investment strategy. The first category was "generals": securities he considered significantly undervalued compared to their intrinsic value. This included most of what one would consider typical value investments—long only investments in companies that are cheap compared to asset values or earnings. There is not a definite timeline for when this undervaluation would be corrected, says Buffett, but over time he expected that on the whole these investments would appreciate. As a result, an investor gets a lot of value for the price paid. His experience was that this category of stocks was correlated with the markets, and hence would decline when the market declined and gain when the market gained. However, given their undervaluation, he expected them to have a significant *margin of safety*; when markets declined, these would decline relatively less than the market.

The second category of investments discussed was "workouts." These were companies where the financial returns depended on corporate actions—mergers, liquidations, reorganizations, spin-offs, and so forth. According to Buffett, this category of investments should be much less dependent on the market, and he expected a fairly steady average return between 10 and 20 percent. As such, this category of investments should significantly outperform a declining market but likely will not match strongly advancing markets. Moreover, these investments (unlike general undervalued events) usually resolve at a determinable timeline, in line with the corporate actions.

The third category of investments that Buffett mentioned were situations in which the partnership can either directly control a company or own a large enough stake to actively influence operations. While these situations might result from one of the previous two categories of investments, Buffett's focus here is on influencing a company to unlock hidden value in assets, working capital, or (later in his career) operational improvements. He called these "control situations."

His overall goal was to use a combination of all three investment types to outperform the market in the long term. His hope, he said, was to incur smaller losses than the market in significantly declining markets, while only matching or slightly underperforming markets that are rapidly advancing. Buffett referred to building a pipeline of opportunities; the best investment type changes depending on market conditions, and the investor must recognize and respond to this flux in order to identify the most promising opportunities.[2] While flexible in the investment types he considered, Buffett remained adamant about his hurdles. When no great public companies could be had for a reasonable price, he invested in more merger arbitrage deals; when those dried up, he looked at private companies. In 1968, when he could not find opportunities in any of those categories, he disbursed his partnership rather than compromise on his investment criteria. If his investment requirement was to have a 50 percent *margin of safety* to intrinsic value for undervalued general investments, then he did not budge until he found such an opportunity. If it meant that he had to have absolute trust in the management's ability to allocate capital wisely, he did not bend on this.

The lesson here is that investors should not force one investment style upon the market. Instead, they should develop expertise in several types of investments that suit different investment environments and take advantage of the opportunities that present themselves. When opportunities seem to be drying up, do not compensate by loosening one's investment criteria.

D. It's All About Management

One aspect of Warren Buffett's approach has remained a constant through the years: his paramount focus on good management. While other renowned value investors (such as Walter Schloss and Benjamin Graham) focused little on assessing management, Buffett spent a huge amount of time understanding and evaluating a company's management. In so many cases—Jack Ringwalt of National Indemnity, Tom Murphy of Cap Cities/ABC, and even John Gutfreund of Salomon, just to mention a few—Buffett had known the management for years before his investment. And when he owns a company, he devotes considerable time to overseeing and supporting management as needed. Even when considered among investors who assess management as part of their investment process, Buffett goes far beyond what I think is the norm.

In assessing management, one criterion Buffett clearly looks for is a history of operational success. Take Jack Ringwalt at National Indemnity. Ringwalt cofounded the business with his brother Arthur in 1940 and built it up from scratch. By 1967, when Buffett invested, he spent over twenty-five years running the company successfully and balancing risks and growth prospects. The same track record of success was apparent in the larger public companies Buffett invested in: American Express's CEO Howard Clark and Coca-Cola's CEO Roberto Goizueta were both proven managers who had been in roles for at least several years. Another similarity among these managers was the detailed and honest annual reports they wrote, which shed unusual insight into their businesses. It was exceptional for Buffett to invest in a company without seeing a history of success from the manager. One notable instance was the *Washington Post*, where Katharine Graham took over the business when Fritz Beebe died unexpectedly. But even in this case, Buffett did get to know the three divisional managers who ran the operations—John Prescott of newspapers, Osborn Elliott of *Newsweek*, and Larry Israel of broadcasting. This was in addition to his extensive mentoring of Graham later on.

Buffett especially seemed to value owner-managers—CEOs who are either an owner in the business or who are otherwise personally devoted or connected to the business. Some cases were very clear cut; Jack Ringwalt at National Indemnity and Rose Blumkin of Nebraska Furniture Mart were owner-managers who founded their businesses. So was Katharine Graham because she was the granddaughter of the founder of the *Washington Post*. In several other instances, the managers were owner-managers by virtue of being incentivized through a direct profit-sharing agreement or being handpicked by Buffett based on a personal relationship to him or to the business. These managers included Harry Bottle at Dempster Mill, Ken Chace at Berkshire Hathaway, Stan Lipsey at *Buffalo Evening News*, and Walter Scott and David Sokol at MidAmerican Energy. Even in the cases where large corporations obviously had professional managers, Buffett invested in companies where those managers had a very long and well-defined history with their company; Tom Murphy at Capital Cities, Carl Reichardt at Wells Fargo, Ronald Ferguson at General Re, and Matthew Rose at BNSF all had been with their various companies for more than ten years, and in some cases over twenty-five years. Buffett preferred owner-managers because they had the same interests as he would have had as a long-term owner of the business.

Buffett had several other criteria for managers. He believed that a manager should have the utmost integrity, otherwise they may hurt investors far more by being smart than by being dumb. He also valued managers with the ability to allocate capital wisely, although he was also willing to teach a manager the conservative approach he espoused rather than insist that they be masters of this approach to begin with. Buffett clearly considered management one of the most important criteria, or even the most iimportant criterion, in finding a good investment. He spent an immense amount of time getting to know, evaluating, and guiding managers, searching for honest people with proven track records of success and who cared deeply about the businesses that they led.

Final Thoughts

Demystifying Warren Buffett is no easy task. Nevertheless, the lessons that can be drawn from studying the activities and strategies implemented by Buffett can be immensely insightful. In this book I have tried to take one specific approach in exploring the details of Buffett's investment fundamentals during several different periods in his career. My focus was foremost on Buffett's role approaching individual investment cases and understanding from a third-party perspective what rationale he or any investor may have seen in each situation. Within this context, I also attempted to present Buffett's evolution as an investor over time. My hope is that the reader can learn from the specific evidence presented in the investment case studies as well as from relating Buffett's evolution as an investor to his or her own unique investing experience.

One question that is frequently asked by investors is to what extent can an individual investor replicate the investments of Warren Buffett? After looking at the twenty investment that I believe were the most significant of his investment career, I would contend that actually a fair number of them would have been possible for a private investor. This is especially true for those investments made in the later part of Buffett's career. And even for those investments, which were private transactions and would have been impossible for most investors to execute, it still is the case that many of the lessons learned in them were often applicable to similar public company opportunities. The primary limitation that I see would be the fact that Buffett found on average only several good investment opportunities each year, and that this was based on exspending a full-time effort. But if one is willing to dedicate significant amounts of time and be patient, I truly believe that one can directly apply many of the lessons in Buffett's investments to improve one's own investment approach.

Appendix A

Performance of Buffett Partnership Limited (1957–1968)

Year	Overall results from Dow (1)	Partnership results (2)	Limited partners' results (3)
1957	−8.4%	10.4%	9.3%
1958	38.5%	40.9%	32.2%
1959	20.0%	25.9%	20.9%
1960	−6.2%	22.8%	18.6%
1961	22.4%	45.9%	35.9%
1962	−7.6%	13.9%	11.9%
1963	20.6%	38.7%	30.5%
1964	18.7%	27.8%	22.3%
1965	14.2%	47.2%	36.9%
1966	−15.6%	20.4%	16.8%
1967	19.0%	35.9%	28.4%
1968	7.7%	58.8%	45.6%
Annual compounded rate	**9.1%**	**31.6%**	**25.3%**

1. Based on yearly changes in the value of the Dow plus dividends that would have been received through ownership of the Dow during that year. The table includes all complete years of partnership activity.

2. For 1957–1961 consists of combined results of all predecessor limited partnerships operating throughout the entire year after all expenses but before distributions to partners or allocations to the general partner.

3. For 1957–1961 computed on the basis of the preceding column of partnership results allowing for allocation to the general partner based upon the present partnership agreement, but before monthly withdrawals by limited partners.

Source: Buffett Partnership letter dated January 22, 1969.

Appendix B

Performance of Berkshire Hathaway
(1965–2014)

	Annual percentage change		
Year	In per share book value of Berkshire	In per share market value of Berkshire	In S&P 500 with dividends included
1965	23.8	49.5	10.0
1966	20.3	(3.4)	(11.7)
1967	11.0	13.3	30.9
1968	19.0	77.8	11.0
1969	16.2	19.4	(8.4)
1970	12.0	(4.6)	3.9
1971	16.4	80.5	14.6
1972	21.7	8.1	18.9
1973	4.7	(2.5)	(14.8)
1974	5.5	(48.7)	(26.4)
1975	21.9	2.5	37.2
1976	59.3	129.3	23.6
1977	31.9	46.8	(7.4)
1978	24.0	14.5	6.4
1979	35.7	102.5	18.2
1980	19.3	32.8	32.3
1981	31.4	31.8	(5.0)
1982	40.0	38.4	21.4
1983	32.3	69.0	22.4
1984	13.6	(2.7)	6.1
1985	48.2	93.7	31.6
1986	26.1	14.2	18.6
1987	19.5	4.6	5.1
1988	20.1	59.3	16.6
1989	44.4	84.6	31.7
1990	7.4	(23.1)	(3.1)

(*continued*)

Year	In per share book value of Berkshire	In per share market value of Berkshire	In S&P 500 with dividends included
1991	39.6	35.6	30.5
1992	20.3	29.8	7.6
1993	14.3	38.9	10.1
1994	13.9	25.0	1.3
1995	43.1	57.4	37.6
1996	31.8	6.2	23.0
1997	34.1	34.9	33.4
1998	48.3	52.2	28.6
1999	0.5	(19.9)	21.0
2000	6.5	26.6	(9.1)
2001	(6.2)	6.5	(11.9)
2002	10.0	(3.8)	(22.1)
2003	21.0	15.8	28.7
2004	10.5	4.3	10.9
2005	6.4	0.8	4.9
2006	18.4	24.1	15.8
2007	11.0	28.7	5.5
2008	(9.6)	(31.8)	(37.0)
2009	19.8	2.7	26.5
2010	13.0	21.4	15.1
2011	4.6	(4.7)	2.1
2012	14.4	16.8	16.0
2013	18.2	32.7	32.4
2014	8.3	27.0	13.7
Compounded annual gain (1965–2014)	19.4%	21.6%	9.9%
Overall gain (1964–2014)	751,113%	1,826,163%	11,196%

Source: Berkshire Hathaway, *2014 Annual Report*, 2, reprinted.

Note: Data are for calendar years with these exceptions: 1965 and 1966, year ended September 30; 1967, 15 months ended December 31. Starting in 1979, accounting rules required insurance companies to value the equity securities they hold at market rather than at the lower of cost or market, which was previously the requirement. In this table, Berkshire's results through 1978 have been restated to conform to the changed rules. In all other respects, the results are calculated using the numbers originally reported. The S&P 500 numbers are *pretax* whereas the Berkshire numbers are *after-tax*. If a corporation such as Berkshire were simply to have owned the S&P 500 and accrued the appropriate taxes, its results would have lagged the S&P 500 in years when that index showed a positive return, but would have exceeded the S&P 500 in years when the index showed a negative return. Over the years, the tax costs would have caused the aggregate lag to be substantial.

NOTES

Part I. The Partnership Years (1957–1968)

1. Buffett Partnership Limited would soon be composed of numerous individual partnerships including Buffett Associates, Buffett Fund, Dacee, Emdee, Glenoff, Mo-Buff, and Underwood between 1956 and 1969.

1. 1958: Sanborn Map Company

1. Sanborn Maps, *Annual Report FY 1966, 1–2*.

2. Wrigley, Robert L., "The Sanborn Map as a Source of Land Use Information for City Planning," *Land Economics*, 25, no. 2 (May, 1949): 216–219.

3. http://www.lib.umd.edu/NTL/Sanbornhistory.html.

4. D. A. Sanborn. *Insurance Map of Boston*. Map. New York: 1867. From Library of Congress, *Sanborn Map Collections*.

5. Wrigley, "The Sanborn Map as a Source of Land Use Information for City Planning."

6. Warren Buffett to Buffett Partnership Limited, January 30, 1961, 10.

7. I assume $100,000 net income based on applying the 27 percent tax rate paid by Sanborn Map Co. in 1959 to its $132,120 operating income from its operating business, and rounding. For the purpose of showing the earnings power of just the operating business, I have excluded the income from investments. Buffett quoted

"after-tax profits of the map business . . . under $100,000 in 1958 and 1959" in his 1960 partnership letter.

8. When looking once more at the Sanborn Map Financial Data box, the Moody's document, a potential investor at the time would have been able to confirm the presence of this investment portfolio, but only if this investor was very detail oriented. In fact, the balance sheet figures merely show investment assets of $2.6 million at cost. One needs to see the footnote that references the market value of these assets of $7.3 million.

9. http://www.sanborn.com.

2. 1961: Dempster Mill Manufacturing Company

1. T. Lindsay Baker, *A Field Guide to American Windmills* (Norman: University of Oklahoma Press, 1985).

2. T. Lindsay Baker (Professor, Chair of Texas Industrial History, Tarleton State University), in discussion with the author.

3. We could make a rough estimate of the percentage of Dempster Mill's revenue stemming from aftersales based on a comment by Buffett in his annual letter. In the letter he stated that when Harry Bottle, his hired manager, raised prices on spare parts, an additional $200K was generated in profits per year. If we assume he raised prices by about 20 percent, which in my experience is possible when a company moves from having no aftersales strategy to having one, we can infer that sales on spare parts would be approximately $1 million. If we assume that an equal amount of service revenue also existed, we can infer that 20 to 25 percent of total revenues came from aftersales— certainly a meaningful amount.

4. There are numerous ways of defining a net-net, and the one I used is to take only the current assets (cash, receivables, inventory, and other current assets), subtract all liabilities, and take two-thirds of this value. By this definition, the math for Dempster would look as follows: net-net value = ([$5491K − $2318K]/60146) * ⅔ = $52.75 per share * ⅔ = $35.17 per share. This is 20 percent above the $28 per share price Buffett paid.

5. Alice Schroeder, *The Snowball: Warren Buffett and the Business of Life* (New York: Bantam, 2008), 246.

3. 1964: Texas National Petroleum Company

1. David Johnson and Daniel Johnson, *Introduction to Oil Company Financial Analysis* (Tulsa: PennWell, 2005), 238–239.

2. Union Oil Company of California Records 1884–2005, UCLA Department of Special Collections.

3. I used the details given in Buffett's annual letter to calculate projected returns based on his acquisition prices. As Buffett had purchased the securities in a span of

a few months, all numbers are estimates based on gains reflecting the average rate of return we are given or specific purchase prices. I also made the assumption that the warrants and common equity were trading similar discounts to the estimated deal price.

4. Specifically on the common equity price, Buffett's average price purchased can be calculated at about $6.92 per share. However, I assume that because he made purchases throughout the period between April and October 1962, the price of the common in April was lower, and by an amount consistent with the overall rate of return.

5. Warren Buffett to Buffett Partnership Limited, January 18, 1964.

4. 1964: American Express

1. Roger Lowenstein, *Buffett: The Making of an American Capitalist* (New York: Random House, 2008), 80.

2. Note that John F. Kennedy was also assassinated during this period, which had a negative impact on stock markets.

3. Lowenstein, *Buffett*, 81.

4. American Express, *1963 and 1964 Annual Reports*. Original annual reports of American Express 1963, 1964 (hardcopies provided by Guildhall Library, London).

5. American Express, *1963 Annual Report*, 2–3.

6. American Express, *1963 Annual Report*, 10.

7. American Express, *Case Study*, 1996.

8. By owner earnings, my preferred measure is cash earnings net of maintenance CAPEX.

9. By capital employed, my preferred measure is total tangible capital and intangible capital excluding goodwill plus net working capital.

10. American Express, *Case Study*, 1996.

11. American Express, *1963 Annual Report*, 27.

12. The term "cigar-butt" as it concerns investments generally refers to the strategy of purchasing poor quality businesses trading at extremely low valuations. Also sometimes referred to as deep value, this investment strategy is often associated with Benjamin Graham.

5. 1965: Berkshire Hathaway

1. Andrew Kilpatrick, *Of Permanent Value: The Story of Warren Buffett* (Mountain Brook, AL: AKPE, 2006), 153.

2. Berkshire Hathaway, *1965 Annual Report*, 11.

3. Warren Buffett to Buffett Partnership Limited, January 20, 1966.

4. My thanks to the Baker Library Historical Collections at the Harvard Business School, who kindly gave me access to its original documents.

5. I calculate the EV by multiplying the shares outstanding (1,017,547) by the share price of $14.69 and adding the net cash at EOY 1965 of $3.68 million from the balance sheet of the annual report. The EV I use is $11.3 million (market cap $14.9 million). Note that during the year, Berkshire had repurchased 120,231 of its own shares in the open market from a year start shares outstanding number of 1,137,778. EPS in 1965 is calculated based on 1,017,547 shares out.

6. Warren Buffett to Buffett Partnership Limited, January 20, 1966.

7. Alice Schroeder, *The Snowball: Warren Buffett and the Business of Life* (New York: Bantam, 2008), 277.

8. To be precise, I should note that this business segmentation is slightly different from DMGT's own segmentation of B2C, which includes a bit more than just the newspaper businesses.

6. 1967: National Indemnity Company

1. Alice Schroeder, *The Snowball: Warren Buffett and the Business of Life* (New York: Bantam, 2008), 302.

2. Robert G. Hagstrom, *The Warren Buffett Way: Investment Strategies of the World's Greatest Investor* (Hoboken, NJ: Wiley, 1997), 7.

3. Warren Buffett to Buffett Partnership Limited, January 22, 1969.

4. Hagstrom, *The Warren Buffett Way*, 6–7.

7. 1972: See's Candies

1. Warren Buffett to Berkshire Hathaway shareholders, March 14, 1984, for year-end 1983.

2. I define ROTCE here as NOPAT/tangible capital.

3. Warren Buffett to Berkshire Hathaway shareholders, March 14, 1984.

4. Warren Buffett to Berkshire Hathaway shareholders, March 14, 1984, 17, appendix.

5. Forty-three percent more is the amount required so that a reduction of 30 percent gets one to 100 percent, i.e., 143 × 0.7 = 100.

6. Richard A. Breadley, Stewart C. Myers, and Franklin Allen, *Principles of Corporate Finance* (New York: McGraw-Hill, 2010), 46.

7. Note that I use the same 10 percent discount rate as implicit with our 10 × PER fair value multiple, which assumes fair value = PV = C/0.1 → fair value = 10×C.

8. 1973: The *Washington Post*

1. Roger Lowenstein, *Buffett: The Making of an American Capitalist* (New York: Random House, 2008), 193.

2. Washington Post, *Annual Report 1972*, 2.

3. The ABI publishes a guideline for share-based incentive schemes that is in line with good practices and what could be considered fair. The latest version is from November 2012. http://www.abi.org.uk.

4. Details of IPO were $15,025,000 raised from the sale of 621,375 Class B shares indicating an IPO price of $24.18 per share or a PE of 15.9 based on the preexceptional diluted eps of $1.52 per share in 1971.

5. Andrew Kilpatrick, *Of Permanent Value: The Story of Warren Buffett* (Mountain Brook, AL: AKPE, 2006), 201–202. Note that Kilpatrick quotes the split-adjusted prices to derive the stock unadjusted price; I multiplied by 4.

6. I calculate the EV by multiplying the shares outstanding by the share price of $22.69 and adding the net debt at EOY 1972 of $7.3 million from the balance sheet of the annual report. The EV I use is $116.3 million (market cap $109 million).

7. Lowenstein, *Buffett*, 193.

9. 1976: GEICO (Government Employees Insurance Company)

1. Andrew Kilpatrick, *Of Permanent Value: The Story of Warren Buffett* (Mountain Brook, AL: AKPE, 2006), 221.

2. Berkshire Hathaway, *2005 Annual Report*, 24.

3. Robert G. Hagstrom, *The Warren Buffett Way: Investment Strategies of the World's Greatest Investor* (Hoboken, NJ: Wiley, 1997).

4. Alice Schroeder, *The Snowball: Warren Buffett and the Business of Life* (New York: Bantam, 2008), 367.

5. Warren Buffett, memo to Carol Loomis, July 6, 1988.

6. David Rolfe, Wedgewood Partners, "GEICO—The 'Growth Company' That Made the 'Value Investing' Careers of Both Benjamin Graham and Warren Buffett," Presented at the Value Investor Conference, Omaha, Nebraska, May 03, 2013.

7. Schroeder, *The Snowball*, 433.

8. Rolfe, "GEICO."

9. The year-end yield on long-term government bonds in 1976 was 7.30 percent.

10. The above scenario is based on 26.6 million shares outstanding. After the preferred convertible share offering brokered by Salomon, there would have been a dilutive effect to the extent of 8.2 million additional shares based on $76 million raised at $9.20 per preferred shares. However, this would also have added capital to the business.

11. Warren Buffett to Berkshire Hathaway shareholders, March 21, 1977.

12. "Insurance: GEICO Pulls Through," *Time*, January 3, 1977, http://www.time.com/time/magazine/article/0,9171,947829-1,00.html.

10. 1977: The *Buffalo Evening News*

1. Buffalo Courier-Express, Inc. v. Buffalo Evening News, Inc., Affidavit of Richard C. Lyons, Jr., 4–5.

2. Roger Lowenstein, *Buffett: The Making of an American Capitalist* (New York: Random House, 2008), 206.

3. Buffalo Courier-Express, Inc. v. Buffalo Evening News, Inc., No. CIV 77-582, U.S. District Court, W.D. New York (November 9, 1977). Exhibit 1 and note on annual gross revenue.

4. Andrew Kilpatrick, *Of Permanent Value: The Story of Warren Buffett* (Mountain Brook, AL: AKPE, 2006), 327.

5. Buffalo Courier-Express, Inc., 1977 U.S. District Court No. CIV 77-582.

6. Calculated based on data in Washington Post, *Annual Report for Year 1977*.

7. Lowenstein, *Buffett*, 215.

8. Buffalo Courier-Express, Inc., 1977 U.S. District Court No. CIV 77-582.

9. Warren Buffett to Berkshire Hathaway shareholders, March 14, 1984.

10. Warren Buffett to Berkshire Hathaway shareholders, 1978–1982.

11. 1983: Nebraska Furniture Mart

1. Barnaby Feder, "Rose Blumkin, Retail Queen, Dies at 104," *New York Times*, August 13, 1998.

2. Warren Buffett to Berkshire Hathaway shareholders, March 14, 1984.

3. Warren Buffett, interview by Linda O'Byron, *Nightly Business Report*, PBS, April 26, 1994.

4. Feder, "Rose Blumkin," *New York Times*, August 13, 1998.

5. Roger Lowenstein, *Buffett: The Making of an American Capitalist* (New York: Random House, 2008), 250.

6. Lowenstein, *Buffett*, 250.

7. Warren Buffett to Berkshire Hathaway shareholders, March 14, 1984.

8. Warren Buffett to Berkshire Hathaway shareholders, March 14, 1984.

9. Larry Green, "At 96, Feuding Matriarch Opens New Business," *Los Angeles Times*, December 18, 1989.

10. Walmart Stores, Inc., *1983 Annual Report*.

11. Walmart Stores, Inc., *1983 Annual Report*. Square footage calculated based on average of 1983 year-beginning square footage of 23.921 million and year-end square footage of 27.728 million.

12. Lowenstein, *Buffett*, 250.

13. The corporate tax rate in 1984 was 46 percent.

14. Alice Schroeder, *The Snowball: Warren Buffett and the Business of Life* (New York: Bantam, 2008), 502.

15. Buffett, interview by O'Byron.

16. Warren Buffett to Berkshire Hathaway shareholders, 1993. Although it was not guaranteed, Nebraska Furniture Mart continued growing for decades to come; by 1993, its pretax earnings had grown to $22 million from $15 million in 1983.

17. Warren Buffett to Berkshire Hathaway shareholders, February 27, 1987.

12. 1985: Capital Cities/ABC

1. Warren Buffett to Berkshire Hathaway shareholders, 1977.

2. By total outreach, the measure used is area of dominance (ADI).

3. The FCC regulation at the time (1961) allowed for a company ownership of a maximum of twelve AM and twelve FM radio stations, with additional limitations on ownership of multiple dominant radio stations in one market.

4. Alice Schroeder, *The Snowball: Warren Buffett and the Business of Life* (New York: Bantam Books, 2008), 898n12.

5. Share price information is given in the 10-year financial summary of the *Capital Cities/ABC 1985 Annual Report.*

13. 1987: Salomon Inc.—Preferred Stock Investments

1. Warren Buffett to Berkshire Hathaway shareholders, February 29, 1988.

2. Alice Schroeder, *The Snowball: Warren Buffett and the Business of Life* (New York: Bantam, 2008), 541.

3. James Sterngold, "Salomon to Sell 12 Percent to Buffett," *New York Times*, September 28, 1987.

4. Warren Buffett to Berkshire Hathaway shareholders, February 29, 1988, 17.

5. Robert G. Hagstrom, *The Warren Buffett Way: Investment Strategies of the World's Greatest Investor* (Hoboken, NJ: Wiley, 1997).

14. 1988: Coca-Cola

1. Warren Buffett to Berkshire Hathaway shareholders (1988 and 1989).

2. Andrew Kilpatrick, *Of Permanent Value: The Story of Warren Buffett* (Mountain Brook, AL: AKPE, 2006), 241–264.

3. The Coca-Cola Company, *1987 Annual Report,* 48.

4. Based on information presented in appendices of the Coca-Cola Company's *1987 Annual Report.*

5. I have adjusted the operating income in 1986 and 1987 to exclude exceptional costs related to provisions and restructuring costs and based my growth calculation on these numbers. The operating income growth based on as-reported (unadjusted) figures would have been 48 percent.

6. Warren Buffett to Berkshire Hathaway shareholders, February 28, 1989, 10.

7. This is because some of the unconsolidated entities are valued at market value but some are valued at cost-basis.

15. 1989: US Air Group

1. US Air Group, *1988 Annual Report*, 21–22.

2. Warren Buffett to Berkshire Hathaway shareholders, February 28, 1997.

3. Warren Buffett to Berkshire Hathaway shareholders, February 27, 1998.

16. 1990: Wells Fargo

1. Wells Fargo, *1986–1992 Annual Reports,* courtesy London Business School Library microfiche.

2. The only assets that may have seemed somewhat higher risk than ordinary loans were quantified as highly leveraged transaction loans (HLTs), which were predominantly senior secured debt used in buyouts, acquisitions, and other corporate transactions. The total exposure to this was $4.2 billion in 1989.

3. Wells Fargo, *1990 Annual Report*, 24. The company reports the range and closing price of its shares in each quarter in 1989 and 1990.

4. Based on FRB's 1992 guidelines; hence Wells Fargo was already in compliance with forward guidelines given but not mandated until 1992 for the industry.

5. Warren Buffett to Berkshire Hathaway shareholders, March 1, 1991.

17. 1998: General Re

1. For those unfamiliar with the term, a reinsurance business is a business that takes on those risks that other insurance companies pass on; hence, it is an insurance company that insures part or all of a risk from other insurances.

2. Warren Buffett 1997 letter to Berkshire Hathaway shareholders, February 28, 1998, 5.

3. Please note that this is a generic description of insurance ratios and insurance accounting. While these metrics and descriptions are generally calculated as described, there are variations in both description and accounting.

4. Swiss Re, "World Insurance in 2000," *Sigma*, no. 6 (2001): figure 5, 13.

18. 1999: MidAmerican Energy Holdings Company

1. Warren Buffett to Berkshire Hathaway shareholders year-end 1999, March 2000.

2. Share buybacks have reduced the share-count even further from the approximate 74 million diluted shares on June 30, 1999.

3. Berkshire Hathaway, press release, October 25, 1999.

4. Warren Buffett to Berkshire Hathaway shareholders, February 28, 2002, 13.

19. 2007–2009: Burlington Northern

1. Union Pacific, 2008 Annual Report, 5, 10.

2. Burlington Northern Santa Fe, 2008 Annual Report, 12–13.

3. BNSF, 2008 Annual Report, Notes to Consolidated Financial Statement no. 7, 54.

4. Based on operational statistics from Association of American Railroads (www.aar.org).

5. Multiples are based on EV and earnings figures based on 2007 year-end report actual figures.

6. Multiples are based on EV and earnings figures based on 2009 year-end report actual figures; EV used was $43.1 billion based on a market cap of $34 billion and a net debt of $9.1 billion.

20. 2011: IBM

1. Sarah Frier, "IBM Granted Most U.S. Patents for 20th Straight Year," January 10, 2013, www.bloomberg.com/news.

2. As reported in the Berkshire Hathaway *2011 Annual Report*, 63,905,931 shares of IBM were purchased for $10.856 billion at cost.

3. As a side note, it was known to investors by the time Buffett announced his stake in IBM that Palmisano was retiring and Virginia Rometty was taking over as CEO.

21. Evolution of Buffett's Investment Strategy

1. Alice Schroeder, *The Snowball: Warren Buffett and the Business of Life* (New York: Bantam, 2008), 673.

22. What We Can Learn from Buffett

1. BlackBerry (formerly known as Research in Motion) had reported revenues of CAD 24.8 billion in 2011 and CAD 4.6 billion in 2014.

2. Buffett discusses the relative abundance of opportunities in the three different categories of investments along with his ability to realize them in several different instances. One instance is the 1961 letter to the Buffett Partnership dated January 24, 1962, in which he discussed realizing relatively more control situations as his increasing capital allowed him to do so.

SELECTED BIBLIOGRAPHY

Altucher, James. *Trade Like Warren Buffett*. Hoboken, NJ: Wiley, 2005.

Buek, Michael. "Why Index Funds Beat Active Strategies." http://www.bankrate.com/finance/financial-literacy/why-index-funds-beat-active-strategies-1.aspx.

Buffett, Warren. Warren Buffett to Shareholders, 1977-2015. Berkshire Hathaway Inc., http://www.berkshirehathaway.com/letters/letters.html.

Graham, Benjamin. *The Intelligent Investor*. New York: HarperCollins, 2006.

Greenwald, Bruce C.N., Judd Kahn, Paul D. Sonkin, and Michael van Biema. *Value Investing: From Graham to Buffett and Beyond*. Hoboken, NJ: Wiley, 2001.

Kilpatrick, Andrew. *Of Permanent Value: The Story of Warren Buffett*. Mountain Brook, AL: AKPE, 2006.

Lowenstein, Roger. *Buffett: The Making of an American Capitalist*. New York: Random House, 2008.

Schroeder, Alice. *The Snowball: Warren Buffett and the Business of Life*. New York: Bantam, 2008.

INDEX